U.S. INSPECTORS GENERAL

U.S. INSPECTORS GENERAL

Truth Tellers in Turbulent Times

CHARLES A. JOHNSON
KATHRYN E. NEWCOMER

BROOKINGS INSTITUTION PRESS
Washington, D.C.

Library of Congress Cataloging-in-Publication Data
Names: Johnson, Charles A., 1948–, author. | Newcomer, Kathryn E., 1949– author.
Title: U.S. inspectors general : truth tellers in turbulent times / Charles A. Johnson, Kathryn E. Newcomer.
Description: Washington, D.C. : Brookings Institution Press, [2020] | Includes bibliographical references and index.
Identifiers: LCCN 2019026907 (print) | LCCN 2019026908 (ebook) | ISBN 9780815737773 (paperback) | ISBN 9780815737780 (epub)
Subjects: LCSH: Finance, Public—United States—Auditing. | Governmental investigations—United States.
Classification: LCC HJ9801 .J63 2020 (print) | LCC HJ9801 (ebook) | DDC 331.7/6135235—dc23
LC record available at https://lccn.loc.gov/2019026907
LC ebook record available at https://lccn.loc.gov/2019026908

9 8 7 6 5 4 3 2 1

Typeset in Adobe Jenson Pro

Composition by Elliott Beard

To our grandchildren, who inspire us every day

for Charles—Grant, Jake, Evelyn, and Walker

for Kathy—Sean, Michaela, Liam, Rose, Finn, and Opal

Contents

Contents

Foreword

In their scholarly and well-informed book *U.S. Inspectors General: Truth Tellers in Turbulent Times*, Professors Johnson and Newcomer provide a detailed accounting of how the federal inspector general (IG) community came to be, what its status is today, and where it might go from here. Their book is timely, since 2018 marked a critically important milestone year for the inspectors general: the fortieth anniversary of the Inspector General Act of 1978, which formally established the IG structure across government lines. President Carter, who signed the legislation into law on October 12, 1978, characterized it as "perhaps the most important new tool in the fight against (government) fraud."

Recent events propel the institution as never before in its core mission of helping to promote public confidence in and understanding of federal government operations in general, and in the various agencies of government in particular. At this very moment, it is hard to scan a newspaper, tune into talk radio, surf the television networks (both traditional and cable), or engage in social media without prominent mention of current IG initiatives. The highly visible and impactful work of the inspectors general (IGs) at the Department of Justice, Veterans Administration,

Department of Homeland Security, and Department of Defense, for example, is frequently "front page, above the fold" material. It seems that almost every day, the IGs are asked to bring their professional expertise to address new or evolving high-profile, controversial matters.

Surprisingly, even after four decades since the enactment of the IG statute, there is a striking lack of familiarity with the IG concept. Despite composite budgets that exceed $2 billion annually and staffing of over 13,000, the work of the IG community is little understood and, in fact, is often misunderstood. Citizens, the media, and even senior elected officials regularly pose fundamental questions about IG operations. What was the genesis of the IG Act? Under what authorities do they operate? How are IG offices structured and staffed? Are the products of IG work publicly available? What is the range of investigatory tools available to an IG in potential criminal matters? These questions and many others are addressed in a comprehensive way in Johnson and Newcomer's book.

Relying on extensive data-gathering techniques, Johnson and Newcomer provide the reader with an insider's sense of what makes the IG world tick. The authors interviewed a broad cross-section of current IG leaders and staff at numerous federal agencies. As reflected in the book's title, the result is an inside look at IG community operations, with an emphasis on aspects that are working well and those that need to be improved. The authors did not, however, limit their data-gathering efforts to those currently in the IG community. In fact, as part of their research, Johnson and Newcomer sought the views of former IG officials and a broad range of other stakeholders, both inside and outside government. Thus, the authors present a realistic view of the IG community, addressing the core elements of IG operations.

There are specific aspects of the book that are of particular importance for the reader. For example, Johnson and Newcomer emphasize the integral role of root cause analysis in the work of an IG. They conclude that if truly useful recommendations for corrective actions are to be provided to agency management, the IG must have a clear understanding of the root cause of the problem. And, the recommendations must address the root cause directly. The authors acknowledge that root cause determination is not always easy. But they recognize that resolving problems is at the core of the IG function and that root cause analysis is a vital part of this effort. I think that Johnson and Newcomer have it exactly right.

The authors explored system stressors that impact IG operations, in particular the challenges of maintaining IG independence and keeping Congress up to date on the current status of operations. These can be among the most significant barriers that IGs must overcome if they are to be successful. Regarding independence, Johnson and Newcomer define the independence concept as it applies to the IG world. They note that an IG who is or is seen to be impaired from an independence perspective cannot be effective. The authors recognize that agency leadership may desire a particular outcome, and that direct or indirect pressure can be applied to obtain such an outcome. Yet, IGs must resist such efforts if they are to maintain their independence. At the end of the day, an independent setting is essential if an IG report is to be viewed by all parties as being objective, impartial, and fair, as well as to serve as a catalyst for corrective action that will improve agency operations.

Johnson and Newcomer address the real-world challenge the IG community faces in managing its unavoidable involvement in the relationship between the executive and legislative branches. The IGs are organizationally part of the executive branch, yet they have a statutory responsibility to report their findings to the legislative branch in a timely fashion. This is a unique relationship that has been characterized as the equivalent of straddling a barbed wire fence. The authors conclude, correctly in my view, that striking the right balance in dealing with these relationships, which often seem entirely incompatible, requires great care on the part of the IG. And, the challenge is further complicated when the IG operates in an environment that is highly partisan and/or when executive and legislative branch relationships are already strained.

Johnson and Newcomer focus on the metrics that the IG community and individual IGs rely on to measure their effectiveness. The authors recognize the unique mission of the IG organization, the role it plays in the federal agency, and the inherent challenges of finding the right metrics to accurately gauge IG success. For example, an IG can recommend corrective actions to address an identified problem, but acceptance of the recommendation is an agency responsibility. In short, actual implementation and execution of corrective actions, which one would think would be the ultimate measure of success, is essentially beyond the control of the IG. This often forces the IG community to rely on output and outcome measures, which I characterize as soft metrics. One such measure, "funds put to better use," is aptly described in the book and is, in my judgment, a less than optimal benchmark of IG achievement. The authors recognize the shortcomings of the range of metrics available to the IG community.

Clearly, like all governmental agencies, IG operations should be subjected to periodic evaluations as a means of ensuring that, for example, the benefits are worth the significant costs. The authors suggest that the IG community would be well served if the current performance metric scheme were enhanced to provide a more definitive confirmation of IG achievement. Professors Johnson and Newcomer provide an analytical basis for a path forward to achieve this goal.

One special note: as part of their interview process, the authors heard what they describe as one singular aspiration expressed by the IGs. When asked how they would measure their own success, the IGs all replied that they would want to see that their office's efforts had improved agency operations. As a longtime member of the IG community, I was pleased but not surprised at this response. In a tumultuous governmental environment, this is just what one would hope for from a group of professionals dedicated to the notion that good government is a realistic and responsible goal.

Finally, much in the spirit of the IG world, the authors provide the reader—and the IG community, for that matter—with a series of constructive recommendations and suggested actions to advance the IG concept and enhance IG operations. These recommendations flowed directly from the analytical data in this book. The recommendations are worthy of serious consideration by the IG community and those stakeholders who have an interest in the work of the community.

To play on a phrase popularized several years ago, Johnson and Newcomer's book is what you always wanted to know about the federal inspector general community but were afraid to ask! By the very nature of their charter, mission, and mandate, the IGs often find themselves in the vortex of a partisan and controversial environment. In these circumstances, it is important that the work of the IG community be transparent and well understood. In their masterfully written book, Newcomer and Johnson provide the reader with an eye-opening view of the IG world that can help to achieve this goal. It is a refreshing and enjoyable read.

The Honorable Gregory Friedman
INSPECTOR GENERAL AT THE U.S. DEPARTMENT
OF ENERGY, 1998–2015

Preface

U.S. inspectors general (IGs) serve as independent government watch-dogs who seek out fraud, waste, and abuse and who promote effective management in federal programs. As of 2019, there were seventy-four IGs who were appointed by the president and confirmed by the Senate or solely appointed by the leadership in the agency within which the IG functions.* Each of these IGs reports findings and makes recommendations to both executive and congressional officials about problems and even scandals they find in federal offices. Their reports frequently lead to front-page news stories in the national media, congressional hearings and legislation, criminal prosecutions and civil actions, and (occasionally) firings or resignations by government officials.

Our experience is that very few public officials have a working knowledge about what IGs actually do, despite the emergence of IGs as key officials in the management of the federal government, major controversies their findings invoke regarding federal executive actions, and IG reports

---

One IG, the Special Inspector General for Afghanistan, is appointed by the president, but does not require Senate confirmation.

identifying significant savings of federal dollars. Moreover, we have observed that this lack of knowledge about IGs also extends to scholars and students studying public administration and public policy, as well as to informed and concerned citizens.

One reason for the low levels of information about these important officers is that there is a dearth of books and articles about IGs. Public administration texts that mention IGs usually reference decade's old scholarship or IG findings of government mismanagement reported in the popular media. This book updates the scholarship about IGs and the work they do, and it provides contemporary information for public officials, faculty, students, journalists, and inquisitive citizens regarding IGs' actions to reduce waste, fraud, and abuse in U.S. government programs.

Acknowledgments

Charles Johnson thanks Texas A&M University, the College of Liberal Arts, and the Department of Political Science for a faculty development leave and seed funding to pursue this project. Fellow political scientists at Texas A&M, including Jon R. Bond, Bill Clark, Robert Durant (formerly at Texas A&M), George Edwards III, Robert Harmel, Kim Q. Hill, Ken Meier, Michelle Taylor-Robinson, Arnold Vedlitz, and Dan Wood—offered encouragement and ideas throughout the project, and conversations with Wendi A. Kaspar, Policy Sciences & Economics Library Professor at Texas A&M, were especially helpful as the research progressed. A grant from the IBM Center for the Business of Government provided valuable funding to support work on the six case studies that are integrated into various chapters of this book.[1] Additionally, thanks go to Dr. Evan Haglund, who is on the faculty of the U.S. Coast Guard Academy, for insightful comments about the project and for co-authoring chapter 3 on the recruitment and appointment of U.S. inspectors general (IGs).

Kathy Newcomer thanks The Honorable Gregory Friedman, George Grob, and Cathy Helm, all exemplary leaders in the IG community, for their many years of instruction on how the IG community really works, as well as her colleagues at The George Washington University for their ongoing support. She also thanks Paul Light for his encouragement and support in following on his work for the past several years.

We also want to acknowledge the advice and assistance of officials at the Council of the Inspectors General on Integrity and Efficiency (CIGIE), and very helpful off-the-record conversations we had with numerous officials about IGs during the course of this project. Additionally, we benefited from the research assistance provided by Angela Allison and Zain-Aamir Maredia (Texas A&M) and Stephen Payne (The George Washington University). Also, John Kamensky, Senior Fellow at the IBM Center, offered encouragement and advice based on his experience in Washington, D.C., that we particularly appreciated. Dr. Edward Jennings, Professor, University of Kentucky, read our draft manuscript and offered immensely helpful comments and suggestions.

We also value the encouragement and support of the editorial staff at the Brookings Institution Press—Bill Finan, Cecilia González, Carla Huelsenbeck, Fred Dews, Yelba Quinn, and Steve Roman—during the many stages of this book's development and production.

Throughout this project, our respective families have been encouraging and patient. Our heartfelt thanks go out to each family member for their wonderful support.

Finally, in extending our deep appreciation to the many, many folks who contributed in a variety of ways to this project, the readers should know that we take sole responsibility for any errors in the design, execution, and conclusions presented in this book. We trust that readers will find this book sufficiently informative that they will knowingly pay attention to future news reports on the scholarly research of IGs. And we hope that some readers will be motivated to pursue additional research on U.S. inspectors general that builds upon or clarifies what we report in this volume.

ONE

Searching for Fraud, Waste, Abuse, and Mismanagement

PATENT OFFICE WORKERS BILKED THE GOVERNMENT
OF MILLIONS BY PLAYING HOOKY, WATCHDOG FINDS[1]

WATCHDOG: IRS ERASED BACKUPS AFTER
LOSS OF TEA PARTY EMAILS[2]

EPA WATCHDOG OPENS A CRIMINAL PROBE INTO
2015 COLORADO SPILL—AGENCY'S INSPECTOR
GENERAL LOOKS INTO INCIDENT THAT TURNED
ANIMAS RIVER MUSTARD YELLOW[3]

WATCHDOG SAYS VA OFFICIALS LIED[4]

—*Story headlines in the national media regarding
reports by U.S. inspectors general*

Family businesses, major corporations, nonprofit foundations, and government agencies actively discourage fraud, waste, abuse, and mismanagement. Similarly, they do all they can to promote economy, efficiency, effectiveness, and accountability. The challenge is how to competently, economically, systematically, and fairly identify the former and embrace the latter.

In the late twentieth century, through the Inspector General Act of 1978 (IG Act of 1978), Congress enacted legislation establishing distinctively new federal offices to meet this challenge—Offices of Inspec-

1

tor General (OIGs). Since passage of the act, these offices have grown in number to cover virtually every major U.S. government agency. The number of officials working in OIGs has increased to over 13,000 federal employees, with a combined budget of $2.7 billion in 2016. The responsibilities of these offices extends into such areas as oversight of financial management plans, guarding civil and constitutional rights, and protecting whistleblowers. Moreover, Congress has expanded the authority of these officials in law enforcement and management consultancy.

Acknowledging the track record of U.S. inspectors general (IGs) and their value to Congress, former Senator John Glenn (R, OH) noted the following in a 2015 letter to members of Congress:

> The Inspector General Act has stood the test of time. The billions of dollars recovered for the government and the increased efficiency and effectiveness of government programs and operation are a testament to the Act's continued success.[5]

Consistent with Senator Glenn's observation, the most recent annual report of the Council for the Inspectors General on Integrity and Efficiency (CIGIE) for fiscal year 2017 showed that OIGs collectively produced $54.6 billion in potential savings and recoveries for the federal government; issued 3,828 audit and evaluation reports; and successfully pursued 14,562 criminal prosecutions, civil actions, debarments of federal contractors, and personnel actions in federal agencies.[6]

Often called watchdogs by the media, IGs regularly make front-page headlines with reports showing scandalous expenditures, foolish executive decisions, and ineffective programs. In fact, IGs and their respective offices are major players in the federal government, doing work that affects day-to-day activities of federal agencies. Congress protects IGs from executive interference and seeks their advice in overseeing federal programs, and with some frequency inspector general (IG) reports draw sufficient attention in the media to reset executive and congressional agendas.

This book takes a comprehensive look at the federal OIGs. It examines the legislation creating these offices, who serves as inspectors general, what IGs do, whether and how they make a difference, and the challenges they face today and in the future because of the legal mandate that they report to both the executive and congressional branches of the federal government. Through case studies of six agencies, a survey of IGs, and analysis of public documents and statistical data, we describe a complex strategic environment in which IGs do their work. We conclude the book with recommendations regarding the operation of OIGs to take advantage of their distinctive skills and authority to improve the operation of U.S. governmental programs.

An Overview of U.S. Inspectors General and the Plan of the Book

The U.S. OIGs emerged in an era emphasizing accountability of government and at a time of heightened concerns about fraud and mismanagement of government programs. The IG Act of 1978 authorizes IGs to (1) pursue independent audits, investigations, or evaluations of agency programs and practices; (2) provide leadership and coordination of policies that promote economy, efficiency, and effectiveness of agency programs; and (3) prevent fraud, waste, and abuse. Distinctive among federal officials, IGs are legally required to report to both the executive and legislative branches of government. Inspectors general are expected to be nonpartisan appointments and to pursue their responsibilities without regard to political interests. The IGs and the offices they manage are expected to be independent, yet they are accountable to both executive offices and to Congress. Chapter 2 reviews the historical development of the 1978 act that institutionalized these features as well as major amendments in 1988, 2008, and 2016, which primarily increased responsibilities, authority, and resources for OIGs.

Consistent with expectations that IGs are nonpartisan appointees holding professional credentials tied to their responsibilities, few IGs have extensive partisan backgrounds. Moreover, except for the presidential transition from Jimmy Carter to Ronald Reagan, IGs typically remain in place through presidential transitions and agency head changes. Since 1989, IGs have not been subject to dismissal during presidential transitions due to the nonpolitical nature of IGs in their respective agencies. The nonpartisan nature of their appointment also strengthens the independence of IGs to pursue audits, investigations, and evaluations despite shifts in political winds.

Chapter 3 reviews the appointment processes for IGs, details who has been appointed to these offices, and discusses challenges associated with open vacancies and allegations against IGs themselves.

The business of government involves the expenditure of trillions of dollars to contractors for buildings, weapon systems, and equipment, and to individuals for government salaries and pensions, Social Security, and tax refunds. Inevitably some of these payments involve fraudulent charges or administrative mistakes. Governing also involves the administration of complex programs requiring the development of regulations and procedures that government officials are expected to implement fairly, in keeping with budgetary and legal guidelines. Here, too, mistakes occur, programs fall short of expectations, and unintended consequences emerge following program implementation. Audits, investigations, and evaluations are the principal means by which IGs identify these shortcomings and make recommendations for their correction. Drawing on a survey of IGs, chapter 4 discusses how OIGs operate, including how audits and investigations are initiated, pursued, and reported upon. The chapter also presents data on how these activities vary across OIGs and what may account for this variation.

In pursuing audits, investigations, and evaluations, IGs must be mindful of their legal obligations to report to both their agency head and to Congress. They must balance expectations regarding their independence and nonpartisanship, their accountability for recommendations to the agency and to Congress, and their timely engagement with federal programs to offer recommendations for making these programs more economical, efficient, and effective. Balancing expectations and dealing with pressure from both executive leaders and Congress is often referred to as walking the barbed wire fence. Chapter 5 reports on case studies involving six IGs, their OIGs, and agency leadership, with a focus on how IGs manage potential clashes between these two principals and across the principles of independence, accountability, and engagement.

Supporters of IGs and the work they do often point to the substantial savings and successful prosecutions by OIGs. This, supporters argue, demonstrates the value of IG work and the difference it makes. Some advocates point out that every dollar invested in OIGs produces a return of $17 in savings and retrieved funds.[7] Of course these measures do not fully capture, and some may overstate, the difference IGs make in their respective agencies. And in many circumstances, the impact IGs have on agencies may not be easily quantified. Chapter 6 examines quantitative measures of the difference IGs make in their agencies and explores more nuanced ways that IGs may impact their respective agencies' policies, practices, and decisions.

Despite positive press and support from Congress and the executive branch, IGs are not without critics. Moreover, the IG community faces challenges on numerous fronts, including increased partisanship in Washington, constrained budgets, and expectations of various groups about their work. Challenges involving management of OIGs themselves and the IG community are also on the horizon, involving delays in filling IG vacancies and auditing programs in policy areas administered by multiple agencies. Chapter 7 outlines several of these major challenges and highlights some of the concerns facing the IG community, executive leaders, and Congress. In the course of discussing these challenges and criticisms, the chapter offers recommendations that could address some of the issues embedded in contemporary discussions of IGs.

Research Methods

Findings and discussion in this volume are based on three principal sources. First, we conducted an extensive literature[8] and document review that included the laws governing OIGs, semiannual reports to Congress, selected individual audits and evaluations, and publicly available data on the occupants of IG offices from 1978 through the end of the Barack Obama administration in January 2017.[9]

Second, during the summer and fall of 2014, we conducted in-depth case studies of six IG offices representing a variety of agencies, including cabinet-level departments and smaller federal agencies. Reflecting the size of their home agencies, the size of the OIGs varied substantially, ranging from several hundred employees to a relatively small OIG with fewer than twenty-five employees. Three of the IGs were appointed by the president and confirmed by the U.S. Senate and are commonly known as PAS IGs, and three were appointed by agency heads or governing boards and are otherwise known as designated federal entities (DFEs). A copy of the general guide for our interviews is included in appendix A.

Third, we conducted an electronic survey of the IG community in fall 2016 to follow up on the findings from our six case studies, broaden our understanding about activities OIGs pursue to fulfill their mission, and identify factors that lead to their success. We pretested the survey with four sitting IGs and then sent the survey to at least five officials in each of the seventy-three IG offices in existence at that time, including the IG. We received responses from a total of fifty-nine IG executives. To ensure that we had comparable responses across OIGs, our analyses in later chapters draw on the twenty-six responses of the IGs representing 35 percent of all OIGs, which is most appropriate since we are primarily focused on interactions between IGs and leadership in the agencies and Congress. Appendix B includes a copy of the questions and instrument used for this survey.

Focusing on the IGs' Strategic Environment

The IG Act of 1978 represents a reform that Beryl Radin, a public administration scholar and former special advisor in the Department of Health and Human Services, characterizes as a one-size-fits-all approach to management reform efforts.[10] To a very large extent, each OIG has the same mission and authority to improve the efficiency of government and to rein in fraud and abuse. In reality, OIGs adapt their organization and activities to programs and policies that differ from one agency to another. These differences are reinforced by differences across the congressional committees to which IGs and their home agencies report. And there are expectations that differ among IGs and individuals with whom they work and to whom they report. Recognizing this aspect of OIGs, we explore the IGs' strategic environment, which is composed of individuals and offices that substantially influence decisions made by IGs, how they conduct their work, and what impact they have on government operations. In very real terms, an IG's strategic environment may significantly influence levels of success for his or her office.

The idea that organizations and government offices operate in an environment that influences their activities is neither new nor surprising. Our conception of an IG's strategic environment draws on James Eisenstein's work on U.S. Attorneys, which describes the relationships central to the operation of local U.S. Attorney offices located in every federal judicial district. Eisenstein's field work on U.S. Attorneys found that their appointment, decisionmaking, and priorities were substantially influenced by Department of Justice (DOJ) offices to whom they technically reported *and* by local officials with whom they interacted regularly, such as federal district judges, elected officials (including U.S. senators from their state), and private attorneys. Eisenstein reveals that, although confirmed by the U.S. Senate and nominally independent of both the DOJ and the local community, U.S. Attorneys pay attention to national and local constituencies as they make investigatory and prosecutorial decisions.[11] Although IGs and U.S. Attorneys do not share the same attributes of independence, both function in an organizational environment that impinges on their day-to-day decisions. In many instances, their respective environments encompass and require contending with conflicting demands and expectations. We believe that understanding this strategic environment is critical to understanding IGs' operations; how their work is accomplished; how their audits, evaluations, and investigations are received; and finally, what impact IGs have on their home agencies.

Our research suggests that an IG's strategic environment is best described as being composed of three sets of elements that are key influences on what IGs do: stakeholders interested in and affected by an IG's work; expectations held by the IG's stakeholders; and system stressors creating challenges and opportunities for an IG. We conclude this chapter with brief descriptions of these three elements, providing a conceptual base for their use in later chapters.

Stakeholders of IGs

Inspectors general have two primary stakeholders with legal authority over them and to whom they officially report—namely, leadership in their home agency and Congress. While statutorily independent, an IG must pay attention to the preferences of and requests from these stakeholders.

We demonstrate in subsequent chapters that both of these stakeholders affect the day-to-day activities of the OIG and significantly impact an IG's long-term success or failure.

A secondary group of stakeholders includes individuals, offices, or groups that hold no statutory authority over an IG but in fact have potential influence because of their expertise, legal authority in allied areas of interest, or power in the political system. These secondary stakeholders can serve as important allies or adversaries for an IG. Perhaps the closest secondary stakeholders to an IG are his or her OIG staff. While an IG has hierarchical authority over his or her staff, OIG staff members are entrusted with considerable responsibilities and have the sort of organizational authority, resources, and expertise that can constrain, alter, or advance an IG's work.

Among secondary stakeholders external to an IG's office, CIGIE holds a distinctive position of speaking for the entire IG community (once there is agreement among the IGs), setting professional standards for IG activities, and providing training opportunities to IGs and their staff. An IG is also likely to encounter other stakeholders in the federal system who have oversight responsibilities and who may be either competitors or partners in audits, investigations, or evaluations. Such stakeholders include the Government Accountability Office (GAO) and the DOJ, which draw their respective auditing and investigating authority from separate statutes. The Office of Management and Budget (OMB) also has a special relationship with IGs, especially since OMB's deputy director for management serves as the executive chair of CIGIE.

Other secondary stakeholders include agency employees whose work IGs often review and upon whom IGs rely for information and for implementation of recommendations. Nongovernmental stakeholders include clients or consumers of an IG's home agency (for example, contractors hired by the agency), groups affiliated with the home agency (for example, professional associations or employee unions associated with the agency), interest groups affected by agency programs, and groups dedicated to oversight of government programs (for example, the Project on Government Oversight [POGO]), all of which have the potential to impact an IG's work—positively or negatively. In addition, the media can affect IG work in at least two ways: first, by reporting on government waste or mismanagement that lead to calls for IG inquiry and, second, by reporting on major findings of fraud or waste, as well as the political consequences of IG reports and recommendations.

Expectations of IGs

In creating OIGs, Congress set a number of expectations in law regarding their operation and their relationships with home agencies as well as with Congress. These responsibilities and authorities are best summarized in three broad areas that we believe shape the activities of an IG and influence how various stakeholders interact with that IG on a day-to-day basis: (1) the independence to initiate, conduct, and report on audits, investigations, and evaluations unencumbered by political constraints; (2) accountability to their home agency and to Congress for their initiatives, findings, and recommendations; and (3) engagement with agency management and with Congress to assure integrity and efficiency in agency programs. In accounting for the decisions of IGs and the operation of OIGs in subsequent chapters, we highlight that IGs and their stakeholders often have differing views about independence, accountability, and engagement. And, importantly, these differences affect the work an IG does and the impact of that work.

INDEPENDENCE

An IG's independence is strongly rooted in the historical development of the IG Act of 1978, and the law provides detailed protections for that independence. For example, an IG is expected to be a nonpartisan appointment with the expertise needed to pursue audits, investigations, and evaluations in the home agency. With few exceptions, there are no terms or time limits for an appointee, which means he or she continues to serve through changes in presidential administrations. Indeed, as discussed in chapter 3, there have been no systematic dismissals of IGs when executive changes occurred, except at the beginning of President Reagan's first term.

The Inspector General Act underscores an IG's independence by providing that he or she is free to initiate and pursue audits, investigations, and evaluations unencumbered by agency management or (less clearly) congressional interests.[12] Agencies are directed to cooperate with an IG and to provide information as needed for audits, investigations, and evaluations. In addition, an IG largely organizes his or her office and hires staff independent of agency management or congressional interests. Finally, unlike virtually all other administrative programs or departments, an IG may independently and publicly comment on budget recommendations for his or her office from agency management, the OMB, and the president; further, the IG may lobby Congress for budgetary support. Given these statutory protections, IGs can reasonably expect considerable latitude in audits, investigations, and evaluations they pursue. However, exercising this discretion may be influenced by organizational or political pressures from stakeholders.

ACCOUNTABILITY

While largely unrestrained in the conduct of audits, investigations, and evaluations, an IG is held accountable for outcomes in these activities, for management of the office, and for relationships with his or her stakeholders. Based on the idea that transparency produces accountability, the 1978 legislation requires IGs to file semiannual reports with agency management and with relevant committees of Congress. These reports detail activities for the past six months and the results of recommendations made in previous semiannual reports. Subsequent legislation also mandated posting individual and semiannual reports on the internet.

While the distribution and posting of reports may not guarantee close review of an IG's work, his or her work is often subject to close scrutiny by agency leadership. This scrutiny may lead agency management to reject an IG's recommendations or undertake a different approach to a problem identified by an IG. In any case, agencies are not legally obligated to accept recommendations, but they must give feedback to IGs on their reports and the status of their recommendations. The Department of Justice provides a check on an IG's investigative activities by deciding whether to prosecute individuals on whom OIG investigators collect evidence of alleged criminal or civil violations. As an ultimate form of accountability to the executive branch, disagreements between an IG and the administration could lead to the IG's dismissal—an action that requires informing Congress about what led to the dismissal. Congress does not have dismissal authority, but it may hold hearings with and about an IG who is considered out of step with congressional views about the IG's work.

While much of the federal budget process is incremental, review of an IG's budget by agency management, OMB, the president, and Congress provides opportunities for review of his or her activities. Budget increases or cutbacks in response to positive or negative views of an IG's record do not occur frequently, but they do occur—and IGs feel this weight of accountability in their respective offices.

An IG may also be held accountable by the community of IGs in two ways. First, the GAO sets government auditing standards and CIGIE issues quality standards for the work IGs do, and conformance with these standards is the subject of peer evaluations. Reports from these peer reviews are shared with an IG, the home agency, and Congress. Second, a CIGIE committee also conducts investigations of any alleged wrongdoing by an IG and makes recommendations regarding the allegations and follow-up actions by the home agency.

ENGAGEMENT

Independence does not mean isolation. The Inspector General Act clearly sets expectations for engagement by an IG with leadership in the home agency. These expectations include making recommendations on proposed legislation or regulations relating to programs and operations of the agency. An IG is also expected to make recommendations about the home agency's relationships with other governmental and nongovernmental entities, and the efficiency of the home agency's programs. Additionally, an IG is expected to keep agency leadership and Congress fully informed about discoveries of serious problems and actions needed to correct the problems. An IG is also expected to report on the progress the home agency has made to implement corrective actions the IG has recommended.

None of these activities occur in isolation, and there is considerable interaction between an IG, the home agency, and Congress—especially if the issue is highly charged. Principals talk with each other, exchanging information before, during, or after an audit, investigation, or evaluation. The challenge is doing so in ways that maintain OIG independence, thereby avoiding concerns about whether the IG is deferential to either agency management or Congress—that is, whether the OIG is "captured" by either entity.

Occasionally, engagement is initiated by an IG's stakeholders. Agency management, for example, might bring an issue to an IG for evaluation or investigation—sometimes to provide an independent review involving a politically hot issue. Similarly, Congress might pass legislation mandating that an IG review an issue, and individual members of Congress might request that an IG inquire into a matter of interest. Wanting to be responsive to these important stakeholders, an IG can work with agency management or Congress to clarify the boundaries of the request and the authority he or she might have to explore the issue.

System Stressors

In the U.S. political system, conflicts are routine between branches of the national government, between national and state governments, between political parties, between interest groups, and between public officials. These conflicts may involve differing views of how to address such matters as tax and spend policies, ending poverty and discrimination, government regulations, or the role of the United States in world affairs. Added to these concerns are occasional major events such as financial meltdowns, terrorist attacks, huge natural disasters, and international conflicts, which heighten stresses regarding government response. These events and pressures create stress for public office holders who balance conflicting interests, hold different priorities, and must account for their decisions (or the lack thereof).

As a high-level public official, an IG is not sheltered from these conflicts, and he or she is not immune from these stressors—they are part of an IG's strategic environment. As is the case with stakeholders in that environment and expectations of IGs, system stressors influence what an IG does and the consequences of those actions. While there may be numerous sources of stress for an IG—some idiosyncratic, some episodic, and some personal—we focus in this book on two system stressors that have routinely influenced OIGs since their creation in 1978: (1) shared powers in the U.S. national government and (2) partisan and particular interests of public office holders.

SHARED POWERS

Constitutional scholar Louis Fisher argues that the "American political system operates primarily on the basis of concurrent powers. One branch can do very little without the support and countenance of the others."[13] Fisher describes stresses created by concurrent or shared powers in a variety of areas, including control of the budget, setting foreign and defense policy, and oversight of the bureaucracy. The essence of his review is that members of Congress, executive officers, and (sometimes) judicial officials must come to an agreement by compromise or combat to settle on policies and actions for the national government.

Congressional and executive branch countenance is required in three major areas that constitute critical elements of an IG's strategic environment: (1) the appointment and continued service of an IG, (2) the specification of an IG's authority and resources, and (3) the follow-up on an IG's findings and recommendations. Disagreements involving these elements often create stresses on IGs, collectively and individually, and influence their audits, investigations, and evaluations. Since an IG reports to both an executive official and members of Congress, conflicts involving these primary stakeholders can be critically important and prompt a careful walk on the previously mentioned "barbed wire fence" between executive and congressional officials.

Stresses stemming from shared powers emerge even before an IG is appointed to his or her office. For example, appointments of IGs that require Senate confirmation may be hastened or held up for a variety of reasons by either the president or Congress, sometimes while that individual serves in an "acting" capacity. At other times, the continued service of an IG is called into question by members of Congress while the IG maintains continued support from executive officials.

The legislation creating OIGs required agreement by Congress and the president, and affected the powers of both institutions. In its final form, the IG Act of 1978 sketched out specific authorities and responsibilities of an IG. However, questions have remained, and changes in expectations over time have led to controversies about an IG's authority and responsibility. For example, the IG Act grants unfettered access to most agency documents, but agencies and IGs have disagreed on whether IGs may have access to particular types of documents (for example, grand jury materials).

Budgets present recurring opportunities for shared influence over OIGs. Addressing these concerns in 2008 amendments to the IG Act, Congress created the means for an IG to disagree with budget decisions by an agency head or the president, granting an IG the power to say for the record that the budget is insufficient to carry out the responsibilities of the specific IG's office.

Access issues and budgets are two examples of where and how an IG may find himself or herself pressed between assertive executive officials and assertive members of Congress—and both have shared powers over OIGs. An IG may influence conversations among executive officials, members of Congress, and other stakeholders, but he or she must live with uncertainties and stresses until the controversies are resolved.

In addition, audits, investigations, and evaluations often result in OIG recommendations to an agency for changes that would address inefficiencies or practices that led to alleged fraud, waste, or mismanagement. The agency might agree with the recommendations and have the authority and resources to implement the recommended changes. On the other hand, an agency might disagree with the recommendations, raising the ire of Congress. Or, the recommendations might require congressional action in the form of increased funding or changes in authorizing legislation. In the latter circumstances, agency leadership and members of Congress engage in discussions, conflicts, and compromises regarding the shortcomings identified in a report. In these instances, an IG faces the stress-inducing prospect of intransigence by agency leadership, inaction by Congress, clashes between executive and congressional branches, or broadened discussion of recommendations by various secondary stakeholders who are interested in the issue.

PARTISAN AND PERSONAL INTERESTS OF PUBLIC OFFICE HOLDERS

Beyond conflicts rooted in shared powers, an IG may face conflicts that simply reflect the partisan divides that routinely affect national political institutions. In 2015, at the end of his two decades of service as IG in the Department of Energy, Gregory Friedman commented that the "largely toxic discourse in Washington" is hindering the work of IGs. Friedman goes on to say, "It's a very, very difficult and challenging climate in which the discourse is not very pleasant. The IGs are part of the scene. It's partisan, it's unpleasant. It seems there's a lack of common purpose that may not be helpful."[14]

In addition to partisan divides, a powerful member of Congress may ask an IG to conduct an inquiry on a matter that the individual representative feels is important. On some occasions, a powerful representative may target an IG for intense scrutiny if, for example, the member of Congress believes the IG failed to be sufficiently critical of an agency, was overly critical of that agency, or ignored a situation the representative thought was particularly important. We will see that IGs pay close attention to demands and requests from Congress, and develop strategies to accommodate, avoid, or gently push back such requests.

An IG can also find himself or herself in conflict with agency leadership, which leads to the OIG being isolated or undercut by agency managers, Congress, or other stakeholders. Public accounts of such conflicts are rare. For example, Clark Ervin, the acting IG for the Department of Homeland Security after its creation in 2003, had a highly conflicted relationship with Tom Ridge, secretary of the newly created department. Ridge and Ervin had very different views of what the department's IG should do and the policies and risks the IG should examine. These disagreements produced personal animosities that resulted in Ridge and Ervin meeting infrequently, and tainted communications between DHS staff and the IG. In the end, Ervin's nomination as the permanent IG appears to have been scuttled in 2004 by mutual agreement of the George W. Bush administration and the congressional committee, which did not act on the nomination for nearly two years.[15]

Conclusion

U.S. inspectors general focus on finding fraud, waste, and abuse, and promoting economy and efficiency. Each year, IGs conduct numerous audits, investigations, and evaluations that assess shortcomings of federal officials and federal programs. Recommendations resulting from these inquiries are shared with the IG's federal agency and relevant congressional committees; those recommendations that do not involve national security are posted on websites for public inspection. With some regularity, IG reports lead to congressional hearings and media reports highlighting questionable actions by federal officials. In pursuing this evaluative mission, IGs report to both executive and congressional leaders. Yet, IGs are also expected to be independent and nonpartisan as well as accountable and engaged. These reporting relationships and expectations create a strategic environment that is rooted in the history of the IG Act of 1978 and its subsequent amendments.

The next chapter discusses the development of the IG Act and how it created a distinctive set of environmental pressures, constraints, and challenges for U.S. IGs.

TWO

The Emergence of Independent Overseers of Federal Funds and Bureaucracy

INDEPENDENT OVERSEERS OF FEDERAL FUNDS AND BUREAUCRACY

Mr. President, this is an enormous package—$700 billion. That ain't chicken feed! That is 17 times what we spend annually on health care for our Nation's veterans. That is 14 times what we spend annually on highways and mass transportation. That is more than the annual defense budget, which supplies our troops and fuels our planes and naval vessels around the globe. That is more than the total amount the Federal Government will spend on homeland security over the next 17 years. And that number actually hides the real potential cost because the Treasury Secretary would be authorized to buy and sell an unlimited amount of these troubled assets in the next 2 years.

It is an enormous amount of money. And it involves granting an enormous amount of authority to the Secretary of the Treasury.[1]

—Comments on the Senate floor by
Senator Robert Byrd (D, WV), October 1, 2008

In the wake of the 2008 financial crisis, Senator Robert Byrd (D, WV), like most members of Congress, saw the potential for mismanagement of $700 billion in funding through the Troubled Asset Relief Program (TARP) and wanted assurance that those dollars would be well spent. Moreover, senators wanted accountability for and transparency of decisions regarding the funds. To oversee TARP decisions, Congress required frequent reports by the secretary of the treasury and the comptroller general; established special oversight panels in Congress and the executive branch; and created a special inspector general (IG) for TARP.

In creating a special IG for TARP (SIGTARP), members of Congress turned to a mechanism they believed would guarantee independent audits, investigations, and evaluations of how $700 billion was spent and to what effect. No one from the George W. Bush administration eagerly endorsed the idea of the special IG, but there were no efforts to block its creation. Accordingly, SIGTARP was created by Congress, and reports from the IG's office provided the kind of inside evaluations of TARP that Congress anticipated.[2]

Creation of SIGTARP provides an important point of departure for understanding the strategic environment of inspectors general (IGs). One of the IGs' principal stakeholders, Congress, desires fully independent assessments of the executive branch's financial management and federal programs, as well as reports of fraud and waste, that are unfiltered or shaped by executive officials. Senators and representatives hold Offices of Inspector General (OIGs) in high regard because they are perceived as producing such assessments. Congress has high expectations for the independent and cogent oversight, analysis, and inside information that IGs can provide. The other principal stakeholders, executive officials, often accept IGs as a mixed blessing. On the one hand, an IG provides information that may reveal fraudulent abuses and suggest program improvements, and serves as someone an executive official may turn when his or her agency needs time or information to manage a crisis. But equally possible, an IG may provide analyses that draw the unwanted attention of the media and Congress, shine an unflattering spotlight on the executive agency, and possibly lead to new restrictive or directive legislation and even criminal prosecutions.

This chapter discusses the legal basis of the strategic environment and relationships between IGs and their two principal stakeholders. As this legal basis developed, Congress typically took the lead in expanding the number of agencies with OIGs and strengthening IG authority. However, IGs are executive officials, and the legislative history outlined in this chapter shows that congressional actions have sought to protect IG independence from executive interference and insulate IGs from administrative pressures and political forces in the executive branch of the government. Executive officials are granted loose supervision of IGs, given opportunities to review reports, and have the right to appoint and dismiss IGs with congressional oversight in both instances. Thus, the strategic environment is very much the product of legislative actions creating and supporting OIGs.

Rationale and Politics in Creating Offices of Inspector General

Inspectors general were established in the 1970s to address financial challenges facing the U.S. government. One challenge cited by many IG proponents is captured in the mission of the OIGs—namely, to ferret out fraud, waste, and abuse in the federal government and to advance efficient and effective administration of federal programs. Long-term trends in presidential-congressional relations also influenced OIG legislation that sought to enhance financial management in the executive branch and engage Congress with the emerging modern administrative state.[3]

INADEQUATE RESPONSES BY FEDERAL EXECUTIVE AGENCIES TO GOVERNMENTAL FRAUD AND WASTE

Virtually every government official acknowledges that in spending billions of dollars for government programs, some of those funds are diverted, stolen, spent unwisely, or simply wasted on unworthy programs, projects, people, or purchases. In the mid-twentieth century, scandals involving federal programs revealed by media investigations and congressional oversight hearings generated pressure for the government to create mechanisms to eliminate fraud and waste. Two scandals in particular underscored the need for reforms and pointed the way for attacking fraud and waste in federal programs: the Billy Sol Estes scandal involving the U.S. Department of Agriculture (USDA) in the early 1960s[4] and a variety of fraudulent activities and ineffective auditing capacities in the Department of Health, Education, and Welfare (HEW) in the mid-1970s.[5] By no small coincidence, Representative L. H. Fountain (D, NC) played a key role in both of these episodes, and he went on to champion passage of the 1978 legislation initially creating inspectors general in twelve federal agencies.

Estes defrauded the federal government of millions of dollars through schemes that involved USDA programs in the 1950s and early 1960s. Representative Fountain's congressional subcommittee held hearings that not only revealed deceptions leading to the fraudulent payments to Estes, but also highlighted the ineffective administrative oversight of programs from which he received those payments. As questions about various expenditures emerged over time, administrative units and various officers were shown to be inattentive and ineffective in seeing the larger picture of the fraud pursued by Estes.

In response to the Estes scandal, President Lyndon B. Johnson's Secretary of Agriculture Orville Freeman offered a multipoint plan that included the creation of an inspector general for the department in 1965.[6] While this IG was not the first to be created in the federal government,[7] the office structure and authority of the newly created USDA inspector general bore many characteristics that shaped the IG Act of 1978. Notable features of the new USDA IG office included reporting directly to the secretary and consolidating audit and investigation activities under the IG's authority. Moreover, the IG had the authority to review virtually any activities in the USDA and engage all parties with whom it had business relations.

The USDA's inspector general was not created by congressional action, but instead was created under the general authority of the secretary to organize the department as he deemed appropriate. Accordingly, the IG could be dismissed by the secretary at any moment for any reason, and the office itself could be eliminated or reorganized by the secretary. Indeed, president Richard Nixon's Secretary of Agriculture Earl Butz eliminated the department's IG position in 1974 and reorganized its auditing and investigation divisions. He undertook these actions despite positive reviews of the IG's actions addressing fraud and waste in USDA, including the support of the General Accounting Office (GAO) and various congressional committees.[8] While Butz clearly had the authority to eliminate the IG's office, "the Agriculture experiment was critical to the evolution of the IG concept, if only to establish the need to give the office some measure of independence."[9]

Fourteen years after revealing fraud and waste in the USDA, Senate and House committee investigations documented substantial fraud and ineffective administrative responses in the HEW. Representative Benjamin S. Rosenthal (D, NY), testifying before a subcommittee of the House Committee on Government Operations, called for the creation of an inspector general for HEW. In doing so, he highlighted congressional findings of fraud and waste:

> Examples abound of HEW mismanagement and abuse. Losses in Medicare and Medicaid programs due to waste or fraud reportedly total as much as $3 billion a year, or 10 percent of these programs' overall outlays. . . .
>
> Moreover, enormous amounts of money have been lost because of program mismanagement and abuse. The Senate Aging Subcommittee on Long-Term Care recently reported that HEW, in a manner of speaking, wasted more than $1 billion in reimbursements for unnecessary surgery. . . .
>
> The Federal student loan program is another HEW activity reportedly crippled by fraud, mismanagement, and abuse. The Office of Guaranteed Student Loans, with a total of $3.3 billion in federal insured loans, experienced an 18 percent default rate in fiscal year 1975. . . . These statistics contrast sharply with the 5 to 8 percent default rate under State-guaranteed student loan programs, and 3 percent delinquency rate for consumer loans generally, and the 1 percent rate for mortgage loan delinquencies.[10]

During these deliberations, Representative Fountain also pointed to the inadequate resources and actions by HEW to identify and address fraudulent activities in many of its programs. In an opening statement for the hearing, he said the following:

> HEW's investigative resources were ridiculously inadequate. Its central investigative unit had only ten investigators with a 10-year backlog of uninvestigated cases.
>
> Information needed by both HEW and Congress for effective action against fraud and abuse was simply not available.
>
> Units responsible for combating fraud and abuse were scattered throughout HEW in a haphazard, fragmented, and confusing pattern, with no single unit having the overall responsibility and authority necessary to provide effective leadership.

Personnel of most of these units lacked independence because they reported to and were hired and fired by officials directly responsible for the programs being investigated. Consequently, honest and thorough reports concerning serious problems might often embarrass their own bosses.

Even when serious deficiencies became known to responsible officials, corrective action was sometimes not taken until literally years later.[11]

Table 2-1 summarizes major elements of the 1976 legislation creating an IG for HEW in the wake of these reports. These elements set the general template for IG Act legislation two years later, creating IGs for a dozen federal agencies.

Importantly, the HEW IG legislation ostensibly created an independent auditing and investigative office that would effectively tackle fraud and waste in HEW, thus meeting Fountain's expectations for the IG post. However, some executive agency officials remained skeptical because of concerns about introducing an independent office for auditing and investigations within the agencies. Critics foresaw considerable conflict between an IG's office and the executive agency in which the office was embedded. To address these concerns and to show the potential effectiveness of inspectors general, in 1977 Representative Fountain's subcommittee (which was considering the creation of additional IG offices) gave the newly appointed HEW IG, Thomas D. Morris, and the secretary of HEW, Joseph A. Califano, the opportunity to discuss whether the HEW IG office created conflicts within the department. Their testimony gave no support to these contentions.[12]

HEW's IG provided evidence of the office's effectiveness in rooting out fraud and waste. In particular, Morris announced an initial effort to tackle Medicaid fraud under an initiative entitled Project Integrity and another initiative to investigate welfare fraud under an initiative entitled Project Match.[13] A later Senate committee report on proposed legislation creating OIGs took note of Project Integrity and its success in identifying 535 cases for full investigation and 554 cases for administrative action. The Senate report also highlighted an IG estimate that "between $6.3 and $7.4 billion in HEW funds have been misspent."[14]

TABLE 2-1

Summary of 1976 Legislation Creating the Office of Inspector General for the Department of Health, Education, and Welfare

- Established an OIG within HEW to investigate fraud and abuse in all departmental programs and to conduct audit activities

- Stipulated that the IG would be a presidential appointee subject to Senate approval; allowed only the president to remove the IG from office and required him or her to inform Congress of the reasons for any such firing

- Allowed the IG to use outside auditors to ensure independent investigations

- Required the IG to set up a separate staff within the IGO to investigate abuses in Medicaid, Medicare, and other health programs

- Required the IG to submit annual reports to Congress and the HEW Secretary detailing significant program abuses, progress in combating such abuses, and the outcome of matters referred to prosecutors for action; required special quarterly reports on corrective steps recommended by the IG that had not been taken by the department

- Required the IG to report serious or flagrant problems or abuses immediately to the HEW Secretary and then to Congress within seven days

- Stipulated that reports by the IG should be forwarded to Congress without any further approval or clearance by HEW or other executive agencies

- Gave the IG access to all HEW materials needed to carry out IG responsibilities; gave the IG subpoena power; required reporting to Congress if the IG found that budget cuts seriously hurt the performance of IG duties; required heads of outside agencies to cooperate with requests for information

- Transferred audit and investigation duties of existing HEW offices to the IGO

Source: "HEW Inspector General," *CQ Almanac 1976*, 32nd ed., 561–63. Washington, DC: *Congressional Quarterly*, 1977 (http://library.cqpress.com/cqalmanac/cqal76 -1187277).

Representative Fountain's subcommittee also offered evidence that mechanisms currently in place to address waste and fraud were not up to the task. In 1977 the subcommittee requested information from several cabinet-level departments regarding their auditing and investigation capabilities, to learn how they pursued fraud and waste. Notably, every department had multiple auditing and investigating units, most of them operating separately rather than as a single, consolidated unit within a department. Often there were additional units engaged in audits or investigations beyond those identified as an agency's principal organizations for those purposes. In most instances, the staff numbers were small or perceived as inadequate, and in virtually all agencies the auditors or investigators reported to an official other than the lead official or deputy in the agency. Responses to subcommittee questionnaires sent to agencies about their auditing and investigation units and testimony before the committee revealed a variety of efforts to ferret out fraud and waste. While all these agencies voiced opposition or significant concerns regarding the legislation to create independent OIGs, some witnesses also acknowledged that greater staff numbers, expanded authority, or more independence might allow auditors and investigators to be more effective. In the end, Representative Fountain concluded that a change was needed:

> The subcommittee found serious deficiencies in auditing and investigative organization, procedures, and resources, such as:
>
> - Multiple audit or investigative units within a single agency, organized in fragmented fashion and without effective central leadership;
> - Auditors and investigators reporting to officials who were responsible for the programs under review or were devoting only a fraction of their time to audit and investigative responsibilities;
> - Lack of affirmative programs to look for possible fraud or abuse; some agencies did not even require employees to report evidence of irregularities;
> - Instances in which investigators had been kept from looking into suspected irregularities, or even ordered to discontinue an ongoing investigation;
> - Potential fraud cases which had not been sent to the Department of Justice for prosecution;
> - Serious shortages of audit and investigative personnel, even though such personnel repay many times their cost in savings and recoveries; and

- Several agencies admitted they had only one-third to one-fifth the number of auditors or investigators needed.[15]

Paul Light rightly draws attention to what he calls the "three horse-men of the IG concept: fraud, waste, and abuse" in accounting for passage of the IG Act of 1978, though he also points to additional factors that promoted its adoption.[16] Clearly, legislative hearings in House and Senate committees revealed extraordinary examples of fraud and waste. More-over, legislators became convinced that as currently structured, executive agencies were not adequately or aggressively addressing the numerous and costly examples of fraud and waste that had been revealed. The success of IGs appointed in the USDA and HEW provided positive examples for legislators and foreshadowed adoption of the IG Act of 1978.

Trends in Presidential-Congressional Relations

Congressional outcry regarding fraud, waste, and mismanagement in the 1960s and 1970s provided a strong impetus for adoption of the inspec-tors general concept at the federal level. A broader perspective, however, suggests that the 1978 legislation is also part of two related efforts to influence executive actions throughout much of the twentieth century: (1) the drive for improved financial management and greater accountabil-ity for federal government operations, and (2) an elevated congressional engagement with executive activities through legislative oversight. There is no evidence of a grand plan by Congress or others to impose greater financial management and oversight of executive actions, but clearly there were common motivations underlying a series of actions by Congress that included passage of the 1978 IG legislation.[17]

IMPROVING FINANCIAL MANAGEMENT
AND ASSURING ACCOUNTABILITY

Most discussions of financial management and accountability at the fed-eral level in the twentieth century begin by highlighting the 1921 Budget and Accounting Act and the 1950 Budget and Accounting Procedures

Act. The former legislation reshuffled the organizational structures that oversaw financial activities of the federal government—a shift that Frederick Mosher characterized as "an innovation of major proportions . . . [for which] there was very little precedent."[18] Changes brought about by the 1921 legislation included (a) granting the President authority to develop the federal budget working through and with the Bureau of the Budget (BoB), forerunner of the current Office of Management and Budget (OMB), and (b) authorizing the GAO to manage accounting processes for congressionally approved appropriations and expenditures by executive agencies. The comptroller general and accompanying accounting responsibilities were moved out of the Department of the Treasury to the independent GAO. The comptroller, as head of the GAO, would be appointed for a fixed term of fifteen years by the president with the advice and consent of the Senate, but could be dismissed by a joint resolution of Congress. The comptroller general and the GAO would primarily report to Congress on the expenditures that followed its appropriation process to assure they were "proper, accurate, and legal."[19]

As the scope and size of federal programs grew in response to the Great Depression and World War II, BoB and the GAO grew in size and responsibility. As the accounting and auditing agency, GAO's workload and number of personnel increased rapidly because the agency had responsibility for overseeing 400,000 different accounts and millions of dollars in expenditures. This workload significantly limited the GAO's ability to look at the larger picture of program effectiveness and overall economy in government operations. The 1950 Budget and Accounting Procedures Act kept BoB and the GAO in operation but reconceived and shifted their responsibilities. BoB (and the president) became more central to the development, organization, and management of the federal budget. Additionally, a new budgeting approach meant that most proposed expenditures "related to larger functions and programs, rather than detailed [appropriations] . . . based on things and services purchased. Attention was directed more to work done and outputs than to prices paid for inputs."[20]

Among changes for the GAO stemming from the 1950 legislation, two were particularly significant with respect to financial management and accountability. First, accounting and auditing responsibilities were shifted to the executive agencies that expended federal dollars and required agency-specific accounting systems for agency managers. Second, while the GAO no longer had responsibility for centralized accounting operations, the 1950 legislation provided that the "Comptroller General, after consulting the secretary of the treasury and the director of the budget, [would] prescribe the accounting principles and standards for agency systems and for integrating them with the general financial requirements of the Treasury Department."[21] In essence, the GAO gave up the detailed accounting and auditing role that its 14,000 employees had assumed under the 1921 legislation in the wake of federal expenditures relating to the Great Depression and WWII. This shift resulted in a much smaller agency that focused on establishing standards for accounting and auditing, and evaluating whether and how well agencies were meeting those standards.[22]

Passage of the 1921 and 1950 legislation set the stage for what Paul Light characterizes as a war on waste that emerged in the 1970s. At mid-twentieth century the executive branch was expected to manage federal expenditures "from appropriation to final audit,"[23] and the GAO set standards that agencies should follow in meeting this expectation. Later actions by the executive branch, Congress, and the GAO created mechanisms for identifying and eliminating wasteful spending, and mismanagement. Ironically, these initiatives revealed how difficult the war on waste was likely to be and the need for further actions to win the war. Adair and Simmons highlight several key events that followed the 1950 legislation relating to internal auditing and investigations that involved Congress and the GAO:

1957 The GAO issues a comprehensive statement of principles and concepts to assist federal agencies in developing internal audit organizations and procedures

1963 The U.S. House of Representatives Committee on Government Operations reports that the internal audit system recommended by the GAO has not been widely adopted and that inadequate staffing compromises this functionality

1966–70 The GAO issues 42 reports on internal audit activities arguing that there was greater need for centralization, more auditors, and closer follow-up to recommendations[24]

These actions by the GAO, and the comptroller's reports on shortcomings in accounting systems throughout the federal government, arguably contributed to what Light[25] identifies as one of four tides of reform aimed at winning the war on waste. As noted previously, IGs in the USDA and in HEW were created in this same period in response to widely publicized reports of financial mismanagement in these agencies. The IG Act of 1978 is one of several congressional initiatives from this era that Light identifies as establishing either new responsibilities or new mechanisms to assure sound financial management. Indeed, by Light's analysis, 37 percent of the thirty reform laws passed between 1975 and 1984 involved the war on waste legislation, followed by 28 percent of forty-five such laws from 1985 to 1994, and 21 percent of twenty-eight laws passed from 1995 to 2002. These percentages are in stark contrast to the period from 1945 to 1964, during which Congress passed virtually no legislation dealing with fraud, waste, or mismanagement.[26]

Between 1974 and 1994, legislation aimed at improving financial management included the 1974 Budget Control and Impoundment Act; creation of statutory IGs in HEW (1976) and the Department of Energy (1977); Inspector General Act (1978); Federal Manager Financial Integrity Act (1982); Whistleblower Protection Act (1989); Chief Financial Officer Act (1990); Government Performance and Results Act (1993); and Government Management Reform Act (1994). Significantly, several laws passed after 1978 assigned new responsibilities to IGs, effectively broadening their authority and continuing the key role of the IGs in financial management plans embraced by war-on-waste legislation. This period also saw legislation that extended the IG concept to all cabinet-level agencies, plus amendments in 1988 that created OIGs in many large-to-moderate-sized noncabinet agencies—essentially doubling the number of statutory OIGs in federal agencies. Table 2-2 lists the agencies receiving OIGs since 1978, including the creation of short-term, specialized offices for major spending programs in Iraq, Afghanistan, and TARP.

In opening remarks at a 1994 Senate committee hearing on government reform, Senator John Glenn (R, OH) captures the coordinated efforts surrounding financial management legislation (and his frustration with the progress to date):

Today the Committee on Governmental Affairs meets, as it has many times before, to discuss improvements to the management and performance of the Federal Government. For many years, the Governmental Affairs Committee has worked to carry out the mandate of improving the efficiency and organization of government. . . .

I believe we have obtained considerable success, including things such as the Chief Financial Officers Act and expansion of the Inspectors General to almost all agencies and departments of government. Now we have to make them work.

With the CFO Act, agencies will, for the first time, give year-end audited statements of what works and what doesn't work. . . .

With the IG, we are doing very well in ferreting out fraud, waste, and abuse. Last year, we had some 2,296 successful prosecutions and recouped about [US]$1 billion, and that is just the start.

While little heralded, I believe these are key building blocks toward any successful revamping of government and are necessary to restore public confidence that tax dollars are wisely and productively spent.

Unfortunately, we still have a long way to go.[27]

ASSERTING CONGRESSIONAL OVERSIGHT OF AND ENGAGEMENT WITH EXECUTIVE ACTIONS

Allied with efforts to improve financial management and reduce fraud in federal programs in the late twentieth century, Congress also sought to limit executive powers and to assert its active engagement with the administration of federal programs. Allen Schick's review of congressional actions during this time leads him to argue that the "[t]he 1970s was a boom period for enactment of limitations on executive power." Schick argues that Congress narrowed executive powers and "also established procedures to monitor or to enforce executive compliance."[28]

Congressional actions in the 1970s were part of that institution's reaction to the widespread view that executive powers had increased dramatically in the early- and mid-twentieth century. David Rosenbloom argues that Congress responded in three ways to "reposition itself in the separation-of-powers system . . . [1] treating agencies as adjuncts for legislative functions; [2] reorganizing itself to enhance its legislative and oversight capacities; and [3] improving its ability to intercede in admin-

TABLE 2-2

Offices of Inspector General (OIGs), Creation Dates, Appointment Type, and Current Status (2019)

Year OIG Created	Inspectors General Nominated by the President and Confirmed by the Senate	Inspectors General Appointed by Agency Head or Other Entity and Senate Confirmation Is Not Required
1976	Health, Education, and Welfare (subsequently brought under the 1978 IG Act with passage of this legislation)	
1977	Energy (subsequently brought under the 1978 IG Act with passage of this legislation)	
1978	Agriculture, Commerce, *Community Services Administration (CSA)**, Health and Human Services (previously established in 1976 under Health, Education, and Welfare (HEW)), Housing and Urban Development, Interior, Labor, Transportation, Environmental Protection Agency, General Services Administration, National Aeronautics and Space Administration, Small Business Administration, Veterans Administration (now the Veterans Affairs Department)	
1979	Education	
1980	*U.S. Synthetic Fuels Corporation**, State	
1981	Agency for International Development	
1982	Defense	
1983	Railroad Retirement Board	
1986	*U.S. Information Agency**	

Year	Agency
1987	*Arms Control and Disarmament Agency**
1988	Justice, Treasury, *Federal Emergency Management Agency**, Nuclear Regulatory Commission, Office of Personnel Management
	*ACTION**, Amtrak, Appalachian Regional Commission, *Board of International Broadcasting**, Commodity Futures Trading Commission, Consumer Product Safety Commission, Corporation for Public Broadcasting, Equal Employment Opportunity Commission, Farm Credit Administration, Federal Communications Commission*, Federal Deposit Insurance Corporation*, *Federal Election Commission, Federal Home Loan Bank Board*, Federal Housing Finance Board** (Succeeded Federal Home Loan Bank Board), Federal Labor Relations Authority, Federal Maritime Commission, Federal Trade Commission*, Government Printing Office, *Interstate Commerce Commission**, Legal Services Corporation, National Archives and Records Administration, National Credit Union Administration, National Endowment for the Arts, National Endowment for the Humanities, National Labor Relations Board, National Science Foundation, *Panama Canal Commission**, Peace Corps, Pension Benefit Guarantee Corporation, Securities and Exchange Commission, Smithsonian Institution, Tennessee Valley Authority*, U.S. International Trade Commission
1989	*Resolution Trust Corporation**, Central Intelligence Agency
1993	Corporation for National and Community Service, Federal Deposit Insurance Corporation (originally DFE OIG)
1994	Social Security Administration, *Community Development Financial Institutions Fund**
1996	U.S. Postal Service
1998	Denali Commission
1998	Treasury Inspector General for Tax Administration
2000	Tennessee Valley Authority (originally DFE OIG)
2002	Export-Import Bank, Homeland Security
2002	Election Assistance Commission
2004	*Iraq Reconstruction** (succeeded Coalition Provisional Authority [2003])
2005	Library of Congress, U.S. Capitol Police

Offices of Inspector General (OIGs), Creation Dates, Appointment Type, and Current Status (2019) (cont.)

Year OIG Created	Inspectors General Nominated by the President and Confirmed by the Senate	Inspectors General Appointed by Agency Head or Other Entity and Senate Confirmation Is Not Required
2007		Architect of the Capitol, Postal Regulatory Commission
2008	Federal Housing Finance Agency (succeeded Federal Home Loan Bank Board and Federal Housing Finance Board (originally DFE OIG)), Afghanistan Reconstruction**, Troubled Asset Relief Program	Government Accountability Office
2010	Office of Director of National Intelligence (IG of Intelligence Community)	Defense Intelligence Agency, National Geospatial-Intelligence Agency, National Reconnaissance Office,* National Security Agency*
2014	National Reconnaissance Office (originally DFE OIG); National Security Agency (originally DFE OIG)	
2016		Committee for Purchase from People Who Are Blind or Severely Disabled (AbilityOne Program)
2018	Federal Communications Commission	U.S. International Development Finance Cooperation

Source: Ginsberg and Green (2016, pp. 15–18). Added to Ginsberg and Green listing is the OIG for Committee for Purchase from People Who Are Blind or Severely Disabled (AbilityOne Program), created by the Consolidated Appropriations Act, 2016, Title IV, Section 401 (P.L. 114–113), and the U.S. International Development Finance Corporation, created by the Better Utilization of Investments Leading to Development Act of 2018 (P.L. 115–254). The FCC OIG was shifted to become a PAS OIG (P.L. 115–141). Current OIGs as of 2019 are listed in Francis (2019a).

*Department, agency, or unit has been eliminated or changed and the associated IG office as originally authorized has been closed (indicated by italics) or the original DFE OIG has been shifted to PAS status (not italicized).

**Presidential appointment only, does not require Senate confirmation.

istrative decisionmaking to promote the specific interests of its members' constituents and districts."[29]

Two legislative acts passed in 1946 asserted Congress's authority over executive agencies and laid the basis for later legislation asserting congressional authority: the Administrative Procedures Act (APA) and the Legislative Reorganization Act (LRA). The APA specified procedures and processes by which administrative agencies were to make rules, enforce and adjudicate those rules, and do so with transparency. With this legislation, Congress asserted its authority to set agency procedures; established statutory expectations for administrative agencies to engage in open processes for rulemaking that allowed interested stakeholders to know of and comment about potential rules; and mandated consideration of those comments emerging from this process.[30]

After passage of the APA, Congress passed additional legislation that enhanced congressional control over executive agencies, the authority those agencies exercised, and processes the agencies were required to follow. Table 2-3 presents Rosenbloom's summaries of key legislation that "reflect[s] the purposes of and strengthen[s]" the 1946 APA. Significantly, Rosenbloom views the IG Act of 1978 as one of those key statutes extending Congress's authority over executive agencies—part of a trend in defining executive-legislative relations in the latter half of the twentieth century.

The Legislative Reorganization Act of 1946 (LRA 1946) focused internally on Congress itself but had the effect of increasing its leverage over the executive agencies. This act restructured the congressional committees and their jurisdictions, and directed that standing committees "exercise continuous watchfulness of the executive by the administrative agencies concerned of any laws, the subject matter of which is within the jurisdiction of such committee; and, for that purpose, shall study all pertinent reports and data submitted to Congress by the agencies in the executive branch of Government."[31]

A key phrase in this section of the act, "exercise continuous watchfulness," set expectations for and clearly established the authority of Congress to oversee administrative actions. Joel Aberbach's review of this legislation leads him to conclude that Congress "set a very high standard

888

for itself" with the expectation that oversight activities "take up a significant share of any committee's time and effort."[32] LRA 1946 also provided staff support for committees, thus allowing them to conduct investigations and initiate legislation independent of the executive branch.[33]

Congress's ability to pursue oversight of federal administrative agencies was further enhanced by the Legislative Reorganization Act of 1970 (LRA 1970). This act specified that "each standing committee shall review and study, on a continuing basis, the application, administration, and execution of those laws or parts of laws, the subject matter of which is within the jurisdiction of that committee."[34] It also required biennial oversight reports from most committees and increased the number of

TABLE 2-3
Illustrative Legislation Furthering Congressional Control
and Leverage over Federal Administrative Agencies

- Freedom of Information Act (1966, significantly amended in 1974)—created a requester model for obtaining government records and mandates timely responsiveness

- National Environmental Policy Act (1970)—required agencies to develop environmental impact statements for major projects affecting the environment

- Congressional Budget and Impoundment Act (1974)—strengthened Congress's role in developing the federal budget and controls presidential impoundment of appropriated funds

- Privacy Act (1974)—limited federal agencies' authority to collect and release information on individuals

- Government in the Sunshine Act (1976)—required commissioners and board members of multiheaded federal agencies to hold open meetings

- Inspector General Act (1978)—established statutory offices of inspector general in 12 federal agencies, regulated appointment and authority of inspectors general, and mandated reporting to Congress

- Regulatory Flexibility Act (1980)—required agencies to assess the impact of potential rules on small businesses

permanent staff members for each standing committee. The 1970 legislation strengthened responsibilities of the GAO and the Legislative Reference Service (renamed the Congressional Research Service) for program evaluation and analysis. The net effect of these expanded responsibilities was to increase independent information provided to Congress for legislative and oversight activities.[35]

Four years later, the 1974 Congressional Budget Act further expanded the authority of committees by permitting them to review and evaluate programs using committee members and staff, by contract, or by requiring the government agency to follow through and report to Congress. Additionally, the 1974 legislation authorized the comptroller general to

---

- Administrative Dispute Resolution Acts (1990, 1996)—established procedures that federal agencies can use to settle disputes by means other than adjudication

- Negotiated Rulemaking Act (1990)—provided mechanism for agencies to negotiate rules with stakeholders

- Government Performance and Results Act (1993)—required agencies to engage in strategic planning with congressional consultation, performance measurement, and performance reporting to Congress

- Congressional Review Act (1996)—created procedures by which Congress can block and overturn agency rules

- Assessment of Federal Regulations and Policies on Families Act (1998)—required agencies to assess the impact of their actions on family concerns

- Data Quality Act (2000)—sought to improve the quality of data on which administrative rulemaking relies

Source: Rosenbloom (2010, pp. 116–117).

conduct program evaluations at his or her initiative or at the request of a congressional committee.[36] Notably, the Congressional Research Service in 1978 developed the "Congressional Oversight Manual" following a three-day workshop on this topic and has continued publishing updated manuals.[37] In particular, the manual details statutory authority, processes, and oversight techniques to inform members of Congress, committees, and staff about oversight activities. The OIGs are listed among the resources available for oversight activities.[38]

An empirical assessment of congressional oversight by Joel Aberbach during this period shows a marked increase in oversight hearings. He reports that in his sample of committee work in the first six months of odd-numbered years from 1961 through 1983, oversight activities increased from 146 to 587 "oversight days." Another measure showed that oversight behavior expanded from 8.25 percent of the total hearings in 1961 to 25.1 percent of the total hearings in 1983. A marked increase in the number and percentage of oversight activities occurred in the mid-1970s. Aberbach's data show an average of 170 oversight days from 1961 to 1971; 290 oversight days in 1973; and an average of 504 oversight days from 1975 to 1983. Similarly, the percentage of total hearings devoted to oversight increased from an average of 7.3 percent from 1961 to 1971; 11.5 percent in 1973; and an average of 20.0 percent from 1975 to 1983.[39]

The increased expectations for oversight and actual oversight activities required increased staffing, as well as greater access to and analysis of information. Congressional staff increased in size during the 1970s, but increases were not dramatically large after 1977. In fact, congressional staff for committees actually decreased from 2,027 staff members in 1979 to 1,164 staff members in 2015.[40] Reflecting the decline during the 1980s, Light reports that staff for subcommittees, where much of the oversight work is done, did not increase commensurate with responsibilities and expectations.[41] He goes on to argue that IGs became vital to the operations of subcommittees pursuing legislative oversight, noting that IG appearances before subcommittees increased substantially from 1977 to 1988. Light quotes a legislative staffer as follows: "The IGs are often the number one or number two witness at the subcommittee level and are always well prepared. With the number of hearings that go on each day up here reaching the dozens, if not hundreds, having a reliable front witness is a big advantage, especially at the subcommittee level where it may be the IG or no one at all."[42] Another key legislative player is quoted by Light as focused on the important role of IGs as officers who were closer to the agencies and who were obligated to keep both the agency head and Congress informed about that agency's activities:

> The IG Act basically moved Congress from retail into wholesale. One of the basic reasons for adopting the idea was that we had been busting our butts to cover even a fraction of our agencies. It wasn't that we couldn't get information, but it was always like pulling teeth. The IGs gave us a middleman in the system, someone who would give us regular input though the semi-annual reports and irregular access through the development of good working relationships. It wasn't our only source of information by any means, but it cut down on some of the spade work we would have to do, and let us go directly to more detailed investigations.[43]

Placing an agent such as an inspector general in the midst of agencies reporting to Congress can be viewed as part of the strategy discussed by Epstein and O'Halloran, by which Congress constrains executive discretion. These researchers found that government had, indeed, expanded its role and scope during the 1947–1991 time frame they analyzed, and that delegated authority had remained relatively constant, but discretion by executive agencies had decreased due to empowering other actors to intervene in decisionmaking. Though not mentioned directly by Epstein and O'Halloran, auditing and investigative organizations such as OIGs and the GAO are rightly viewed as components of Congress's strategy to export watchfulness and to limit executive agency discretion.[44]

Provisions of the IG Act of 1978 required that the IG be a nonpolitical appointment; provided that the IG could conduct audits and investigations unencumbered by agency leadership; guaranteed access to information from within the agency; and required that the IG keep the agency head *and* Congress informed through semiannual and, as appropriate, immediate reports. Though these provisions may not have been aimed at providing a source of support for oversight activities, they clearly contributed to these efforts and reflected the prevailing trend of congressional actions seeking to counter the perception or reality of an executive branch operating solely under the direction of the chief executive.

Contemporary OIG Authority, Responsibility, and Organization

U.S. Offices of Inspector General have grown in number, size, and complexity since their initial authorization in 1978 and major amendments to the original legislation in 1988, 2008, and 2016. The net effect of this legislation has been the institutionalization of IGs as watchdogs for fraud, waste, and abuse, and promoters of efficiency, economy, and integrity in government. Moreover, the independence of OIGs from the politics and agency control that marked creation of these offices has also been strengthened in later legislation, and their responsibilities and authority have increased relative to their respective agencies.

Table 2-2 lists the agencies for which IGs were created by year. The original 1978 legislation created IGs for eleven cabinet-level agencies and incorporated two previously created IGs from the Department of Energy and the HEW under the statute. The departments of Justice, State, and Defense held off the creation of IGs in their respective agencies for a few years, arguing that constitutional issues and the departments' distinctive roles precluded establishment of OIGs in their agencies. In the following decade, however, these three departments and several major agencies were given IGs despite their opposition to or lack of enthusiasm for creation of OIGs in their organizations.[45] All of these IGs were appointed by the president and confirmed by the U.S. Senate.

Major legislation in 1988 introduced a new group of IGs in noncabinet-level agencies and designated a new process by which these IGs were appointed. These new OIGs were created for large to moderately sized, noncabinet-level federal agencies that were termed "designated federal entities" by the legislation and the IGs in those agencies are referenced as DFE IGs. A total of thirty-four DFE agencies were assigned new OIGs, of which twenty-five remain largely in place.[46] Under the 1988 legislation, DFE IGs are not appointed by the president, but instead they are appointed by their agency head and the appointment does not require Senate confirmation. Thus there are currently two different groups of IGs—presidentially appointed, senate confirmed IGs (PAS IGs) and agency head appointed IGs (DFE IGs)—each with essentially the same authority and responsibility.

After the 1988 legislation, several PAS and DFE IGs were added to the roster of OIGs as listed in table 2-2. Several of these new additions were authorized in legislation separate from the IG Act of 1978, but essentially had the same responsibilities and authority.[47] Additionally, several OIGs were eliminated (identified in table 2-2 in italics) because their home agency was eliminated or changed, resulting in the closing of the IG office. Finally, on several occasions Congress enacted legislation redesignating several DFE OIGs as PAS OIGs, which means that instead of having the agency appoint the IG, he or she is now appointed by the president and confirmed by the Senate.

Both PAS and DFE IGs are appointed "without regard to political affiliation and solely on the basis of integrity and demonstrated ability in accounting, auditing, financial analysis, law, management analysis, public administration, or investigations."[48] With a few exceptions written into statutory language regarding IGs for specific agencies, IG appointments are open ended. That is, IGs leave office only by their own decision to resign or by dismissal by the president (for PAS IGs) or by the agency head (for DFE IGs). If an IG is dismissed, the president or the agency head must inform Congress of this action and state the reasons for the removal. Legislation in 2008 changed this reporting requirement to mandate that the president or the agency head inform Congress 30 days in advance of any terminations or shift of an IG from his or her position.

AUTHORITY

IGs are members of the executive branch, but they are granted substantial freedom to pursue their work independent of direction from or interference by any executive official—including the president or their respective agency head. Table 2-4 summarizes the statutory authority granted to OIGs, effectively making these offices independent within their respective agencies. (Some OIGs have special legislative provisions regarding their authority, as with the special IG for TARP.)[49]

In addition to the grants of authority listed in table 2-4, OIG independence is enhanced by the statutory provision that "each Office of Inspector

TABLE 2-4

Key Statutory Authority and Responsibilities of U.S. Inspectors General

AUTHORITY:

- Have access to all records, reports, audits, reviews, documents, papers, recommendations, or other material available to [the home agency] which relate to programs and operations with respect to which that Inspector General has responsibilities under this [legislation]

- Make such investigations and reports relating to the administration of the programs and operations of {the home agency] as are, in the judgment of the Inspector General, necessary or desirable

- Request such information or assistance as may be necessary for carrying out the duties and responsibilities provided by this Act from any Federal, State, or local governmental agency or unit thereof

- Require by subpoena the production of all information, documents, reports, answers, records, accounts, papers, and other data in any medium (including electronically stored information, as well as any tangible thing) and documentary evidence necessary in the performance of the functions assigned by this [legislation]

- Administer to or take from any person an oath, affirmation, or affidavit, whenever necessary in the performance of the functions assigned by this [legislation]

- Have direct and prompt access to the head of the establishment involved when necessary for any purpose pertaining to the performance of functions and responsibilities under this [legislation]

- Select, appoint, and employ such officers and employees as may be necessary for carrying out the functions, powers, and duties of the Office

- Upon request of an Inspector General for information or assistance . . . the head of any Federal agency involved shall . . . furnish to such Inspector General, or to an authorized designee, such information or assistance; . . . Whenever information or assistance requested [under this legislation] is, in the judgment of an Inspector General, unreasonably refused or not provided, the Inspector General shall report the circumstances to the head of [the home agency] involved without delay

- Each Inspector General, any Assistant Inspector General for Investigations under such an Inspector General, and any special agent supervised by such an Assistant Inspector General may be authorized by the Attorney General to . . . carry a firearm while engaged in official duties . . . ; make an arrest without a warrant while engaged in official duties . . . ; [and] seek and execute warrants for arrest, search of a premises, or seizure of evidence issued under the authority of the United States upon probable cause to believe that a violation has been committed

RESPONSIBILITIES:

- Provide policy direction for and to conduct, supervise, and coordinate audits and investigations relating to the programs and operations

- Review existing and proposed legislation and regulations relating to programs and operations of such establishment

- Make recommendations in the semiannual reports required by [this legislation] concerning the impact of such legislation or regulations on the economy and efficiency in the administration of programs and operations administered or financed by [the home agency] for the prevention and detection of fraud and abuse in such programs and operations

- Recommend policies for, and to conduct, supervise, or coordinate other activities carried out or financed by [the agency] for the purpose of promoting economy and efficiency in the administration of, or preventing and detecting fraud and abuse in, its programs and operations

- Recommend policies for, and to conduct, supervise, or coordinate relationships between such establishment and other Federal agencies, State and local governmental agencies, and nongovernmental entities with respect to (A) all matters relating to the promotion of economy and efficiency in the administration of, or the prevention and detection of fraud and abuse in, programs and operations administered or financed by such establishment, or (B) the identification and prosecution of participants in such fraud or abuse

- Keep the head of such establishment and the Congress fully and currently informed, by means of the reports required by [this legislation] and otherwise, concerning fraud and other serious problems, abuses, and deficiencies relating to the administration of programs and operations administered or financed by [the home agency], to recommend corrective action concerning such problems, abuses, and deficiencies, and to report on the progress made in implementing such corrective action

Source: Inspector General Act of 1978, amended; items quoted directly from sections 4 and 6.

General shall be considered to be a separate agency." This authority gives IGs substantial administrative control to create positions, make appointments, and carry out duties that are routinely held by agency heads.[50] Legislation in 2008 enhanced this administrative flexibility by granting IGs increased authority in personnel matters, including direct access to the Office of Personnel Management (OPM) instead of working with their respective agency's human resources office on personnel matters.[51]

Each OIG has a separate budget, and an OIG's funding cannot be easily altered by agency leadership after enactment of the federal budget. The 2008 legislation elevated the visibility of OIG budgetary needs by alerting every organization in the budget-making process. As before, OIG budget requests are subject to review and adjustment by the agency head, OMB, and the president, but the original budget request by an OIG is now reported throughout the process and to Congress. Moreover, the IG may now comment about any reductions in funding levels if the president's recommended budget "would substantially inhibit the Inspector General from performing the duties of the office."[52] This special treatment of OIG budget requests is unlike virtually all such requests from bureau or division directors in the federal government.

Significant authority and independence stem from sections in the IG Act providing that an IG may initiate inquiries and issue reports "relating to programs and operations [of that IG's home agency] as are, in the judgment of the Inspector General, necessary and desirable."[53] Moreover, the IG Act holds that an IG has "access to all records, reports, audits, reviews, documents, papers, recommendations, or other material available to [the home agency] which relate to [the agency's] program and operations" and may request or subpoena information and "administer to or take from any person an oath, affirmation, or affidavit" that is necessary to pursue IG-initiated investigations.

Access to government records, on the other hand, has been a source of much controversy, with conflicting interpretations of the extent to which an IG may gain access to sensitive agency documents.[54] In an August 5, 2014, letter signed by forty-seven inspectors general and directed to the chairs and ranking members of the Senate and House oversight committees, the IGs claimed that interpretations of the law by agency officials challenged that authority, constrained the IGs' ability to conduct their work, and interfered with their independence as specified by the IG Act of 1978. The letter pointed to restrictive interpretations in three agencies—the Peace Corps, the Environmental Protection Agency (EPA), and the Department of Justice (DOJ)—which the IGs argued "represent potentially serious challenges to the authority of every Inspector General and our ability to conduct our work thoroughly, independently, and in a timely manner."[55]

Discussions surrounding the charges that agencies were narrowly interpreting IG access to documents led to congressional hearings and eventual adoption of provisions in the Inspector General Empowerment Act of 2016.[56] These provisions affirm "timely access" to information held by the agency. Additionally, section 5 outlines processes an IG may undertake if he or she is denied access to federal grand jury documents by an agency or the DOJ—a point of contention raised by DOJ IG Michael Horowitz in earlier testimony before the House Committee on Oversight and Government Reform on September 10, 2014.

OIGs also have investigation authority that may lead to criminal prosecutions by the DOJ and U.S. Attorneys. This authority has been enhanced over time by granting OIG investigative agents the authority to carry weapons and make arrests under some circumstances. The Homeland Security Act of 2002 clarified and extended these privileges to most OIG investigators. When joined with OIG authority to investigate agency activities and personnel, the expanded law enforcement authority of OIGs may in some respects exceed the authority of other federal law enforcement agencies.[57]

RESPONSIBILITIES

To assure that IGs are accountable to both their agencies and to Congress, a major responsibility of IGs is to keep their agency heads and Congress "fully and currently informed" about OIG work (see table 2-4). Thus, IGs are guaranteed to "have direct and prompt access to the head of [the agency] when necessary for any purpose pertaining to the performance of functions and responsibilities" detailed in the IG Act. Additionally, IGs are required to file semiannual reports to Congress through their respective agency head. Over time, amendments to the IG Act have detailed what information IGs must provide about their work, including problems they discover in their audits, investigations, and evaluations; recommendations they make to resolve the problems; and whether their recommendations are adopted by the agency.[58] Additionally, detailed statistical information is required about cost savings, recommended funds put to better use, the number of investigations and prosecutions, and disbarments of contractors doing business with the agency. Agency heads must review the report regarding their respective agency; the agency head cannot change the report but may add comments as he or she submits the report to Congress. Finally, amendments in 2008 to the Inspector General Act expand the transparency of what IGs do by requiring that semiannual reports to Congress (SARCs) and individual audit reports be posted on the OIG website. This public posting requirement was seen as increasing accountability to the groups interested in the agency's work and to the general public.

Additional responsibilities call on IGs "to provide policy direction for and to conduct, supervise, and coordinate audits and investigations related to the programs and operations" of the agency; to recommend policies that promote "economy and efficiency" in the agency and in its relations with other governmental units; and to review existing and proposed legislation and regulations. IGs are instructed to comply with auditing standards promulgated by the GAO and to avoid duplicating its activities. IGs are also instructed to "report expeditiously to the Attorney General [of the United States] whenever the Inspector General has reasonable grounds to believe there has been a violation of Federal criminal law."[59]

In addition to the responsibilities outlined in the 1978 statute and later amendments, IGs have been assigned responsibilities by Congress in major legislation passed. These additional responsibilities include directing IGs to perform or oversee audits within their respective agencies for financial statements required under the Chief Financial Officers Act of 1990 and the Government Management Reform Act of 1994.[60, 61] Implementing the Federal Financial Management Improvement Act of 1996, the OMB directed IGs (and agency chief financial officers) to assist with determining whether the financial management systems comply with federal laws and regulations. Legislation in 2000, the Reports Consolidation Act, requires that IGs identify the most serious management and performance challenges facing their respective agencies and discuss how their agency is addressing those challenges.[62] And the Federal Information Security Management Act of 2002 requires that IGs perform independent annual evaluations of their respective agency's IG cybersecurity.[63]

The Whistleblower Protection Act of 2012 instructs IGs to "designate a Whistleblower Protection Ombudsman" to inform agency employees about their rights as whistleblowers and protections against retaliation.[64] This act strengthens a provision in the original 1978 legislation, which authorized IGs to "receive and investigate complaints or information from an employee [of the agency] concerning the possible existence of an activity constituting a violation of law, rules, or regulations, or mismanagement, gross waste of funds, abuse of authority, or a substantial and specific danger to public health and safety."[65] The 2008 legislation also requires that OIG websites include a link for individuals to report fraud, waste, and abuse. Once again, OIGs were given clear authority to receive information from (and perhaps to encourage) whistleblowers in an agency and to act on that information under the umbrella of independent authority granted by the original 1978 legislation.

While IGs are held to account by the requirement that they report fully and currently to the agency head and to Congress, this requirement also provides an important tool for IGs to draw attention to issues that need immediate attention. To assure that Congress is informed of such issues, the IG Act of 1978 provides that if an IG encounters difficulties performing his or her duties and the issue requires immediate attention, the IG may send what is known as a "seven-day letter" to the agency head, who must share the letter with Congress within seven days, thus underscoring the urgency and seriousness of the matter. However, a report by the GAO in 2011 found that seven-day letters are rarely used by IGs because urgent issues are usually settled informally within the agency. Nevertheless, the option of sending a seven-day letter constitutes a potent instrument to prompt action by agency leadership.[66]

MISSION AND APPROACH

Legislation creating and expanding the number of IGs, and increasing their authority and responsibilities, retained a common understanding about a central mission of these offices—to ferret out fraud, waste, and abuse in federal programs. In pursuit of this mission, IGs are authorized to conduct audits, investigations, and evaluations (inspections). This mission is often referred to as compliance accountability, compliance auditing, or compliance monitoring, and it speaks to an approach that focuses most efforts on identifying *ex post facto* violations of rules or laws by government agencies. This approach was challenged in the 1990s by the Bill Clinton administration, especially in the National Performance Review led by Vice President Al Gore.

Critiquing contemporary IG work, the National Performance Review argued that the prevailing IG reports—identifying noncompliance with laws, regulations, or financial management standards—created disincentives for administrative entrepreneurship and innovation. Additionally, the National Performance Review (hereafter cited as NPR) stated that IG reports led to adversarial relationships between OIGs and their home agencies. Consequently, NPR recommended that IGs "should see their mission as not only to identify problems, but to get them solved." NPR urged that "[IGs] need to build a collaborative, not adversarial, relationship with the staffs being audited." The recommended action was that IGs change their emphasis "from compliance auditing to evaluating management control systems," which would focus on assessing an agency's management systems for evaluating their own programs.[67]

IGs responded to NPR's assessment through a self-study conducted jointly by two IG organizations previously created by executive action: the President's Council on Integrity and Efficiency (PCIE) for PAS IGs and the Executive Council on Integrity and Efficiency (ECIE) for DFE IGs—two separate councils that are discussed later in this chapter and that were combined and replaced by the Council of the Inspectors General for Integrity and Efficiency (CIGIE), which was created in 2008 by congressional action. PCIE and ECIE worked together on a vision statement issued after meetings with NPR officials, congressional staff, and "outside government experts."[68] This statement aims to broaden the approach taken by IGs to "place greater emphasis on identifying underlying vulnerabilities, recommending ways to prevent fraud from recurring, and, where appropriate, offering advice to management as management makes necessary improvements."[69]

The vision statement excerpt in table 2-5 is a list of actions and commitments that underscore a proactive approach to IG work that is not precluded by the IG Act but clearly sets new expectations about the scope and manner of IG work. Thus, the IGs set new expectations for themselves by using phrases such as "work with our agency head and the Congress," "use our investigations and other reviews to increase Government integrity and recommend improved systems," "build relationships with program managers," and "work together to address Government-wide issues." Following up on this statement, Kathryn Newcomer surveyed OIGs regarding their actions after the vision statement was issued. Asking about the relative emphasis on traditional versus performance audits, Newcomer finds a shift to performance audits in many OIGs, especially in contrast to a similar survey in 1992, before NPR and the IG vision statement.[70]

INTERNAL ORGANIZATION OF OFFICES
OF INSPECTOR GENERAL

The IG Act of 1978 specified a basic organization for OIGs that has remained largely in place over time. Each inspector general is to appoint an assistant inspector general for auditing and an assistant IG for investigations. Additionally and importantly, each IG is authorized "to select, appoint, and employ such officers and employees as may be necessary for carrying out the functions, powers, and duties of the Office. . . ."[71] Section 6 basically authorizes IGs to organize their offices as they deem appropriate, and in virtually every instance the IG has appointed a deputy IG to be second in command of the office. Various OIGs have added assistant IGs or senior officials for inspections or evaluations, for management or administration, or for other areas specific to the agencies they serve, such as a chief engineer in the National Aeronautics and Space Administra-

---

TABLE 2-5

Excerpt from Inspectors General Vision Statement (1994)

STATEMENT OF REINVENTION PRINCIPLES

We will:

- Each work with our agency head and the Congress to improve program management

- Maximize the positive impact and ensure the independence and objectivity of our audits, investigations and other reviews

- Use our investigations and other reviews to increase government integrity and recommend improved systems to prevent fraud, waste and abuse

- Be innovative and question existing procedures and suggest improvements

- Build relationships with program managers based on shared commitment to improving program operations and effectiveness

- Strive to continually improve the quality and usefulness of our products

- Work together to address government-wide issues

Source: Rivlin (2008, p. 11).

---

tion (NASA) OIG. Additionally, some OIGs have regional offices that roughly correspond to regionalized offices of the home agency.

Light's summary of the increased size, scope, and organizational layers in OIGs argues that these increases added to the independence of the offices relative to their home agencies.[72] These increases enhanced the capacities of OIGs to conduct audits and investigations, and also expanded OIG functions to include program evaluation, or inspection of agency programs. Creation of deputy IG positions, according to Light, served to make OIGs similar in structure to other federal agencies and provide opportunities to mentor future candidates for IG appointments in the home agency or other federal agencies.

Beginning in the 1990s, an important change for OIGs concerned who provides legal advice for IGs. Whereas they relied primarily on agency general counsel for legal advice during early stages of OIG existence, this practice created conflicts of interest for an agency's general counsel and potentially compromised the independence of OIGs from their agencies. To assure that OIGs were receiving legal advice independent of agency interpretation, a few of them hired their own legal advisors. The 2008 legislation authorized all IGs to appoint their own counsel to the IG, or to rely on counsel provided by another IG office or the Council of the Inspectors General on Integrity and Efficiency (CIGIE). After adoption of this provision, IGs were no longer dependent on legal advice from home agency legal counsel, which further enhanced independence from their home agencies. With only a few exceptions, all OIGs now rely on in-house counsel for legal advice.

ORGANIZATION AND COORDINATION OF THE IG COMMUNITY

Coordination among IGs was not addressed in the 1978 or 1988 legislation, although two organizations were created by presidential orders— namely, the President's Council on Integrity and Efficiency for PAS IGs and the Executive Council on Integrity and Efficiency for DFE IGs, in 1981 and 1992 respectively. After several years of lobbying by members of the IG community, the IG Reform Act of 2008 included provisions creating the Council of the Inspectors General on Integrity and Efficiency (CIGIE), thereby replacing PCIE and ECIE.[73] CIGIE is composed of all PAS and DFE IGs plus the controller of the Office of Federal Financial Management from OMB, deputy director for management from OMB; deputy director of OPM; DOJ's special counsel from the Office of Special Counsel; a senior level official of the Federal Bureau of Investigation designated by the director of the FBI; and director of the Office of Government Ethics. OMB's deputy director serves as executive chair of CIGIE, and council members elect the council chair for a two-year term.[74]

The legislation creating CIGIE highlights two missions, both of which aim to strengthen the IG community: first, "to address integrity, economy, and effectiveness issues that transcend individual Government agencies," and second, "to increase the professionalism and effectiveness of personnel by developing policies, standards, and approaches to aid in the establishment of a well-trained skilled workforce in the offices of the Inspectors General."[75] In pursuing these missions, CIGIE is authorized to perform three critical functions that contribute to professionalization in the IG community. First, CIGIE is to develop plans and programs that promote the work of inspectors general within and across federal agencies. This does not authorize CIGIE to direct the work of individual IGs, but CIGIE is expected to coordinate activities and develop standards for operation to help guide the IG community collectively and individually. Second, CIGIE is authorized to develop professional training programs for "audits, investigators, evaluators, and other personnel" so as to maintain a "corps of well-trained and highly skilled" individuals in IG offices. And third, CIGIE is to oversee an Integrity Committee to "receive, review, and refer for investigation allegations of wrongdoing" that involve IGs and senior OIG staff. The Integrity Committee conducts these investigations and makes recommendations to either the president (PAS appointments) or an agency head (DFE appointments), with copies of the recommendations also sent to Congress. The president or the DFE agency head makes the final determination about allegations and any subsequent sanctions, and the decision is conveyed to Congress soon thereafter.[76]

As authorized by the 2008 legislation, CIGIE issued quality standards in the four areas of digital forensics (2012), investigations (2011), inspection and evaluation (2012), and more generally, federal offices of inspector general (2012).[77] The quality standards for the latter three areas largely incorporate statements previously developed by PCIE or ECIE, but the 2008 legislation provided a statutory basis for their adoption, as compared with being previously based on authority granted in an executive order. Finally, the quality standards for auditing are set by the "Yellow Book" prepared by the comptroller general and GAO.

The 2008 legislation also authorized CIGIE to "submit recommendations of individuals to the appropriate appointing authority for any appointment to an office of Inspector General . . . " Under this authority, CIGIE created the IG Candidate Recommendation Panel, which solicits and reviews potential IG candidate and makes recommendations to appointing authorities. However, those authorities are not required to accept the recommendations, and there has been no publicly available accounting of how recommendations from CIGIE have fared in the process.[78]

Following the broad mission outlined in the 2008 legislation, CIGIE has also created a series of committees to make recommendations and oversee various activities of the council. These standing committees are in the areas of audit, professional development, information technology, inspection and evaluation, investigations, and legislation, in addition to the Integrity Committee and IG Candidate Recommendation Panel. Various ad hoc working groups are also created for specialized activities, and their accomplishments are detailed in annual reports.[79]

The statutory creation of CIGIE provided a legislative foundation that further strengthens the independence of IGs. In particular, the legislation contributes to independence by authorizing the setting of standards for the IG community, creating recruitment avenues for IGs and their staff, and affirming existing procedures that give the community first review and evaluation of allegations of misconduct by IGs and senior staff.

COORDINATION AMONG SELECTED OFFICES OF INSPECTOR GENERAL

Individual organizations comprising multiple IG offices have been created in response to major challenges that involve multiple executive agencies. Two of these organizations came together at the IG community's initiation, and three were created by Congress. PCIE created the first multi-IG in 2005 as a special working group of IGs to address homeland security issues, with the IG of the Department of Homeland Security serving as the group's chair. Later that year, in the aftermath of Hurricane Katrina and the passage of federal programs with massive funding dedicated to recovery from this disaster, the group focused its efforts on fraud, waste, and abuse that might accompany those programs. By the fall of 2005 this ad hoc group consisted of IGs from 21 agencies with major funding associated with relief and reconstruction. The group met regularly to focus resources on audits and investigations, offer advice on controls and policy to avoid duplication of effort, and bridge oversight involving multiple agencies.[80]

A second council, organized by SIGTARP in 2009, also attempted to focus IG resources to oversee federal programs dedicated to recovery and relief from the 2008 fiscal crisis. Neil Barofsky, SIGTARP's first IG, created this council, chaired by himself and including IGs from eight agencies responsible for TARP funds, plus the U.S. comptroller general. Barofsky's aim was to coordinate audits and investigations associated with TARP-funded programs. SIGTARP's initial report in February 2009 referenced creation of this group, and subsequent reports by SIG-TARP through April 2010 mention the council.[81] The fiscal year 2013 SIGTARP budget request references this group as a coordinating council and indicates that it meets "as needed to discuss developments in TARP and coordinate interconnected audit and investigative issues."[82] Overall, however, it appears that the council did not meet regularly and was not particularly effective in coordinating the efforts of several OIGs. Notably, Barofsky's account of his service as the first special IG for TARP reports considerable friction between SIGTARP and other OIGs involved with the program, especially the IG in the Treasury Department, regarding the independence of their respective offices and, in particular, their independence from SIGTARP.[83]

Passage in 2009 of the $787 billion American Recovery and Reinvestment Act (ARRA) generated concern among members of Congress that the rapid expenditure of those funds would create vast opportunities for fraud and waste. This concern prompted creation by Congress of the Recovery Accountability and Transparency Board "to coordinate and conduct oversight of covered funds to prevent fraud, waste, and abuse."[84] This board, which did not include and was not connected to the council organized by SIGTARP's Barofsky, was composed of eleven IGs from agencies receiving the majority of ARRA funding. Initially chaired by Department of Interior IG Earl Devaney, the board oversaw ARRA expenditures by working through agency IGs and their staff. The board acquired a staff of 80 individuals, many on loan from existing federal IG offices, to coordinate its activities and develop a website making ARRA expenditures transparent (Recovery.gov). The board's authority was expanded under the Consolidated Appropriations Act of 2012 to include all federal funding, and in 2013 the board was mandated by Congress to provide oversight for disaster funding surrounding Hurricane Sandy. However, the board closed its operations in 2015 after Congress did not provide additional funding or extend the board's authorization.

A major activity of the Recovery Accountability and Transparency Board was the creation of the Recovery Operations Center (ROC), which developed and maintained a database of ARRA contracts and grants, and developed data analytic tools to scan the database for potential instances of fraud. In 2013, the chair of the board, Kathleen S. Tighe (who was also the IG for the Department of Education), testified about the key function of the ROC:

> The ROC's strength is the ability to rapidly aggregate and analyze large, complex volumes of data to screen for potential risks or identify targets and to provide deeper investigative information, such as link analysis and discovery of non-obvious relationships, in the support of preventative activities, audits, investigations, or prosecutions. Customers are supported through collaborative work with ROC analysts, thus benefiting from the Board's infrastructure, skilled workforce, multiple advanced analytical tools, and proven tactics to quickly detect fraud in federal funding.[85]

Despite positive evaluations, ROC and its analytical tools lapsed when the board's activities ceased.[86]

Another statutorily multi-IG council created in the wake of the 2008 financial crisis was established in 2010 as part of the Dodd-Frank Wall Street Reform and Consumer Protection Act.[87] The Council of Inspectors General on Financial Oversight (CIGFO) coordinates the work of IGs relating to financial sector regulations. As a multi-agency council, CIGFO reports to the newly created Financial Stability Oversight Council (FSOC) and is chaired by the Treasury IG. CIGFO's membership included all of the IGs for the agencies that were represented on the Financial Stability Oversight Council as well as the IG for SIGTARP. This IG council meets quarterly, publishes meeting minutes, and issues annual reports primarily devoted to accounts by each IG of the activities within his or her agency that relate to financial regulations.

Passage of the 2013 National Defense Authorization Act for fiscal year 2013 authorized creation of an IG oversight group for "an overseas contingency operation that exceeds 60 days."[88] This group would be led by a Lead Inspector General (Lead IG) for Overseas Contingency Operations who would be appointed by the chair of CIGIE in consultation with the IGs in the Department of Defense, Department of State, and the United States Agency for International Development (USAID). The Lead IG would be one of the three IGs consulted by the chair of CIGIE. The Lead IG would coordinate oversight of overseas contingency operations that would be carried out by the OIGs whose agencies were involved in the military action. As of 2019, this provision has been used to designate Lead IGs for military operations in a number of foreign countries, including Afghanistan, Iraq, Pakistan, the Philippines, and Syria, as well as for operations that are not tied to specific countries. The legislation requires bi-annual and quarterly reports to Congress about investigations and evaluations tied to the military operation.[89] The Lead IG's responsibilities and overall coordination end one year after the total amount appropriated for the contingency operation is less than $100 million.

Reorganization of the national intelligence community after the September 11, 2001 (9/11), attacks in New York and Washington eventually led to legislation in 2010 creating an IG for the Intelligence Community (IG IC) and a multi-IG council for the intelligence community.[90] Reporting to the director of national intelligence, the IG IC is appointed by the president and confirmed by the Senate (PAS). The IG IC exercises the powers normally assigned to inspectors general except that the director of national intelligence may limit IG IC activities for national security reasons. Additionally, the IG IC has the distinctive authority to conduct inquiries across the intelligence community and serves as chair of a statutorily created multi-IG organization—the Intelligence Community Inspectors General Forum.[91] The forum, which is composed of the IGs for each agency included in the intelligence community,[92] serves as an information-sharing organization, and may assist in resolving jurisdictional disputes among intelligence community IGs. If such disputes are not settled with assistance of the forum, the issues are submitted to the director of national intelligence and the head of the agency affected by the particular dispute. Except for assistance in resolving conflicting initiatives or jurisdictional disputes, the forum has "no administrative authority over any inspector general [in the IC community]."[93]

An important point about these multi-IG councils—two created by IGs themselves, and three by congressional mandate, and one authorized by Congress on a contingency basis—is that none are authorized to impinge on the independence or the work of member IGs. However, the Intelligence Community Inspectors General Forum is statutorily authorized to assist in resolution of jurisdictional disputes between that community's IGs. While the group of IGs conducting audits and other reviews of federal operations associated with recovery efforts following Hurricane Katrina appears to have coordinated relatively well among themselves and with other offices, the SIGTARP council appears to have met considerable resistance to coordination among its members. Reports from the statutorily created CIGFO suggest that the group shares information, but there are few coordinated efforts documented in official materials.[94] The Recovery Accountability and Transparency Board received generally positive reviews for its overall effort overseeing ARRA funds, but the system it created to identify potential areas of fraud was allowed to lapse. Information about the IG IC and the Intelligence Community Inspectors General Forum is subject to considerable secrecy due to its central interest—intelligence and national security—so we know little about how, and how well, this group operates.[95]

Conclusion

In the late twentieth century, as the U.S. government's executive branch increased in size and federal budgets and programs expanded, so too did opportunities for fraud, waste, and abuse in federal programs. During this time, reports and investigations of executive misconduct and poorly managed programs led to public outrage, executive embarrassment, and congressional hearings and outrage. Using their administrative authority, a few executive agencies created inspectors general to oversee agency finances and activities, but legally and practically these IGs were wholly creatures of the executive branch. The push toward statutorily independent OIGs emerged in the 1970s when the USDA created an OIG under the Lyndon Johnson administration in response to an administrative scandal, and the Nixon administration that followed dismantled the office despite strongly felt congressional support for the operation. Congress's desire to increase its oversight of the executive branch and the need for informed, independent analysis also fed congressional interest in IGs. So despite pushback from executive agencies, Congress passed the Inspector General Act of 1978, which set the legal foundation for today's IGs embedded in every major federal agency.

This chapter reviewed the 1978 act's early development, noting that it laid the basis for the strategic environment discussed in the opening chapter. Under this act, IGs serve two major stakeholders—the executive branch and Congress. All IGs are executive appointments, with Senate confirmation for presidentially appointed IGs. The IGs report to the head of their respective home agency, but they are obligated to file semiannual reports to Congress and are authorized to contact Congress if the agency interferes with their work. Executive agencies and the president set OIG budgets, but they are also reviewed by Congress. In these and other provisions outlined in this chapter, IGs are clearly placed betwixt and between the executive branch and Congress, and either stakeholder could boost or undermine their activities.

The original 1978 act and subsequent amendments established expectations, especially congressional expectations, regarding three key elements of an IG's strategic environment—independence, accountability, and engagement. Accordingly, IGs make independent decisions about the organization of their offices and what to audit, investigate, or evaluate; IGs have access to any individual or document in their agency that they deem necessary to pursue their work; and IG reports are shared with and commented on by agency officials but not edited, limited, or censured in any way. IGs themselves are appointed based on their experience in auditing, investigations, or similar job-related expertise—not partisan connections or political stance. Although the president or agency head can fire or reassign an IG, Congress must be advised of the decision, and there are no set terms limiting their appointment. IG independence from Congress is less well detailed, except that Congress cannot hire or dismiss an IG. But Congress can decide on OIG budgets, summon IGs before congressional hearings for praise or criticism, and strengthen or weaken their authority through legislative actions. On balance, IG independence from executive interference is clearly more detailed and secure than their corresponding independence from Congress.

Though independent, IGs under the 1978 act are accountable for their actions to both stakeholders. Audit and evaluation reports are submitted to executive officials for review and comment, and those officials may accept or reject any final recommendations. Those reports are now posted on the internet for any interested party to review. And semiannual reports to Congress highlight significant IG reports and give summary statistics about audit and evaluation findings, whether the agency rejected or accepted recommendations, and the status of their implementation. For investigations that find evidence of criminal misconduct, IGs rely on the discretion of the Department of Justice to make the final decision about whether to prosecute a case. Summary statistics about investigations are reported to Congress in the IG's semiannual report. IGs are held to account by agency leadership through budget recommendations and, ultimately, through dismissals; Congress, on the other hand, can only hold hearings, complain to the president or agency head, or publicly criticize an IG or the IG's work. However, as we discuss in chapter 3, congressional actions appear to account for more voluntary departures of IGs than official executive dismissals.

The IG Act of 1978 sets very few boundaries on what IGs may audit, investigate, or evaluate; IGs are authorized to engage agency heads at any time and may reach out to Congress if they believe agency officials are interfering with their work. IGs must follow the auditing process detailed in the so-called Federal Yellow Book prepared by the comptroller general and GAO, which calls for engagement between auditors and the program officials they are auditing. Evaluations carry the same expectations, and IG investigators are expected to follow standards set for federal law enforcement personnel. In practice, if not precisely authorized in law, agency heads can call upon IGs to look into suspected fraud, waste, or abuse or to offer evaluations of programs. And members of Congress have exercised their oversight of IGs by requesting or legislatively mandating inquiries regarding their home agencies. The IG Act does, however, specifically prohibit IGs from becoming engaged with program design or implementation. IGs may make suggestions, but they are not policymakers or policy implementers.

So the IG Act of 1978 and significant amendments in 1998, 2008, and 2016 establish who an IG's stakeholders are and lay the legal foundation for the stakeholders' expectations regarding independence, accountability, and engagement. This legislation and specific responses to system stressors have also shaped or reshaped the IGs' strategic environment. For example, the 2016 IG Empowerment Act resolved the highly visible and contentious stressor regarding the expectations about IGs' access to information they requested for legitimate audits, investigations, and evaluations. That legislation also pushed the IG community to review allegations of misconduct by IGs and OIG senior leadership more quickly. Similarly, frustrations with the presidential appointment process and problems stemming from delayed nominations for open IG posts were cited for review by the GAO.

While amendments to the 1978 act did not address every stressor IGs or their stakeholders felt over time, the changes did focus on several major issues highlighted by the IG community and in doing so, mostly strengthened the independence of IGs. Significantly, Congress took the initiative for much of this legislation at the behest of the IG community. One stressor regarding expectations of IGs came from the National Performance Review during the Clinton administration, where IGs were taken to task for allegedly focusing on small-scale audits and investigations, and in the process missing the larger picture of helping to improve government programs. As a result of this executive intervention, IGs adopted an approach that embraces proactive work and closer engagement with executive officials. As we discuss in chapter 5, operationally this approach is shaped by the give and take between agency managers and their respective IGs.

THREE

Appointments, Career Tracks, and Controversies

October 15, 2008

Mike Garcia, U.S. Attorney for the Southern District of New York, in a phone call to Neil Barofsky, Assistant U.S. Attorney in Garcia's office: "You got a minute . . . C'mon up."

Minutes later, Garcia: "Did you know that when they passed TARP [the Troubled Asset Relief Program] they also created a $50 million law enforcement agency to oversee it?"

Barofsky: "No, I had no idea."

Garcia: "So, you think you'd be interested?"

Barofsky: "In what?"

Garcia: "In the job."

Barofsky: "What job?"

Garcia: "The special inspector general job."

Barofsky: I recall being stunned by the question.

October 23, 2008

Lou Reyes, attorney in the White House Office of Presidential Personnel, in a phone call to Barofsky after he interviewed the previous week with officials in Washington: "I've got some news for you. . . . This morning Joie Gregor [head of the White House Presidential Personnel Office] will recommend to the President that you be nominated as the special inspector general for the Troubled Asset Relief Program."

This chapter is co-authored by Charles A. Johnson, Kathryn E. Newcomer, and Evan T. Haglund. Professor Haglund is an assistant professor of public policy at the U.S. Coast Guard Academy.

December 8, 2008
Barofsky was confirmed by the U.S. Senate to be the Special Inspector General for TARP, otherwise shortened to SIGTARP.[1]

Neil Barofsky's book on his IG service, *Bailout*, offers one of the few public accounts of the appointment process for a presidentially appointed and Senate-confirmed inspector general. He describes an out-of-the-blue contact about the IG position, prenomination interviews, and background checks by the White House and the Federal Bureau of Investigation (FBI); coaching by White House personnel; meetings with Treasury and TARP officials, senators, and their staffs; dealing with leaks to the media and their subsequent inquiries; and testifying at Senate hearings.

Supplementing Barofsky's account, interviews with IGs offered varied accounts about how they became IGs. Some received out-of-the-blue calls; some hoped to be appointed to an administrative position in a particular presidential administration and were offered an IG appointment; and others specifically sought an IG appointment, informally or through formal processes. By all accounts, pathways to an inspector general appointment vary across administrations, agencies, and moments in time. Nevertheless, understanding the appointment process is critical to understanding the IG community, since this process has the potential to significantly influence who becomes an IG, what an IG does in office, and how he or she relates to the IG's strategic environment.

This chapter focuses on the IGs appointed by Presidents Carter, Reagan, G. H. W. Bush, Clinton, G. W. Bush, and Obama. We discuss the processes leading to appointment of IGs, as well as their backgrounds and career tracks. Additionally, the chapter explores challenges and contemporary issues regarding the appointment, review, and removal of IGs.

Inspectors General as Major Executive Appointments

Of the more than 2.6 million civilian employees in the executive branch, presidents directly control only 3,000–4,000 appointees across cabinet departments, independent agencies, boards, and commissions.[2] From highly visible appointments to the Supreme Court to low-profile schedulers or confidential assistants, these presidential appointments are, in fact, considered political appointments. About 1,000 of these appointments are at the senior level—such as cabinet secretaries, deputy and assistant secretaries, directors of major agencies, and members of independent regulatory agencies—and require confirmation by the U.S. Senate. Most other appointees who do not require Senate confirmation are either non-career Senior Executive Service (SES) appointments or Schedule C appointees under the U.S. civil service system.[3]

With few exceptions where specific terms are set statutorily, none of the president's political appointments are considered permanent. Indeed, most appointees to these offices resign or are forced out of office when the president or the appointing senior official leaves office. Members of Congress expect turnover with a change in administration, and presidents generally have a free hand in "changing the guard" and shaping their administrations by appointing their own executive officials. By all accounts, growth in the number, spread, and intrusion of these appointments into all levels of the federal bureaucracy—and the expected turnover with a change in administration—allow the president to assert leadership of, and give direction to, the executive branch.[4]

Every U.S. Inspector General appointment is an executive appointment—either by the president (with Senate confirmation) or an agency head. However, three features distinguish IG appointments from the thousands of other appointments made by presidents and their senior officers.

First, the law creating these offices states explicitly that IG appointments should be made "without regard to political affiliation and solely on the basis of integrity and demonstrated ability in accounting, auditing, financial analysis, law, management analysis, public administration, or investigations."[5]

Second, except for a few IG positions specified in federal law, IG appointments are open ended, with no designated term or end date. Moreover, while an IG may be dismissed by the president (or agency head for those appointed by agencies without Senate confirmation), currently there are no norms dictating that IGs resign or leave as administrations change. Thus, IGs leave office only by their own decision (though sometimes under pressure from the administration, the media, Congress, or other political actors) or by being fired. If an IG is dismissed by the president or agency head, that official must notify Congress regarding the circumstances surrounding the removal.

Third, IGs are oversight or watchdog positions without significant policymaking authority. Unlike many other senior executive positions, the primary function of which is to make or influence policy directly, IGs are focused on monitoring how other appointees and careerists are making and implementing policy. Although general counsels or chief financial officers share some similar oversight functions,[6] they also hold policymaking authority or other roles that IGs do not.

These three differences create distinctive effects on the appointment processes by which IGs are selected, the strategic environments in which they operate, and their independence as they pursue their responsibilities.

Appointing U.S. Inspectors General—Process and Politics

The IG positions created by the original Inspector General Act of 1978 are presidentially appointed and Senate confirmed (PAS). These IGs, and those subsequently created that require presidential appointments, are usually referred to as PAS or establishment IGs.[7] The 1988 amendments to the IG Act of 1978 created IGs in a host of generally smaller federal agencies, which are referred to as designated federal entities (DFEs) in the legislation. In contrast to PAS IGs established under the 1978 legislation, these IGs are appointed by agency heads, boards, or commissions without Senate confirmation and are usually referred to as DFE IGs. Since 1988, nearly all newly created IG positions use one of these two appointment methods, and a few IGs have been shifted from one category to another.[8] While the responsibilities and authorities of PAS IGs and DFE IGs are essentially the same, their appointment processes differ in important and potentially consequential ways.

PRESIDENTIALLY APPOINTED AND SENATE CONFIRMED (PAS) INSPECTORS GENERAL

The IG Act of 1978 gives no guidance to presidents regarding how to identify candidates for Senate review and confirmation. Absent this guidance, the prenomination processes adopted by Presidents Carter, Reagan, and G.H.W. Bush set the general parameters later used by Presidents Clinton, G.W. Bush, and Obama in developing nominations for PAS IGs.[9]

Paul Light reports that President Jimmy Carter's search for twelve inspectors general created in the 1978 legislation began—quoting a White House staffer—with calls to "'bar associations, accounting firms, inside players, a lot of seasoned folks, some of the national groups—looking for women and minorities.'" The Office of Management and Budget (OMB) played a significant role in gathering and vetting suggestions, which resulted in a list of "roughly 25 candidates," and thereafter "every agency was given two to three names per slot." Light indicates that "departments and agencies did have a say in the final choices," although a second White House staffer is quoted as saying "it made no sense to put people in a job where the agency was completely opposed. But we never gave the agencies carte blanche. They could tell us if they were uncomfortable, but had no veto."[10] Whether candidates were interviewed by agency officials is not reported by Light, but he implies that the final decision as to who was nominated rested with the White House Presidential Personnel Office (PPO).[11] Despite White House leadership of the process, most candidates learned of their selection as the nominee from a department or agency official, not a White House or OMB official.[12]

President Ronald Reagan's dismissal of all inspectors general—including those with permanent PAS appointments and serving as acting IGs—on the first day of his administration (an action discussed later in this chapter) set in motion prenomination processes under the guidance of Edwin Harper, OMB's deputy director under Reagan. Harper also carried the title of assistant to the president, which meant that he reported to the OMB director, David Stockman, and Edwin Meese, Counselor to the President for Policy (and a high-ranking White House advisor to President Reagan). Harper was considered a key link between the White House and OMB.[13] Acting quickly after Reagan's address to Congress on February 18, 1981, which included a pledge to "appoint as inspectors general highly trained professionals," Harper created a new search process for prospective nominees in which OMB "took charge . . . [and] often had the final say." OMB's relationship with the IG community had also been enhanced by Reagan's creation of the President's Council on Integrity and

Efficiency (PCIE) on March 26, 1981, composed of all IGs and chaired by OMB's deputy director.[14]

Harper's successor in the Reagan administration, Joe Wright, introduced an additional feature to the selection process, by creating "an informal [three-person] recruiting committee composed of only IGs to screen names and recruit candidates." While OMB was clearly in charge, the White House gave candidates a "cursory political check." Additionally, departments and agencies continued to have a limited veto, as was the case in the Carter administration.[15] Thus, an IG nominee needed the support of OMB, clearance by PPO, and acceptance by the home agency. In the prenomination process established by Harper and Wright, however, agencies "had only one option if they did not like the initial candidate: Draw another name, which was likely to resemble the first one, from the IG-generated list."[16]

The succeeding George H. W. Bush administration inherited an expanded number of IG positions as a result of Congress's creation of IG posts in all cabinet-level departments and several major agencies after passage of the IG Act of 1978.[17] In 1981, the transition from Carter to Reagan resulted in the dismissal of all IGs on the first day of the Reagan administration. In similar fashion, President Bush is reported to have sent the IGs "the standard letter all the PASs [presidentially appointed, Senate confirmed executive appointees] got reminding them to resign." Most IGs, however, refused to resign, "citing the independence of their office"—a view supported by Senate and House committees overseeing federal inspectors general.[18]

President Bush did not press the issue, and most of the previously appointed IGs remained in their posts unless they decided to leave voluntarily. Modified appointment processes emerged, however, which shifted the locus of decisionmaking from the OMB to the White House and slowed the process for filling vacancies. While the informal screening committee remained in place, at least initially, Light reports that "it had little influence."[19] Finally, as leadership in G. H. W. Bush's OMB placed a lower priority on IGs and their mission, the appointment process for PAS IGs guided by the White House "allow[ed] greater input from secretaries and administrators" and "occasional marginal candidates [were allowed] as a political favor."[20]

Processes for appointing PAS IGs remained largely the same in the Clinton, G. W. Bush, and Obama administrations. The only change in these processes occurred after establishment of the Council of the Inspectors General for Integrity and Efficiency (CIGIE) in the 2008 amendments to the IG Act. The 2008 legislation authorized a practice used by Presidents Reagan and G. H. W. Bush, formally calling on CIGIE to compile names of individuals interested in being appointed to a PAS IG position and to organize a panel of IGs that would examine the credentials of those individuals. However, it is unclear if CIGIE serves either as a recruiting agency for specific PAS IG positions or as a placement tool of specific candidates for PAS IG offices.[21]

Since the G. H. W. Bush administration, the White House Office of Presidential Personnel (PPO) has guided the process for appointment of PAS IGs. Typically, there is no call for nominees. However, since vacancies among PAS IGs are well known to the IG community and to groups with particular interest in the specific agency, the White House may receive nominations from congressional representatives, interest groups, and friends of the president (or of the potential nominee). CIGIE may offer recommendations or comments on prospective nominees if requested to do so by PPO. Whether and when a department secretary or agency head advances names for an IG in his or her agency is unknown, but there are no legal rules prohibiting such recommendations. Interviews by the coauthors of this volume in confidential or off-the-record conversations suggest, however, that a department's leadership is more likely to be consulted by the White House after there is a short list of candidates or a final prospective nominee is identified—rather than to initially lobby for a particular choice for a department's IG.

Prospective PAS IGs are subject to the clearance processes used by PPO for virtually all PAS executive appointments. This means prospective nominees must provide substantial background information, including employment history, tax information, and connections with political, business, or social interests. Prospective nominees are asked if anything in their background, career, or family might embarrass the administration or the agency for which they are being considered. Additionally, the FBI performs an extensive background check on prospective IG nominees, as with all presidential appointees. Depending on the agency, nominees also undergo the background checks required for national security clearance. Once there is a sign-off by the White House and agency leadership, a prospective nominee is presumed to meet the expectations set forth in the Inspector General Act regarding his or her ability to fulfill the role of IG in the particular agency. The focus at this point in the process is whether the nominee can survive the confirmation process.

It is unclear when (or whether) the names of prospective IG nominees are floated by the Senate committee chairs, ranking members, or senior committee staff who would be key to securing Senate confirmation. Doubtless, informal contacts with Senate officials vary with the history of the specific Office of Inspector General (OIG) and the agency in question, the congressional committee that reviews the nomination, and the political dynamics of the president and Congress. When the nomination is formally sent to the Senate, committees have their own processes for vetting PAS nominees. These processes also apply to IG nominations and include having the nominees provide written responses to questions similar to those raised by the White House PPO in the prenomination phase. After their formal nomination, IG nominees are guided by the White House through interviews with key senators or their staff. If committee leadership agrees, then there are hearings.

While most PAS appointments are referred to a single committee, some executive departments and agencies are overseen by multiple Senate committees, and thus, several committees become involved in the appointment process. There is usually a predominant committee to which the nomination is initially referred, and other committees receive the nomination sequentially. In 2007, the Senate agreed that IG nominations would be "referred to the committee having primary jurisdiction of the department, agency or entity, and if and when reported in each case, then to the Committee on Homeland Security and Government Affairs."[22] Thus, most PAS IG nominations are reviewed by at least one policy committee overseeing the executive department or agency, and by the Committee on Homeland Security and Government Affairs.[23]

DESIGNATED FEDERAL ENTITY INSPECTORS GENERAL

Legislation in 1988 amending the original IG Act of 1978 created thirty-three new inspector general positions in a variety of government agencies, commissions, and corporations.[24] Unlike PAS IGs, these DFE IGs are appointed by either the agency head or a designated hiring authority, such as a commission or corporate board, and do not require Senate confirmation.

Paul Light reports that while Congress intended that DFE IGs would have the same functions, protections from agency management interference, and authority of PAS IGs, "the lack of Senate confirmation meant that these small agency IGs would be different from their Executive Level peers. Most would be career officers; many would be buried in small agencies almost unknown to most members of Congress, as well as the White House."[25] Also, consistent with the diminished involvement of OMB in the appointment of PAS IGs, there is no evidence that OMB leadership is involved with the recruitment, vetting, or appointment of DFE IGs. Nor is there any evidence that the White House is involved in DFE IG appointments.

Initial appointments of DFE IGs in the G. H. W. Bush administration included four permanent DFE IGs holding IG-like appointments in similar posts; sixteen permanent DFE IGs appointed by their respective home agencies in the first four months of the administration; and nine permanent DFE IGs (plus one replacement) appointed by the end of 1989. The four remaining DFE agencies filled their IG posts with permanent appointments in 1990 or 1991.

The 1988 statute mandates that "the Inspector General shall be appointed by the head of the designated Federal entity in accordance with the applicable laws and regulations governing appointments with the designated Federal entity."[26] All evidence suggests that DFE IG appointments under Clinton and subsequent administrations were handled largely by the agencies themselves without any apparent review by PPO or OMB.

Legally and practically, DFE IG appointments are handled like career appointments in the agency, commission, or other entity. Thus, at the hiring agency's discretion or official policies, DFE IG positions are posted on various internet websites for government positions; some appointment processes are organized by the Office of Personnel Management (OPM) or follow its rules for such appointments; and other appointments receive the same treatment as SES appointments within the agency. These varied processes also mean that recruitment and vetting of candidates may be undertaken by the hiring authority or by OPM, following criteria set by a DFE for the position. CIGIE maintains a file of individuals interested in IG positions and, if requested by a DFE, forwards the names of individuals expressing an interest in the open IG position. There is no systematic evidence about whether the hiring authority receives recommendations from congressional sources, interested parties outside of government, or friends of the DFE. Because DFE IG positions are posted federal positions, individual candidates formally apply for DFE IG positions and provide materials required by federal law and agency policies.

Discussions with sitting DFE IGs suggest that prospective candidates rely on networking in the IG community or the agency to test their chances for appointment to an open position. Once interested applicants are placed on a short list, these candidates are interviewed by some combination of the DFE agency head (or commissioner) and a search committee whose membership may include representatives from the agency, OPM, CIGIE, or other interests. Once a candidate is selected, the appointment process follows the procedures for that particular agency, commission, or entity. The norm is that final appointments proceed without White House or OMB approval.

IG VACANCIES, APPOINTMENTS, AND DEPARTURES FROM 1978 TO 2016

Using data from CIGIE, the Congressional Record, and other information sources, we have compiled a data set of both PAS and DFE IGs from 1978 to 2016, their entry and exit dates, the duration of vacancies, and the time from exit to successor nomination by the president and confirmation by the Senate. Data reported in table 3-1 highlight increased vacancy durations over time and show how presidential delays in nominating new IGs account for more of the vacancy duration than does senatorial delay in confirming them once nominated.

TABLE 3-1

PAS IG Presidential Nominations and DFE IGs Agency Head Appointments, 1978–2016

	PAS IGs					DFE IGs	
	Successful Nominations	Failed or Withdrawn	Average Vacancy Duration (mos.)	Average Nomination Delay (mos.)	Average Confirmation Delay (mos.)	Appointments by Agency Heads	Average Vacancy (mos.)
Carter	16	0				0	0
Reagan	36	0	9.30	5.96	1.93	5	15.25
G.H.W. Bush	14	1	12.25	8.17	2.75	36	8.48
Clinton	35	5	13.05	8.81	3.45	27	6.22
G.W. Bush	30	14	14.57	8.90	5.04	37	6.69
Obama	24	17	26.06	17.67	5.79	33	4.50
Total	155	37	14.60	9.53	3.79	138	7.60

Source: Nomination and confirmation data from Congress.gov; resignation and vacancy dates from CIGIE Inspector General Historical Data tables, agency press releases, leader biographical data, and newspaper archives.

Note: This table counts IGs formally nominated to PAS positions by the president that were successfully approved by the Senate and those that did not receive Senate confirmation (failed) or were withdrawn before a final vote by the Senate. Five IG appointments are excluded from this table: three Special Inspectors General for Afghanistan (SIGAR) and Iraq (SIGIR) who were appointed by the president, but did not require Senate confirmation; and Clark Ervin's recess appointment as the DHS IG, which was not voted on by the Senate and is counted as "failed" (see, Ervin, 2006). Also not included in the table is an unknown DFE appointment (if one was made) for the Community Development Financial Institutions Fund (CDFIF) in the U.S. Department of the Treasury.

After President Reagan's initial decision in January 1981 to fire the IGs previously appointed by President Carter, most of the positions were filled within five to six months. That gap of a few months between an incumbent's exit and a successor's entry into an IG position has steadily grown. For the Clinton and G. W. Bush administrations, the typical IG position remained vacant for about a year before getting a confirmed successor in place; that doubled in the Obama administration, with several IG slots going empty for more than four years. While some of this was due to a slower Senate confirmation process—from an average of around two months under Reagan and G. H. W. Bush to more than four months under G. W. Bush and Obama—a greater portion of the delay was from slower nominations coming from the White House. From the late 1980s under G. H. W. Bush through the Clinton and G. W. Bush administrations, the White House took just over eight months on average to nominate a replacement. This jumped to almost eighteen months during the Obama administration.

As we report in table 3-2, the average vacancy duration was less than a year for just four cabinet department IGs: Energy (3.8 months), Transportation (8.7), Housing and Urban Development (10.9), and Treasury (10.9). Lagging far behind were Health and Human Services (18.3 months), State (19), Defense (19.3), and Homeland Security (22.3). Among smaller agencies, the National Aeronautics and Space Administration (NASA) and the U.S. Information Agency (before it merged with State) had vacancies averaging 5.5 months, while the Federal Deposit Insurance Corporation, Tennessee Valley Authority, and Export-Import Bank all approached vacancies averaging more than two years.

By contrast, the DFE IG positions—for which agency heads make the appointment—remained vacant on average only 7.6 months and the median vacancy was 4 months. Just over 17 percent of DFE IGs had a successor ready to start prior to the incumbent's departure, while barely 5 percent of PAS IGs had a successor confirmed by departure. Interestingly, the Obama administration was the quickest with its DFE appointments, with an average vacancy around 4 months.

With congressional and media scrutiny of vacancies in appointed positions generally and, more recently, vacancies in OIGs specifically,

Congress mandated that the Government Accountability Office (GAO) look into IG appointments and vacancies. In the IG Empowerment Act, passed in December 2016, Congress included a requirement that the GAO "conduct a study of prolonged vacancies in the Offices of Inspector General during which a temporary appointee has served as the head of the office that includes—(A) the number and duration of Inspector General vacancies; (B) an examination of the extent to which the number and duration of such vacancies has changed over time; (C) an evaluation of the impact such vacancies have had on the ability of the relevant Office of Inspector General to effectively carry out statutory requirements; and (D) recommendations to minimize the duration of such vacancies."[27]

The GAO report, issued in March 2018, focused on the sixty-four active OIGs that specifically fall under the IG Act of 1978 (amended). Examining vacancies for these offices, the GAO found that twenty-six out of thirty-two PAS OIGs "experienced at least one vacancy during the 10-year period with the cumulative duration ranging from 25 days to 5 years and 258 days." Among the thirty-two DFE OIGs, twenty-seven offices "experienced at least one vacancy during the 10-year period with the cumulative duration ranging from 13 days to 3 years and 67 days."[28]

The GAO also surveyed individuals who served as acting IGs during this 10-year period, OIG staff who worked under an acting IG, and permanently appointed IGs, regarding whether lengthy vacancies had an impact on OIG operations or on the acting IGs themselves. Answering various questions about planning and conducting work, interacting with agency management, and managing OIG personnel, most of the respondents reported that acting status had no impact on their work or the impact was positive. However, a sizable number of respondents raised questions about whether an acting IG was or was possibly viewed as having less independence or being less proactive in office.[29] The GAO's analysis did not include evaluation of the decisions and recommendations of acting IGs versus permanently appointment IGs—an analysis not requested by Congress in its 2016 legislation.

The Barofsky nomination for SIGTARP, described at the chapter's beginning, is perhaps the exception that reaffirms the dominant trend of limited attention to and the glacial pace of IG nominations. First, TARP

TABLE 3-2

Average Vacancy Duration for PAS IGs by Agency and Non-Cabinet vs. Cabinet Status

	Average Vacancy (mos.)	Cabinet Department
National Aeronautics and Space Administration	5.53	No
U.S. Information Agency	5.66	No
Troubled Asset Relief Program	7.15	No
Resolution Trust Corporation	7.67	No
Social Security Administration	8.36	No
Small Business Administration	9.56	No
General Services Administration	9.81	No
Nuclear Regulatory Commission	10.20	No
Central Intelligence Agency	11.41	No
Director of National Intelligence	13.20	No
Federal Emergency Management Agency	13.57	No
National Reconnaissance Office	13.80	No
National Security Agency	13.80	No
Treasury IG for Tax Administration	15.35	No
U.S. Synthetic Fuels Corporation	15.60	No
Railroad Retirement Board	15.67	No
Office of Personnel Management	15.83	No
Corporation for National and Community Service	17.91	No
Federal Housing Finance Agency	19.53	No
Agency for International Development	20.54	No
Federal Deposit Insurance Corporation	27.18	No
Tennessee Valley Authority	27.70	No
Export–Import Bank of the United States	30.14	No

and the broader financial crisis that gave rise to it were highly salient to both political elites and the American public generally. The money involved was astronomical for any one program—$700 billion, higher than the Department of Defense's annual budget—and the potential for corruption, or at least the perception of it, seemed perfectly suited for making a high-profile IG appointment to combat any waste, fraud, and

	Average Vacancy (mos.)	Cabinet Department
Energy	3.81	Yes
Transportation	8.69	Yes
Housing and Urban Development	10.91	Yes
Treasury	10.93	Yes
Justice	14.22	Yes
Agriculture	14.80	Yes
Environmental Protection Agency	15.33	Yes
Veterans Affairs	15.64	Yes
Commerce	15.81	Yes
Interior	16.89	Yes
Education	17.40	Yes
Labor	17.85	Yes
Health and Human Services	18.34	Yes
State	18.99	Yes
Defense	19.25	Yes
Homeland Security	22.25	Yes

Note: Nomination and confirmation data from Congress.gov; resignation and vacancy dates from CIGIE Inspector General Historical Data tables, agency press releases, leader biographical data, and newspaper archives.

abuse. Similarly, some IG positions garner attention from the media and the public because of scandals, making those positions a priority for both presidents and Congress.

But most IGs are not so visible to important stakeholders or the general public. This lack of visibility could translate into less impetus for an incoming administration to exert the effort to find, vet, and appoint

IGs. A newly elected president is focused on policy plans and outcomes, and the positions that can implement the presidential agenda. Newly appointed agency heads are less likely to be pushing for the quick appointment of IGs compared with the need for deputy and assistant secretaries to fill out their leadership ranks. And in the search process, the number of high-profile or politically connected IG candidates might be more limited. Prospective IGs generally have auditing or investigative backgrounds, experience that does not put them at the forefront of agency leadership or in prominent policymaking positions that are more familiar or visible to political elites. Though CIGIE does provide recommendations, there is a much deeper and eager pool of potential appointees for policy-oriented positions drawn from friends of the president, campaign and congressional staff, prominent politicians, and policy experts.

It is also clear that IGs are different from other classes of appointments that have consistent, powerful advocates outside the administration to push for swift nomination and confirmation. While the cry for IGs to be put in place occurs during and after scandals, this is situation dependent rather than a constant force. As a counterexample, another appointment class, the U.S. Attorneys, have attentive advocates who are always ready to ensure swift nomination and confirmation: the home state senators who recruit and vet potential nominees, push their names to the White House, and then shepherd their confirmations quickly through the Senate. And because of U.S. Attorneys' direct effect on policy outcomes—exercised through prosecutorial discretion, public relations about important cases and policies, and success or failure in the courtroom—senators as well as presidents are more interested in getting these appointments made quickly, especially compared with IG positions where the policy effects are generally less noticeable or direct.[30] Though some individual IG nominees might have a few powerful advocates, especially when a high-profile scandal has drawn significant publicity and political scrutiny to an agency or program, IGs as a class of appointees do not have institutionally embedded advocates like U.S. Attorneys do.[31]

In addition to the general trend of increased delays in nomination and confirmation, the evidence shows that the Obama administration was different from prior presidents—slower to nominate IGs and slower to get them confirmed by the Senate. Was this due to a specific choice not to prioritize IGs by the administration and a corresponding increase in Senate obstructionism? Or was it simply a question of volume? As one Obama PPO director noted, too many nominations all at once make the problem of confirmation worse.[32] The last-minute nominations for four IGs by President Obama in late 2016 suggests some combination of several factors: a lack of urgency or prioritization; greater Senate obstructionism as the Democratic majority shrank and then disappeared after the 2014 midterm elections; the sheer volume of nominations faced by PPO; and a disconnect between CIGIE and the White House on finding qualified appointees.

POLITICS AND IG PERSONNEL

Statutory language for both PAS IGs and DFE IGs appointed by their respective processes indicate that their appointment should be done "without regard to political affiliation and solely on the basis of integrity and demonstrated ability in accounting, auditing, financial analysis, law, management analysis, public administration, or investigations."[33] Throughout the six presidential administrations since passage of the IG Act of 1978, however, hints and suspicions have surfaced regarding the role of politics in the appointment and dismissal of IGs. President Reagan's firing of all sitting IGs on the first day of his administration—all of whom were appointed by President Carter—raised concerns about the politicization of the IG community. These dismissals were characterized by the Reagan administration as an effort to strengthen the IGs by appointing "'meaner junkyard dogs.'"[34] Reagan later reappointed six of the IGs who were previously confirmed by the Senate under President Carter. While Reagan's subsequent appointments were not notably "political," and despite the strong negative reactions to the mass dismissals, his actions reminded the IGs that they were subject to dismissal by the president and that their performance needed to be in keeping with Reagan's pledge to reduce waste, fraud, and abuse.[35]

In the wake of strong negative reactions from Congress and the press to Reagan's firing of IGs, and the pushback that G. H. W. Bush received to his request for resignations from sitting IGs, President Bill Clinton evidently ignored advice from his staff "to find a way to fire the political IGs, nearly all of whom had been appointed by Reagan or Bush."[36] Similarly, Presidents George W. Bush and Barack Obama evidently did not issue letters to sitting IGs, or to individually targeted IGs, requesting that they submit their resignations at the beginning of the respective presidential terms. President Donald Trump's post-election transition team reportedly contacted several sitting IGs to inform them they would be replaced. These phone calls received coverage in the *Washington Post* and resulted in Michael Horowitz, Department of Justice (DOJ) IG and chair of CIGIE, contacting members of Congress regarding the transition team's calls. A few days after the initial phone calls, senior members of the Trump transition team reversed course and countermanded the original calls.[37]

Taking a broader view of whether transition politics lead to dismissals or forced resignations, table 3-3 provides a systematic overview of the number of departures and new appointments for each president since 1978. Aside from the mass firing at the beginning of the Reagan administration, these data show that IGs did not depart in substantially greater numbers in the first year of a president's term of office compared with later years in the administration's term. Though the number of departures for any specific year is small, comparatively larger numbers of departures occurred in the first year of Clinton's, G. W. Bush's, and Obama's second terms in office.

While politics may not routinely force wholesale turnovers in the IG community, there have been occasional charges that politically driven decisions led to some PAS IG appointments. For example, the congressional staff of former representative Henry A. Waxman (D, CA) issued a report entitled "The Politicization of Inspectors General," which argued that President George W. Bush's IG appointments had substantial political backgrounds. This report compared the backgrounds of thirty-two PAS IGs appointed by Clinton from 1993 to 2000 with the backgrounds of eleven PAS IGs appointed by Bush from 2001 to 2004. The report indicates that "two-thirds of President Clinton's appointments had prior audit experience, while fewer than one-fourth had prior political experience. These figures are reversed for President Bush's appointments: ap-

TABLE 3-3

*Departures and Appointments of U.S. Inspectors
General by Year of President's Term*

(*Includes PAS and DFE IGs*)

Presidential Term	Departures				Appointments			
	1st year	2nd year	3rd year	4th year	1st year	2nd year	3rd year	4th year
Carter	0	0	0	5	2[a]	1[b]	12	1
Reagan I	11[c]	2	3	1	16[c]	1	5	0
Reagan II	2	6	2	2	4	6[e]	6	3
G.H.W. Bush	3	5	2	8	28[d]	14[d]	4	4
Clinton I	7	11	8	4	5	9	7	10
Clinton II	10	10	11	3	6	10	10	5
G. W. Bush I	5	10	6	7[f]	6	9	6	7
G. W. Bush II	10	6	9	6	11	9	12	10
Obama I	10	1	10	6	6	7	10	5
Obama II	13	8	6	6	10	9	5	6

a Department of Health and Human Services and U.S. Agency for International Development—both later incorporated into the Inspector General Act of 1978.

b Department of Energy—later incorporated into the Inspector General Act of 1978.

c President Reagan dismissed all permanent and sitting IGs after his inauguration and then appointed new IGs—including several who were initially dismissed on his first day in the office. One Reagan appointee departed in 1981.

d Includes new appointments resulting from creation in 1988 of DFE OIGs in 33 federal agencies.

e Includes appointment of Patrick Conklin, a carryover appointment after legislation created PAS OPM IG.

f Includes departure of recess appointment not confirmed by Senate.

Note: This table includes the appointments of three Special IGs for Afghanistan and Iraq, and the recess appointment for the DHS IG. Excluded is the IG for the CDFIF for which there is no documentation of an appointment.

Source: Nomination and confirmation data from Congress.gov; resignation and vacancy dates from CIGIE Inspector General Historical Data tables, agency press releases, leader biographical data, and newspaper archives.

proximately two-thirds . . . had prior political experience, while fewer than one-fifth had prior audit experience." The report goes on to highlight decisions by three Bush appointees that are characterized as reflective of "politicization," which the report's authors maintain substantiated the charge that such appointments were increasingly placing political agents in IG positions.[38] Notwithstanding this congressional staff report, there is no systematic evidence that IG appointments and their decisions have been politicized, though additional research is needed to confirm or disconfirm a possible relationship.

Leaving Office—Retiring, Resigning, and Being Dismissed

Permanently appointed IGs in office between 1978 and 2016 served an average of (median) 3.8 years (PAS IGs) and 4.7 years (DFE IGs). Twenty-five percent of the PAS IGs served only 2.1 years or less, while another 25 percent served 7.0 years or more. DFE IGs served longer terms for these percentiles—25 percent served 3.1 years or less and 25 percent served 8.6 years or more.[39] Importantly, the overwhelming majority of these IGs left their office by their own decision—not by being fired or dismissed.

DISMISSALS AND RESIGNATIONS

The IG Act of 1978 (amended) provides that PAS IGs "shall report to and be under the general supervision of the head of the establishment involved or, to the extent such authority is delegated, the officer next in rank below such head," and that DFE IGs "shall report to and be subject to supervision of the head of the designated Federal entity, but shall not report to, or be subject to supervision by, any other officer or employee of such designated Federal entity."[40]

What constitutes "shall report to" for all IGs, "general supervision" of PAS IGs, and "supervision" of DFE IGs is not addressed in detail by the IG Act of 1978. A 2014 CIGIE publication summarizing the authority and activities of IGs takes a nearly absolute position on the matter: "The IG Act specifically prohibits agency management officials from supervising the IG."[41] This view is clarified in a subsequent paragraph: "There is no statutory definition of 'general supervision.' However, the IG Act is clear that supervision is limited and may not be exercised in a way that would inhibit an IG's full discretion to undertake an audit or investigation, issue subpoenas, and see these matters through to conclusion."[42]

Citing both the IG Act and a federal appeals court decision in *United States Nuclear Regulatory Commission v. Federal Labor Relations Authority* [25 F.3d 229 (4th Cir. 1994)], CIGIE's publication reports that the court's decision "reviewed the legislative history of the 'general supervision' language and described the agency head's supervisory authority over the IG as 'nominal.'"[43] The term *nominal* is not specifically defined, but after reviewing the legislative history of the IG Act, the court decision indicates "we cannot conclude that Congress intended for the 'general supervision' granted to agency heads to include any authority to compromise the investigatory rights conferred on Inspectors General."[44]

Even if supervisory authority is nominal, IGs are subject to dismissal—the ultimate exercise of supervisory authority and enforced accountability. In the case of PAS IGs, only the president can dismiss an IG, though presumably this could be at the recommendation of the agency head; for DFE IGs, the agency head can dismiss the organization's IG without presidential approval. In either case, both houses of Congress must be informed in writing regarding the reasons for removal or transfer of the IG. The original IG Act of 1978 anticipated that Congress would be informed after the personnel action. The IG Reform Act of 2008 specified that the notification must be thirty days before the actual dismissal.[45]

In fact, dismissal procedures mandated by the IG Act are rarely invoked by the president or agency heads. Among all the permanent IGs appointed by Presidents Carter through Obama, only thirteen have been fired by a president—twelve by President Reagan after his inauguration in January 1981, and one by President Obama in June 2009. The latter case, involving Gerald Walpin, Corporation for National and Community Service IG, brought criticism from Congress that the firing was politically driven and that President Obama did not follow amendments to the IG Act requiring thirty days' notice before dismissing an IG. Walpin filed suit in federal court, but the DC Court of Appeals panel unanimously ruled that Walpin's dismissal was lawful.[46]

Dismissals may be rare, but forced resignations or retirements can and do occur. For example, the G. W. Bush administration reportedly forced two IGs to resign their posts in February 2001. Luise S. Jordan, IG for the Corporation for National and Community Service, reported being summoned to a meeting with Ed Moy, associate director of the White House

PPO, and being told that "the corporation had decided to get a new IG."
On the same day, NASA's administrator, Sean O'Keefe, informed the IG
for NASA, Roberta L. Gross, that "'the White House was in the process
of selecting somebody else' for the IG job. . . . It was time to move on."
Both instances were considered resignations, not dismissals.[47]

Of course, IGs leave their posts for a variety of reasons. An internet
search in mainstream media using the names of each permanently appointed IG and such words as *resign, fired,* or *dismissed* produced the following findings based on published reports:

- Two IGs reportedly left under pressure from the White House

- Eight IGs reportedly resigned under pressure from the agency

- Sixteen IGs reportedly resigned in the wake of pressures from Congress

- Five IGs reportedly left office in response to an official investigation
  by PCIE, CIGIE, or GAO finding fault with their work

A few news articles suggest multiple sources of pressure to resign. Ex-
cluding the Senate-confirmed IGs dismissed by Presidents Reagan and
Obama, this survey of mainstream media stories produced articles for
about 10 percent of the permanently appointed IGs. This relatively small
number suggests that forced departures may not occur very often or they
may not be newsworthy—or that IGs who are forced to leave office simply
choose to remain silent even if they receive a push from any source.

INVESTIGATIONS OF IGS AND THEIR SENIOR STAFF

At least five resignations by IGs resulted from allegations of misconduct
that were evaluated by an official investigation.[48] With one exception, these
investigations were organized by the Integrity Committee of CIGIE (or by
PCIE or the Executive Council on Integrity and Efficiency/ECIE prior to
the creation of CIGIE). The original IG Act of 1978 and the 1988 amendments did not include sections regarding the treatment of allegations of
wrongdoing by IGs or their staff. Filling this gap, President Clinton issued

an executive order in 1996 creating a single Integrity Committee to evaluate noncriminal allegations of misconduct by IGs and senior OIG officers under the then-existing PCIE and ECIE organizations.[49]

The 2008 IG Reform Act incorporated processes developed under the 1996 executive order, giving statutory authority to an Integrity Committee under CIGIE. Owing to congressional concerns about significant delays in starting, pursuing, and closing investigations,[50] the 2016 IG Empowerment Act retained most of the provisions in Clinton's executive order for handling allegations, but placed specific deadlines on opening, assessing, and closing investigations.[51]

Composition of the Integrity Committee also changed slightly under the 2016 legislation, with the committee now electing one of the IGs to serve as chairperson. The Integrity Committee comprises an official from the FBI who serves as the FBI's representative on CIGIE; four IGs appointed by the chair of CIGIE; the special counsel from the Office of the Special Counsel; and the director of the Office of Government Ethics. The chief of the Public Integrity Section of the Criminal Division of the DOJ serves as the committee's legal advisor.

The 2008 legislation authorized the Integrity Committee to issue policies and procedures detailing processes for handling allegations of wrongdoing.[52] These policies and procedures provide considerable detail for a variety of circumstances and contingencies. At the outset, the Integrity Committee determines whether a complaint is within its authority. Allegations not within the committee's authority may be referred to an IG if they involve a staff member not covered by the law. If the complaint is adjudged to be within the committee's authority, then a series of steps are undertaken to determine whether a formal investigation by the Integrity Committee is warranted. Such an investigation involves requesting a response to the allegations by the IG or named staff member, and possibly enlisting another IG to undertake an investigation at the request of the committee. The IG that conducts the investigation issues a report to the committee, which shares the report with the individual under investigation for review and comment, after which the committee makes a decision and recommends disciplinary action if the facts support the allegation. Thereafter, the CIGIE executive chair, the CIGIE chair, the president (for PAS IGs) or the relevant agency head (for DFE IGs), and committees in the House and Senate are informed of the recommendation.

Data on allegations and responses by the Integrity Committee are reported annually to the president and Congress. Table 3-4 summarizes key data for committee actions from these reports and notes that fiscal year 2013 was an anomalous year, with 312 allegations received from two complainants concerning allegations previously reviewed and closed. Setting aside anomalous figures for 2013, table 3-4 reveals that a slight majority of allegations were closed with no referrals and about 20 percent of the total pool of allegations were referred to another agency for handling. Allegations that involve similar charges and the same individual or OIG are consolidated for administrative review and referral. Accordingly, the thirty-five cases referred to the committee chair for investigation likely involve more than thirty-five allegations. For these cases, the committee's annual reports summarize fourteen final reports, involving seven IGs, two acting IGs, and nine OIG senior staff (see table 3-5). The allegations were sustained after investigations regarding six individuals—two IGs, one acting IG, and three unspecified individuals. One of these IGs resigned after the investigation, another continued serving as IG, and the acting IG was replaced by a permanent IG at the time the report was released.

Backgrounds and Career Tracks of Inspectors General

Paul Light's analysis of the career backgrounds of the thirty-three PAS IGs appointed during the Reagan administration revealed that most (thirty-one) were affiliated with a federal executive department and only two were outside the executive branch prior to their appointment as IGs. Moreover, a significant number (n=20) had experience in OIGs prior to their appointment—although some appointees in the first term were IGs who were reappointed after Reagan's firing of all IGs on his first day in office. Nevertheless, by Reagan's second term, most newly appointed IGs (twelve of fourteen) were drawn from a cadre of individuals with experience as IGs, deputy IGs, or assistant IGs. This pattern, Light observes, demonstrates that the IG community had substantial influence over the recruitment and selection process, and effectively limited appointments

TABLE 3-4

Integrity Committee Annual Investigative Workload, 2009–2018

Fiscal Year	Allegations Received	Allegations within IC Purview	Allegations Closed	Allegations Referred to Committee Chair for Investigation	Allegations Referred to Appropriate Agency	Allegations Pending Review	Final Reports Noted in Annual IC Report
2009	43	38	36	2	5	0	1
2010	44	43	36	1	1	6	1
2011	51	28	22	1	23	5	1
2012	44	19	8	3	25	8	1
2013[a]	390[b]	29	361[b]	12	16	1	3
2014[c]	72	35	30	4	15	1	1
2015	65	40	30	0	5	1	3
2016	68	41	36	1	5	4	0
2017	59	39	33	6	6	1	1
2018	86[d]	63	47	5	18	10	2

Sources: Table draws from Congressional Research Service, "Oversight of the Inspector General Community: The IG Council's Integrity Committee," September 21, 2015, for 2009 through 2014 (https://www.everycrsreport.com/files/20150921_R44198_ceaead39431704eb909c0a3e07c8bfb1a7c492c.pdf). For CRS report and for data from 2015 through 2018, Annual Integrity Committee reports for 2009 through 2018 (https://www.ignet.gov/content/integrity-0).

a Figures reported by CRS for 2013 are revised by the authors: "Allegations within IC Purview" are revised from 374 to 29 in accord with the Integrity Committee report for that year.

b Data on allegations received and closed include 312 concerning allegations previously reviewed and closed.

c Figures reported by CRS for 2014 are revised by the authors as follows: "Allegations Closed" revised from 30 to 36, "Allegations Referred to Committee Chair" revised from 4 to 0, and "Allegations Referred to Appropriate Agency" revised from 37 to 15 in accord with the Integrity Committee report for 2014.

d The Integrity Committee received 385 "communications" that were consolidated into 86 complaints by the Allegation Review Group of the Integrity Committee. See 2018 IC annual report posted at https://ignet.gov/sites/default/files/files/2018_IC_Annual_Report.pdf.

TABLE 3-5

Reported Outcomes of IC Investigations (2009–2016)

Year	Agency	Position Held by the Accused Individual	One or More Allegations Sustained
2009	Securities and Exchange Commission	IG	No
	Securities and Exchange Commission	Deputy IG	No
2010	Commodity Futures Trading Commission	IG	No
2011	U.S. Postal Service	IG	No
	U.S. Postal Service	Assistant IG	No
	U.S. Postal Service	Deputy Assistant IG	No
	U.S. Postal Service	(former) Deputy Assistant IG	No
2012	Federal Communications Commission	IG	No
	Federal Communications Commission	Assistant IG	No
2013	Agriculture	Assistant IG	No
	Interior	Acting IG	No
	National Reconnaissance Office	IG	No
2014	National Archives and Records Administration	IG	Yes
	National Archives and Records Administration	Counsel to the IG	No

	National Archives and Records Administration	Assistant IG	No
2015	Homeland Security	Acting IG	Yes
	National Labor Relations Board	IG	Yes
	Defense	Deputy IG	No
2016	None listed		
2017	Commerce (carried over from previous year)	Not given	Yes
2018	Federal Election Commission	Not given	Yes
	Farm Credit Agency	Not given	No

Sources: Table draws from Congressional Research Service, "Oversight of the Inspector General Community: The IG Council's Integrity Committee," September 21, 2015, for 2009 through 2014 (https://www.everycrsreport.com/files/20150921_R44198_ceaead39431704eb909c0a3e07c8bf-b1a7c492c.pdf). For CRS report and for data from 2015 through 2018, Annual Integrity Committee reports for 2009 through 2018 (https://www.ignet.gov/content/integrity-0).

of non-IG administrative office holders. A consequence of this influence was that IGs "gained greater independence from their home departments and agencies."[53]

We have updated Light's analysis by examining the career tracks of the 297 PAS and DFE IGs permanently appointed to their respective posts from 1978 through January 2017.[54] This number counts as separate appointments the twenty-seven IGs who have served in multiple OIGs during the course of their careers, including six IGs fired by Reagan in 1981 and subsequently rehired as the IG in the same agency (n=3) or in a different agency (n=3). Notably, two IGs have held multiple permanent IG positions in more than two agencies: June Gibbs-Brown with four appointments (Department of Labor [1979–1981], NASA [1981–1985], Department of Defense [1987–1989], and Department of Health and Human Services [1993–2001]) and David C. Williams with five appointments (Nuclear Regulatory Commission [1989–1996], Social Security Administration [1996–1998], Department of the Treasury [1998–1999], Treasury Inspector General for Texas Administration [1999–2002], and U.S. Postal Service [2003–2016]).[55]

To construct a portrait of the IG community during the Carter, Reagan, G. H. W. Bush, Clinton, G. W. Bush, and Obama administrations, we searched for biographical and career information in publicly available sources, including various Who's Who volumes, the Leadership Directories,[56] the Washington Post, the New York Times, published Senate confirmation hearings (for PAS appointments), and biographies posted by the IGs themselves. In particular, we collected information regarding dates of service, whether the IG had a law degree, and his or her gender, race/ethnicity, and position at the time of confirmation or appointment.

DEMOGRAPHICS

The IG community from its inception through 2016 is predominantly male and white. The greatest proportion (76percent) of IGs are male, with only a slight difference between PAS IGs (79 percent male) and DFE IGs (73 percent male). On average across administrations, higher percentages of IG appointees were male in Republican administrations (89 percent for PAS and 79 percent for DFE appointees)[57] versus Democratic administrations (67 percent for PAS and 67 percent for DFE appointees). A majority of appointees in all administrations were white, although there are also differences between Republican and Democratic administrations. Precise percentages are difficult to calculate due to missing information on fifty-two appointees (18 percent of the total) where race or ethnicity could not be verified. Nevertheless, on average across administrations, Republican appointees were more predominantly white (78 percent for PAS and 71 percent for DFE appointees) versus Democratic appointees (63 percent for PAS and 64 percent for DFE appointees).[58] Among the minority thirty-six PAS or DFE appointees, twenty-five were African American, five were Hispanic, and six were Pacific Islanders or Asian. Most of these appointments (nineteen PAS IGs and eleven DFE IGs) came in the Clinton, G. W. Bush, and Obama administrations.

Light's survey of PAS IGs serving through the late 1980s asked about their career focus and yielded the finding that most identified as either auditors (n=12) or investigators (n=16).[59] His data also show that six respondents indicated that they had law degrees, all but one of whom were investigators. Light's focus on auditors and investigators reflected discussions surrounding the IG Act of 1978, which mandated the merging of investigative and auditing units in federal agencies under newly created OIGs. Light goes on to argue that the trend for IGs in the first dozen years after passage of the 1978 act reflects a shift from audits to investigations. A listing of DFE appointees that included backgrounds was later compiled by the ECIE for eighty-six DFE appointments through January 2007. These data show that most DFE IGs identified as auditors (43 percent), followed by attorneys (29 percent), investigators (15 percent), management analysts (9 percent), and other backgrounds (4 percent).[60] This listing of DFE IGs distinguishes attorneys from investigators, auditors, and others, and so it is not fully comparable to Light's survey.

Our efforts to identify career focus by using the publicly available sources mentioned previously were unsuccessful. In many cases, biographical information was incomplete, did not give undergraduate majors, or did not give a detailed description of full responsibilities of positions held prior to an IG appointment. In other cases, the IGs' positions indicated experiences that were rooted in auditing and investigations.

Our interviews within the IG community suggested IGs increasingly came to office holding a law degree. The proportion of IGs with legal backgrounds has always been significant with PAS appointees—Carter (50 percent), Reagan (33 percent), G. H. W. Bush (36 percent) and Clinton (40 percent)—but the percentages increase substantially with appointees under G. W. Bush (61 percent) and Obama (76 percent). The percentages of DFE IGs holding law degrees is smaller when compared with PAS IGs, with an overall average of 33 percent having legal backgrounds—G. H. W. Bush (18 percent), Clinton (32 percent), G. W. Bush (42 percent), and Obama (38 percent)—although this finding is constrained by missing information for nearly a quarter of DFE IG appointees. Nevertheless, these data confirm that attorneys and IGs with legal backgrounds are increasingly prominent in the IG community—especially among PAS IGs.

CAREER TRACKS

Inspectors general differ from many executive officials in that legislation creating their office specified that they should be appointed "without regard to political affiliation and solely on the basis of integrity and demonstrated ability in accounting, auditing, financial analysis, law, management analysis, public administration, or investigations."[61] Light's analysis of Carter and Reagan appointees shows that most IGs appointed by these two presidents had career tracks that fit comfortably within these parameters.[62] Light's analysis also points to an unspecified but potentially consequential attribute of the appointees—namely, that most (95 percent) had extensive careers in the executive branch and many (50 percent) had experience within an IG office.

The data for IGs appointed from 1978 through 2016 indicate that, indeed, most IGs have prior federal service and that many IGs emerge from a previous position in an OIG. The percentages of PAS IG appointments with prior federal service range from 69 percent for G. W. Bush appointees to 89 percent for Clinton appointees, and the overall percentage for PAS appointees holding federal positions prior to appointment as IG is 81 percent. The percentages of DFE IGs with federal service immediately prior to their appointment as IGs is general higher except for Clinton appointees, with a range from 79 percent for G. H. W. Bush to 97 percent for Obama. Overall, these data show that 88 percent of the DFE IGs stepped into their IG appointment from a prior position in the federal government.

Among all PAS IGs, 42 percent assumed their IG appointment from a previous position in an OIG and 39 percent came from a federal position but not in an OIG. PAS appointees from OIGs varied substantially from one administration to another—Carter (19 percent), Reagan (61 percent), G. H. W. Bush (14 percent), Clinton (49 percent), G. W. Bush (31 percent), and Obama (62 percent). Notably, 25 percent of G. W. Bush PAS appointees were drawn from the private sector, with much lower percentages for the remaining presidents serving in private business or as private attorneys—Carter (6 percent), Reagan (9 percent), G. H. W. Bush (7 percent), Clinton (9 percent), and Obama (14 percent). Finally, we found very low percentages of PAS IGs stepped into their positions from non-OIG positions within the federal agency whose IG position they assumed (5 percent), a U.S. Attorney's office (1 percent), the armed forces (2 percent), a state-level office (3 percent), or a nonprofit organization (2 percent).

Inspectors general in DFEs are more likely to have an immediately prior position in the federal government (88 percent versus 81 percent for PAS IGs) and a substantially greater proportion stepped into their position from within their agency's OIG (30 percent versus 17 percent for PAS IGs). Like PAS IGs, about one-quarter of the DFE IGs have previously served in another agency's OIG. However, DFE IGs show an increasing percentage of appointees coming from other agencies' OIGs— G. H. W. Bush (13 percent), Clinton (28 percent), G. W. Bush (34 percent), and Obama (35 percent). This increase may be a consequence of a larger pool of candidates and the development of a career ladder for DFE IGs. Finally, it is noteworthy that very few DFE IGs come directly to their office from outside federal executive offices, and in the Clinton, G. W. Bush, and Obama administrations, only a small percentage of the appointees emerged from non-IG offices in the home agency.

Conclusion

When most IGs step into the office as either presidential appointments or agency appointments, they also enter the strategic environment described in the opening chapter of this volume. Accounts of appointment processes and data reported in this chapter show that the IG community significantly affects the recruitment, training, and socialization of IGs. This occurred initially through OMB's stewardship of IG selection, which used an IG committee to identify and review prospective PAS IG nominees. Thereafter, the IG community itself became a major source for PAS IGs and, after the creation of DFEs in 1988, for DFE IGs. Notably, over 60 percent of the DFE IGs appointed by Presidents Clinton, G. W. Bush, and Obama stepped into their executive offices from an office of inspector general. Links to the IG community among PAS IGs appointed by Presidents Clinton and Obama are slightly weaker in terms of percentages with immediately prior positions in OIGs, and President G. W. Bush's appointments with prior OIG appointments were significantly less—although prior OIG experience is the model career track for his PAS appointees.

Having a large number of IGs with substantial roots in the IG community means that the values and norms of inspectors general are likely to be reinforced with each replacement appointment, regardless of what political party or president leads the executive branch. Specifically, the IG community's view about the importance of independence from agency interference is likely to be widely and deeply held, and will remain a guiding principle for future appointees.

For PAS IGs, the pulls and tugs of Congress and the executive branch are revealed during a confirmation process in which nominees are vetted by at least two sets of protagonists—congressional representatives who view IGs as important agents in their oversight of the executive branch, and executive officials who may view IGs with some suspicion as executive officers with congressional allies, statutory independence, and authority unlike any other members of their administration. While selection processes for DFE IGs may appear to be more bureaucratic and do not involve senatorial review, many will have prior experience in the IG community that doubtless includes stories of tensions between Congress and executive agencies. Our interviews with PAS and DFE IGs suggest that all were attentive to expectations and intrusions of both Congress and their home agencies, and sought to protect their office from the ill effects of such pressures.

While attributes of the appointment process clearly reinforce IG independence, there are fewer stages or opportunities where discussions might occur regarding accountability and engagement. Interviews with congressional sources and IGs suggest that conversations with PAS nominees are intended to emphasize the importance of IG accountability to Congress and independence from agency influence. Our interviews with agency officials and IGs suggest that conversations between prospective IGs and agency officials may cover notions of independence and accountability, but not in any great depth. A few DFE IGs reported that their interviews included conversations about audits, investigations, or evaluations that the agency believed needed to be done, but discussions about accountability simply emphasized the need to keep agency leadership informed. By all accounts, there were very few discussions about whether and how IGs might be engaged with either Congress or agency officials in terms of problem solving.

FOUR

Conducting the Work

INVESTIGATIONS, FINANCIAL AUDITS, AND PERFORMANCE AUDITS

This week is reserved for the congressional grilling of OPM Director Katherine Archuleta. Members of the House and Senate want answers to questions about the digital data breach that resulted in the theft of personal information belonging to more than 4 million current and former federal employees. Archuleta endured antagonistic questioning at the House Oversight and Government Reform Committee last week and she is scheduled for three more hearings this week.

On Tuesday she faced the Senate Appropriations financial services and general government subcommittee. Though the senators treated her relatively gently, their hearing set the stage for what could be a more aggressive session when Archuleta returns to the House panel Wednesday. Then it's back before the Senate on Thursday for the Homeland Security and Governmental Affairs Committee hearing.

Archuleta has defended her agency's program to protect its computerized records and her initiatives to improve systems since she entered office. "Over the last 18 months, OPM has undertaken an aggressive effort to upgrade its cybersecurity posture," she said.

But not long before she took her seat at the witness table in 124 Dirksen Senate Office Building Tuesday, OPM's inspector general released a "flash audit alert" that sharply criticized her agency's management of a project to overhaul its technical infrastructure.

For House members who like their red meat raw, this latest report will be a full plate.

"In our opinion, the project management approach for this major infrastructure overhaul is entirely inadequate, and introduces a very high risk of project failure," Inspector General Patrick E. McFarland wrote in the flash audit. . . . The flash audit, however, is pointedly critical of management problems in [Donna] Seymour's Office of the Chief Information Officer (OCIO). The second paragraph of the audit minces no words: "Our primary concern is that the OCIO has not followed U.S. Office of Management and Budget (OMB) requirements and project management best practices. The OCIO has initiated this project without a complete understanding of the scope of OPM's existing technical infrastructure or the scale and costs of the effort required to migrate it to the new environment."

Although McFarland said he agrees in principle with OPM's IT plans, he lambasted the implementation. OPM, he wrote, has not "identified the full scope and cost" of the project, has "not prepared a 'Major IT Business Case'" as required and OPM's "overall project management process is missing a number of critical artifacts considered to be best practices by relevant organizations."

—Report in the Washington Post, June 23, 2015, on a Senate hearing regarding the hacking of OPM's computer system at which an IG report criticizing the agency was referenced in the hearing

Sometimes an inspector general participates in criticizing agency operations publicly and refers to recommendations that his or her office made but that were not followed, as IG Patrick McFarland did in June 2015 regarding the publicized digital data breach at the U.S. Office of Personnel Management (OPM). But that is rare and virtually never the preferred course of action for IGs. In fact, extensive background efforts and deliberations are typically undertaken by IG offices to prioritize their work, collect relevant data, develop actionable recommendations, and then support actions made by agency staff to make the recommended changes.

In this chapter we describe how IG offices conduct work to improve agency operations, processes, and programs through investigations, audits, and the development of actionable recommendations. First, we discuss the way that IG offices set their agendas for work and describe the resources devoted to IG work across the federal government. Second, we describe the typical flow of the work for investigations. Third, we discuss the processes that the IG offices use to focus audits (both financial and performance) and develop recommendations. We then discuss the challenges and opportunities that IG offices face in getting their recommendations implemented. Finally, we discuss how IG auditing and investigative work is affected by and may affect the IG's stakeholders, expectations held by those stakeholders, and system stressors in the IG's strategic environment.

Setting the Agenda

Inspectors General are expected to accomplish broad objectives in improving government—by both detecting and preventing fraud, waste, and abuse through recommendations to improve agency systems and operations. Originally the work of OIGs was focused almost solely on investigations and financial audits—detection of wrongdoing. In 1986, Mark Moore and Margaret Gates examined the work of the IG community and noted that what they called the second generation of IGs in select federal agencies—that is, U.S. Department of Agriculture (USDA), Health and Human Services (HHS), and Labor—had started working more on the prevention objective, and they had established new divisions called Inspections Offices or Inspections and Evaluations Offices. By 1993 over half of the large IG offices had set up such divisions,[1] and by 2017 virtually all IG offices were conducting other work focused on improving program management, in addition to financial audits and investigations.

When we interviewed inspectors general as part of this research, we heard one singular aspiration voiced by all IGs from across the federal government. When asked how they would measure their own success, they all replied they would want to see that their office's efforts had improved their agency's operations. Not one IG told us that monetary savings for the agency was his or her personal goal, despite the very public nature of that performance measure.[2] But achieving success through improving agency operations is not a clear nor easy process.

Federal inspectors general consistently work to identify appropriate targets—or problems—to fix or improve, and then marshal appropriate and adequate resources—both monetary and in terms of skilled staff—to investigate where improvements are needed. Since IGs must engage in a positive manner with both Congress and their agency leadership to secure adequate support, the IGs are vigilant in scanning the priorities voiced by both. But while all IG offices seek input from their agency leadership and their congressional contacts on potential audit targets, our interviews suggest that most IG work is targeted through internal scanning and by fires that flare up unexpectedly, for example, through calls to IG hotlines.

All IG offices develop work plans each year. They proactively solicit ideas for preventive work with their agency leadership and relevant congressional staff. In addition, the U.S. Government Accountability Office (GAO) issues a High Risk List every two years, in which it identifies weaknesses within agencies that an IG may target, and each IG compiles his or her own annual management risk list as well. The annual work plan prioritizes IG work to be undertaken, and it is also populated with legislative requirements. However, unanticipated work arises that may crowd out planned work.

A great deal of reactive work undertaken by IG offices is initiated in response to complaints brought in through the hotline each IG maintains. Other potential risks and allegations of wrongdoing may be brought to light by the media and congressional calls. Figure 4-1 outlines how IG offices are prompted to undertake fact-finding to clarify the type of action they will initiate, for example, an investigation or audit.

The nature of the work of an agency affects where OIGs are likely to focus their efforts. For example, in agencies where contracting out for goods and/or services is common—such as the departments of Defense and Energy—procurement and contracting processes are likely to draw more attention from the IG than in agencies where contracting is less common, such as the Department of Justice (DOJ) or the Securities and Exchange Commission (SEC). On the other hand, there are some similarities in focus across OIGs. For example, virtually all federal agencies are vulnerable to cybersecurity and information technology challenges.

The resources that IG offices bring to bear on their work also affects their work plans and priorities for action. The budgets and number of personnel in IG offices vary greatly across the federal government, as seen in

FIGURE 4-1

Prompts for IG Action and Type of Action Taken

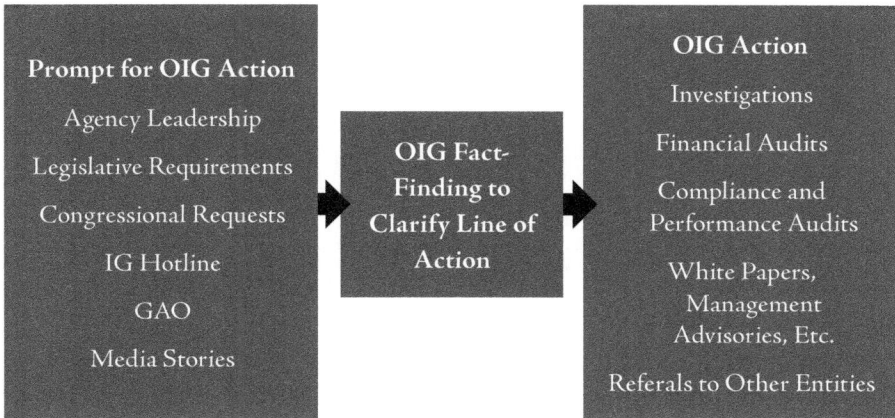

table 4-1, which presents data from fiscal year 2012. Agency-specific cir-cumstances affect the way that IG personnel are allocated. For example, the large amount of money paid to contractors for products and services at the Department of Defense (DoD) and the Centers for Medicare and Medicaid Services (within HHS) explains in part why OIGs for DOD and HHS have large numbers of employees. The differences between the budgets for some IG offices and the amounts actually spent—for ex-ample, in the Social Security Administration (SSA) and HHS—reflect other sources those offices rely on for funding. And while the size of the IG offices in the large departments is impressive, half of the offices have budgets below $13 million. Control over IG budgets is a key lever of con-trol that Congress may threaten to use, as we will discuss below.

Conducting Investigations

Within each IG office there is an assistant IG for investigations who over-sees a staff that is deployed to investigate alleged wrongdoing by employ-ees of the government or by nonfederal entities such as contractors to the government.[3] Many instances of alleged wrongdoing are flagged via

TABLE 4-I

Budgets and Number of Personnel in IG Offices Vary Greatly (FY2012)

Largest IG Offices	FY 2012 Budget (millions)[a]	FY 2012 Outlays (millions)[a]	FY 2012 FTEs[b]	Number of Agency Employees[c] per OIG FTE
Department of Defense	$339	$329	1,575	487
Postal Service	$241	$241	1,136	531
Internal Revenue Service	$152	$153	807	112
Department of Homeland Security	$141	$154	676	283
State Department	$129	$114	233	174
Department of Housing and Urban Development	$124	$129	655	14
Department of Veterans Affairs	$112	$116	638	498
Department of Agriculture	$86	$92	545	164
Department of Justice	$84	$104	465	251
Department of Transportation	$80	$86	413	136
Department of Health and Human Services	$50	$101	1,773	41
Social Security Administration	$29	$109	569	115
Median-Sized IG Offices				
National Science Foundation	$14	$15	78	19
Nuclear Regulatory Agency	$11	$10	58	68
Smallest IG Offices (with at least $100 million budgets)				
Commodity Futures Trading Commission	—[d]	—[d]	4	172
Farm Credit Administration	$1.2	—[d]	5	58

a Data drawn from budget justifications for IG offices in each agency, FY14, Appendix, Budget of the U.S. Government, Office of Management and Budget, 2013. This budget document gives actual budget authorizations and outlays for FY12 in addition to information on FY13 budget authority and the proposed FY14 budget.

b FOIA response from Mark Jones, Executive Director, CIGIE, December 6, 2016, regarding FTE totals for OIGs in FY 2012.

c The number of agency employees was obtained through the Office of Personnel Management, "Employment and Trends—March 2012," Table 2, "Comparison of Total Civilian Employment of the Federal Government by Branch, Agency, and Area as of December 2011 and March 2012."

d Budget outlays not given for small agencies in Appendix for FY14 budget.

the agency hotlines, and other IG staff members may also flag issues that they uncover while undertaking audits or inspections. IG investigators are highly trained agents of the government, with the authority to issue subpoenas and carry firearms, much like Federal Bureau of Investigation (FBI) special agents. While IG investigators collect evidence, they then transfer the evidence to the DOJ or to state or local attorneys to prosecute, as is shown in figure 4-2.

Virtually every IG office needs to prioritize the investigative work that

FIGURE 4-2
Typical OIG Investigation Stages

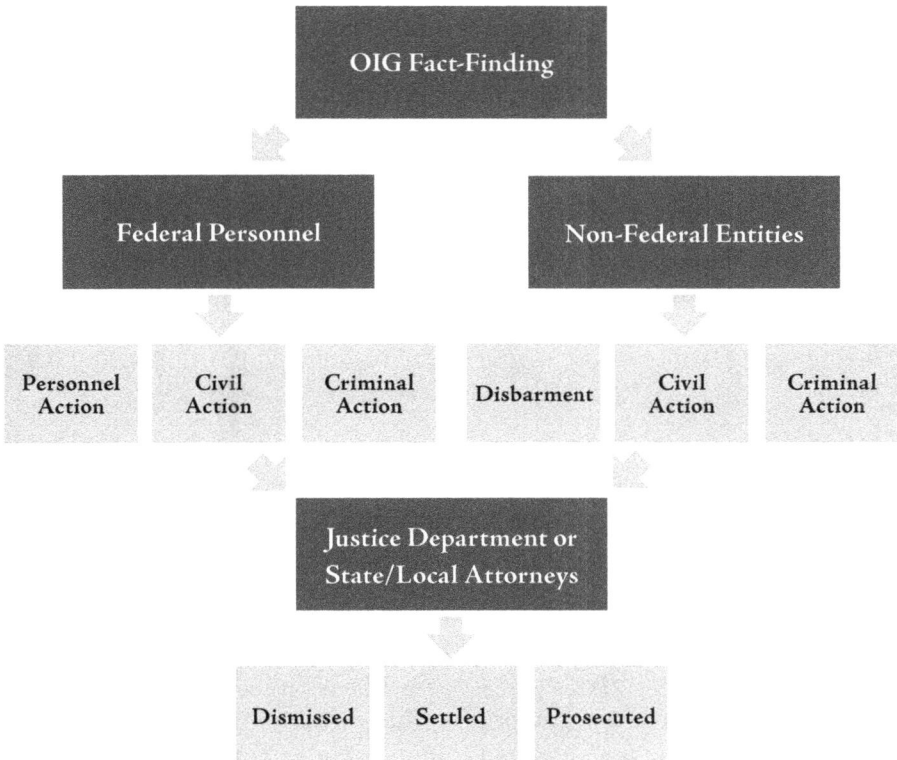

it can take on, due to limited resources. The cases that are pursued reflect the level of financial fraud involved in the case, as well as the priorities of the inspector general, agency management, the IG office's congressional contacts, the DOJ, and/or the U.S. Attorney's office that would handle the case. IG staff members are mindful that they must provide sufficient evidence to convince prosecutors that the case is worth pursuing, so the perceived strength of the evidence in the case matters. Media interest in the case or issue area may also affect IG interest. When alternatives to prosecution—such as civil settlements, or suspensions, debarment, or personnel actions—are available, IG investigators may quickly relinquish their role in the matter.

IG investigators also work in concert with a variety of other federal law enforcement agencies on criminal cases that cross over jurisdictions. For example, Department of Transportation (DOT) IG investigators worked closely with the FBI on a case in which a citizen flew a drone over federal airspace in the Washington, DC, area. U.S. Postal Service IG investigators are likely to work with state and local law enforcement agencies on postal fraud cases. Many participants, including IG investigators, personnel from other law enforcement agencies, and federal, state, or local attorneys, are involved in cases that were initiated by IG investigators, so it is difficult to attribute successful prosecutions or settlements to IG action alone. But IG offices monitor closely the number of personnel actions, disbarments, civil cases, and criminal cases filed each year.

Planning and Conducting Audits

Unlike investigations, IG financial and performance audits are typically initiated and concluded without the involvement of other federal agencies. By statute, each IG office has an assistant IG for financial audits. In many offices the staff in that unit undertake both financial audits and performance audits, which are process evaluations or compliance audits of programs. Some IG offices have established a separate unit, called Inspection Offices or Inspection and Evaluation Offices, to house the staff that conducts performance audits. But the process for both financial and performance audits is similar and is outlined in figure 4-3. Throughout the process there is much back and forth between the IG staff and the agency's staff in the part of the agency that is targeted for the audit. The audit findings and recommendations are eventually released to the agency leadership and Congress simultaneously.

Targeting processes or programs where IG recommendations are likely to result in substantial improvements and cost savings is a priority for an IG. Marshaling adequate resources, especially audit teams with appropriate skill sets, is critical, as is working well with the agency staff in the targeted area to gain the knowledge and data needed to ascertain what changes are necessary. Ensuring access to needed information is likely to be affected by how well the IG is received by the rest of the agency. A reputation for fairness and integrity helps IG teams secure the cooperation they need to research issues, offer credible findings, and develop recommendations that result in improvements.

By statute, all IG offices conduct financial and performance audits in accordance with requirements set forth in *Government Auditing Standards*, which is published by the GAO and typically referred to as the Yellow Book. For every finding that an IG office offers as a result of their work, they must describe four things: (1) the condition they studied—typically because there was reason to believe that the condition was undesirable; (2) the criteria they applied to assess how deviant the condition was from the desired state, for example, as per a law or regulation; (3) the effect or potential effect of the existing condition, such as undesirable outcomes; and (4) the cause, or the reason or factor responsible for the difference between the current condition and the desired state. Table 4-2 provides the *Government Auditing Standards* language for these requirements.

Before potential corrective actions can be envisioned and recommended, IGs must first identify the underlying causes of the undesirable condition. As *Government Auditing Standards* notes, the potential causes for undesirable conditions may include "poorly designed policies, procedures, or criteria; inconsistent, incomplete, or incorrect implementation; or factors beyond the control of program management." Factors outside of the control of program management that constitute the cause of undesired conditions may well include poorly or vaguely written legislation,

FIGURE 4-3

The Process Through Which Federal Investigators Plan and Conduct Audits to Improve Management Systems and Operations in Their Agencies

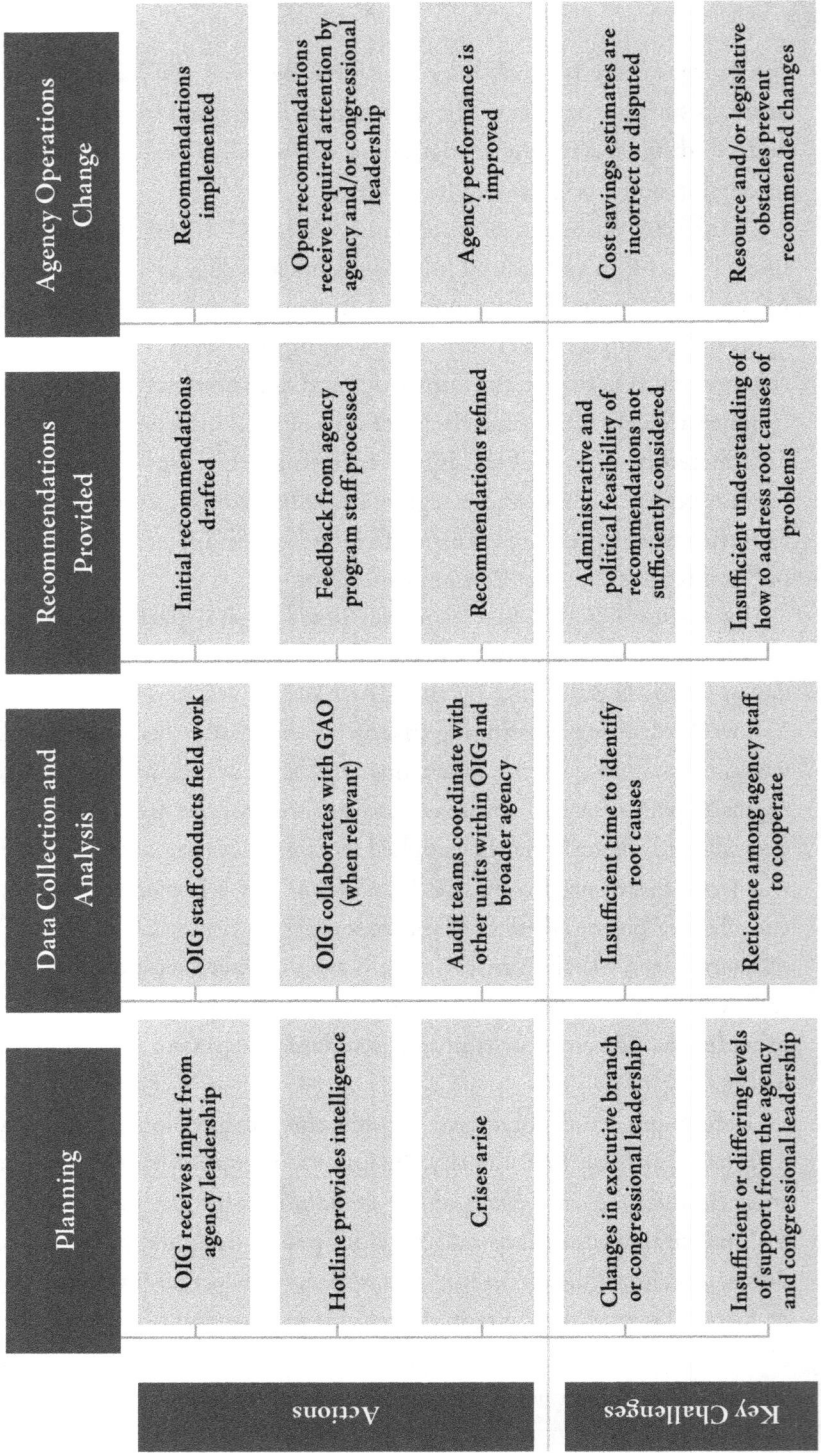

	Planning	Data Collection and Analysis	Recommendations Provided	Agency Operations Change
Actions	OIG receives input from agency leadership	OIG staff conducts field work	Initial recommendations drafted	Recommendations implemented
	Hotline provides intelligence	OIG collaborates with GAO (when relevant)	Feedback from agency program staff processed	Open recommendations receive required attention by agency and/or congressional leadership
	Crises arise	Audit teams coordinate with other units within OIG and broader agency	Recommendations refined	Agency performance is improved
Key Challenges	Changes in executive branch or congressional leadership	Insufficient time to identify root causes	Administrative and political feasibility of recommendations not sufficiently considered	Cost savings estimates are incorrect or disputed
	Insufficient or differing levels of support from the agency and congressional leadership	Reticence among agency staff to cooperate	Insufficient understanding of how to address root causes of problems	Resource and/or legislative obstacles prevent recommended changes

---

TABLE 4-2

Required Elements of OIG Audit Finding: Criteria, Condition, Cause, and Effect

Criteria: The laws, regulations, contracts, grant agreements, standards, measures, expected performance, defined business practices, and benchmarks against which performance is compared or evaluated. Criteria identify the required or desired state or expectation with respect to the program or operation. Criteria provide a context for evaluating evidence and understanding the findings.

Condition: Condition is a situation that exists. The condition is determined and documented during the audit.

Cause: The cause identifies the reason or explanation for the condition or the factor or factors responsible for the difference between the situation that exists (condition) and the required or desired state (criteria), which may also serve as a basis for recommendations for corrective actions. Common factors include poorly designed policies, procedures, or criteria; inconsistent, incomplete, or incorrect implementation; or factors beyond the control of program management. Auditors may assess whether the evidence provides a reasonable and convincing argument for why the stated cause is the key factor or factors contributing to the difference between the condition and the criteria.

Effect or potential effect: The effect is a clear, logical link to establish the impact or potential impact of the difference between the situation that exists (condition) and the required or desired state (criteria). The effect or potential effect identifies the outcomes or consequences of the condition. When the audit objectives include identifying the actual or potential consequences of a condition that varies (either positively or negatively) from the criteria identified in the audit, "effect" is a measure of those consequences. Effect or potential effect may be used to demonstrate the need for corrective action in response to identified problems or relevant risks.

Source: U.S. GAO, *Government Auditing Standards*, 2011 Revision, paragraphs 4.11 through 4.14, pp. 76–77.

---

and/or insufficient funding appropriated by Congress. However, IG findings are unlikely to simply point the finger at Congress as a cause.

Finding Root Causes during Financial and Performance Audits

Identifying the fundamental, or root, cause for the undesirable conditions that an IG office describes is likely to be challenging and will require contextual wisdom about the policy or programmatic setting, adequate time to devote to studying the problem, and the resources and ability to sort through factors that contribute to existing conditions. To recommend corrective action, the IG must have some certainty that if the root cause is removed or changed, then the undesirable events or outcomes will not recur. Plus, the IG team must identify specific actions or steps that the agency can take within existing resources to reduce the negative outcomes from the faulty processes or procedures that the OIG has characterized as the cause.

OIG staff are very cognizant that the recommendations they offer need to be deemed feasible and on target to address the root cause by the agency management. Once received, agencies may decline to accept a recommendation for a variety of reasons. For example, some recommendations may require changes in the legislative or regulatory requirements of the program, many of which are outside the control of agency management. Agencies may find such recommendations are not credible or doable, but may request legislative or programmatic changes based on the IG report. On other occasions, agency management may simply disagree with the recommendations and decline to adopt the recommendation because they question the data or the data analysis that led to the recommendation.

In addition, the number of recommendations that are implemented constitutes one performance measure for IG offices, as well as for the GAO; thus, there may be some pressure internally within an IG office to develop recommendations that are implementable. IG offices can claim credit when conditions improve because the recommendations that the OIGs offered produced the desired corrections. Thus, developing recommendations is an extremely critical task that typically entails a quite deliberative and laborious process for IG audit teams.

Developing Actionable Recommendations

It takes time to ensure that IG staff develop a sufficient understanding of the context and can identify mitigating factors that have contributed to the visible problems they have observed. The IG audit team needs to strategize and balance a variety of priorities as they develop recommendations. Through interviews with leaders in six IG offices, we identified a large number of potential factors that IG staff consider when they develop recommendations; we then surveyed the broader community of IGs to gain their perceptions on the relative weights of the many factors.[4] Table 4-3 lists fifteen factors that IG staff identified and how frequently they are important considerations in the recommendation development process.

The most significant factors affecting IG deliberations regarding how to frame recommendations relate to the mission of the agency and of the OIG. As table 4-3 shows, advancing the agency's objectives (that is, mission) is the most important driver for recommendation development, with 73 percent of the IGs noting it is always key. Virtually all of the IGs responding to the survey (96 percent) report it is key in 75 percent or more of the cases. In line with the IG mission, providing efficiencies in agency operations is a close second-most important consideration when developing recommendations, with 72 percent of the responding IGs reporting that it is always a key consideration. Relatedly, ensuring compliance with federal laws and polices is noted to be a key consideration in all cases by over 70 percent of the responding IGs.

Reflecting the great diversity in the work of the agencies in which IGs are located, there is less consensus among the survey respondents on the relative importance of the twelve other factors that sometimes affect the development of recommendations—factors that emerged previously in interviews for the six case studies that are reported in chapter 5.[5] A somewhat surprising finding is that anticipated reactions from the affected agency managers or from Congress on the "reasonableness, cost, importance and/or challenges in implementation" are not consistently considered important factors affecting the development of recommendations by the responding IGs, with over 40 percent responding that they are considered 25 percent of the time or less. Relatedly, anticipated reactions from agency clienteles and agency leadership on the "reasonableness, cost, importance and/or challenges in implementation" are considered important factors affecting the development of recommendations only about half the time. And in another surprise, given that the number of recom-

TABLE 4-3

Considerations Important for OIG Staff When Developing Recommendations

Using the scale listed below, what percentage of the time are the following factors important considerations when you are developing draft recommendations? (n=26)

Answer Options	Never, 0% of the time	About 25% of the time	About 50% of the time	About 75% of the time	Always, 100% of the time
			Responses		
How the recommendation will advance the agency's objectives	0.0%	3.8%	0.0%	23.1%	73.1%
How the recommendation will provide efficiencies in agency operations	0.0%	0.0%	8.0%	20.0%	72.0%
Bringing the agency's actions into compliance with federal laws and policies	0.0%	8.3%	8.3%	12.5%	70.8%
Bringing the agency's financial practices into alignment with general accounting standards	8.3%	8.3%	8.3%	20.8%	54.2%
Administrative feasibility of the recommendation	0.0%	11.5%	7.7%	34.6%	46.2%
Projected cost/benefit ratio	0.0%	16.0%	12.0%	28.0%	44.0%
Views of IG regarding what the agency should be doing to achieve its mission	8.3%	20.8%	29.2%	8.3%	33.3%
Significant budgetary increases or additional funding will be required	8.3%	20.8%	12.5%	25.0%	33.3%
Statutory changes or authorization will be required	12.5%	20.8%	20.8%	16.7%	29.2%

Anticipated agency clienteles' perspectives on the reasonableness, cost, importance, and/or challenges in implementation	12.5%	29.2%	16.7%	20.8%	20.8%
Anticipated agency leadership's perspectives on the reasonableness, cost, importance, and/or challenges in implementation	4.2%	25.0%	16.7%	33.3%	20.8%
Priorities or goals of IG or OIG	20.0%	32.0%	12.0%	16.0%	20.0%
Anticipated reactions of affected agency managers on the reasonableness, cost, importance, and/or challenges in implementation	8.3%	29.2%	8.3%	37.5%	16.7%
Anticipated congressional perspectives on the reasonableness, cost, importance, and/or challenges in implementation	22.7%	18.2%	22.7%	27.3%	9.1%
The OIG's assessment that the recommendation will not be fully implemented	25.0%	29.2%	16.7%	20.8%	8.3%

Source: Electronic survey of the IG community in the fall of 2016 by the co-authors. See Appendix B, this volume, for the questionnaire.

mendations not implemented (called "open") is a measure that attracts publicity to IG offices, the IG's assessment that a recommendation "will not be fully implemented" is the factor rated as the least important of the fifteen factors, with over half of the reporting IGs saying it is a consideration in 25 percent or less of the cases. One-fourth of the IGs reported that they never even consider the likelihood of full implementation when initially developing recommendations.

We asked IGs to estimate how often the various factors affect internal deliberations regarding how to develop recommendations. The conditions that an audit examines vary across processes and programs even within the same agency. Some factors affect certain audits but not others. The unique characteristics of the problem or condition uncovered, along with the challenges faced in identifying both the root causes and ways to address those root causes, vary greatly. Sometimes agency clienteles or Congress may be alert to and interested in the issues being addressed, and sometimes they may not be at all.

Before recommendations are finalized, IG teams share draft recommendations and solicit input from both agency officials outside of the IG office and from managers within the IG office. Through this vetting process, IG staff may uncover likely obstacles to implementation that lead them to revise or even drop draft recommendations. Sometimes the IGs themselves simply rewrite or delete a recommendation when the draft report reaches them. Table 4-4 provides the assessments by responding IGs of the factors that are important considerations when they finalize recommendations. Again, factors listed in the survey were initially identified during interviews with IGs in our case studies.

The feasibility of implementing the recommendation is an important consideration when recommendations are being finalized. As seen in table 4-4, recommendations may well be revised or deleted when they are considered vague, inappropriate, or unreasonable, or are deemed by some to simply not identify root causes. Again, interestingly, the view that the recommendation will not be accepted by agency management is not an overriding consideration even at the final stage, with 50 percent of the IGs noting that they never worry about that. The responses in table 4-4 indicate that IGs do pay attention to questions raised by the

TABLE 4-4

Considerations Important for OIG Staff When Finalizing Recommendations

Using the scale listed below, what percentage of the time are the following factors important considerations when you are finalizing recommendations? (n=26)

			Responses		
Answer Options	Never, 0% of the time	About 25% of the time	About 50% of the time	About 75% of the time	Always, 100% of the time
Comments from agency officials regarding a recommendation's vagueness or poor writing	12.5%	4.2%	16.7%	12.5%	54.2%
Comments from agency officials about the appropriateness and reasonableness of recommendation	3.8%	15.4%	23.1%	19.2%	38.5%
Comments from agency officials that the report does not identify the root causes sufficiently or correctly to offer a reasonable recommendation	20.0%	4.0%	20.0%	20.0%	36.0%
Views of IG regarding what the agency should be doing to achieve its mission	4.3%	26.1%	30.4%	13.0%	26.1%
Priorities or goals of IG or OIG	28.0%	20.0%	16.0%	16.0%	20.0%
Conclusion by the OIG that the recommendation will not be fully implemented for any number of reasons	38.5%	38.5%	3.8%	7.7%	11.5%
Conclusion by the OIG that a recommendation will not be accepted by agency management	50.0%	30.8%	0.0%	11.5%	7.7%

Source: Electronic survey of the IG community in the fall of 2016 by the co-authors. See Appendix B, this volume, for the questionnaire.

agency regarding whether the root cause has been identified. But once the IG believes he or she has identified the root cause and provided reasonable recommendations to address the issue, concerns about acceptability from agency leadership are secondary. Only two of the responding IGs reported that likely acceptance from agency management is always a consideration for their work.

Getting IG Recommendations Implemented

Recommendations are intended to provide agency staff with explicit actions that they may take to correct deficiencies or fix problems that IG audits identify. But not all recommendations are viewed as readily implementable by the affected agency staff. Given the variety in the types of recommended actions offered, as well as the circumstances in which the responding agency staff operate, there is not one simple reason that can explain when and why recommendations are not implemented. Building on the factors that we uncovered in our qualitative research, we asked IGs to rate the frequency of various factors in explaining why IG recommendations are not implemented. Table 4-5 displays the variety of reasons IGs provided for why they believe their recommendations are not implemented.

Not surprisingly, a lack of resources within the affected agency office is the most frequent obstacle cited by IGs as to why their recommendations are not implemented. Agency leadership interest matters as well. Over one-third of the responding IGs reported that "Insufficient support from agency leadership" hinders recommendations from being implemented more than 50 percent of the time.

Factors that are not viewed as obstacles to getting recommendations implemented include congressional intervention and "Current negative relationships between your IG office and agency management." Our interviews with OIG staff suggest that cultivating positive relationships with Congress and agency leadership helps both at the front end, when initiating IG audits, and at the back end, when trying to get IG audit recommendations implemented. As a result of these OIG efforts, there may be few occasions when agency managers and OIG staff have negative relationships that affect implementation of OIG recommendations.

TABLE 4-5

Factors that Explain Why OIG Recommendations Are Not Implemented

Using the scale listed below, what percentage of the time do the following factors account for recommendations not being implemented by agency management? (n=26)

			Responses			
Answer Options	Never, 0% of the time	About 25% of the time	About 50% of the time	About 75% of the time	Always, 100% of the time	
The affected agency office requires additional resources to take recommended actions	8.7%	34.8%	21.7%	30.4%	4.3%	
The recommended change requires longer to accomplish than 2 years due to the need to coordinate with external entities	33.3%	23.8%	19.0%	23.8%	0.0%	
Insufficient support from agency leadership to implement the recommended actions	26.1%	39.1%	17.4%	17.4%	0.0%	
Managers in the affected agency office do not agree that the recommendations will enhance operations	21.7%	52.2%	17.4%	8.7%	0.0%	
The affected agency office requires additional authority to take recommended actions due to legislative or regulatory constraints	45.5%	40.9%	9.1%	4.5%	0.0%	
Insufficient vetting of the feasibility (political, administrative, or financial) of implementing the recommendation by the IG team who conducted the audit or inspection	54.5%	36.4%	4.5%	4.5%	0.0%	
Lack of clarity in the recommendations as written	62.5%	25.0%	8.3%	4.2%	0.0%	
Congressional interest or intervention that works against implementation of the recommendation	85.7%	9.5%	4.8%	0.0%	0.0%	
Current negative relationships between your IG office and agency management	91.3%	8.7%	0.0%	0.0%	0.0%	

Source: Electronic survey of the IG community in the fall of 2016 by the co-authors. See Appendix B, this volume, for the questionnaire.

OIG staff members work proactively to get their audit recommendations implemented. As shown in table 4-6, OIGs employ a variety of strategies and tools to implement recommendations that remain "open" for more than a year. Setting deadlines for responses from the affected program offices is undertaken virtually all of the time. Both formal and informal conversations with affected program staff and agency leadership are typically held to discuss open recommendations as well. And over half of the time, an OIG will bring up open recommendations formally to Congress and to the audit liaison office within their agency.

According to our research, the vast majority of federal agencies have an office or official outside of the OIG that works with the OIG to get open recommendations implemented; this office or official is typically referred to as the audit liaison. When asked, "Does your host agency have a designated official or office responsible for following up on OIG reports and recommendations?," almost all (92 percent) of the respondents replied yes. Virtually all large federal agencies have someone who reports to the agency leadership and is tasked with keeping an eye on progress made on implementing open recommendations.

The priority given by agency leadership to getting IG recommendations implemented varies across agencies. The professional experience and knowledge of internal auditing, and the relationship an agency develops with its IG, all shape agency perceptions about the urgency of closing open IG audit recommendations. For example, when Anthony Foxx became Secretary of Transportation in July 2013, he appointed an official in his office, Jeff Marootian, to focus on getting the more than 200 open IG recommendations at the department closed under his watch.[6]

Given the visibility of the performance measure of closing IG recommendations that have been open for one year or more, we asked whether the percentage of closed recommendations was used as a criterion on the performance appraisals of top managers in the IG offices. We found that this is not typically the case. In our survey, only 19 percent of the IGs replied that this was customary. Given the many factors that affect whether recommendations are closed and that are outside the control of the OIG—in fact, even outside the control of the affected program managers—it is hard to clarify accountability for implementation in all cases.

TABLE 4-6

Activities Undertaken by Federal Inspectors General to Get Open Recommendations Implemented

How frequently does your office use activities listed below to follow up on recommendations that have been open for over 12 months, and have these activities resulted in recommended changes? (Please check all that apply) (n=26)

Answer Options	Frequency of Activities		Perceived Results of Activities[a]	
	Happens frequently	Does not happen frequently	Has resulted in recommendation being implemented	Has *not* resulted in recommendation being implemented
Having target deadlines for a response from the affected program office	100.0%	0.0%	61.5%	15.4%
Informal conversations with agency staff in offices affected by the recommendations	84.6%	15.4%	61.5%	11.5%
Raising the issue with agency leadership	72.0%	28.0%	48.0%	8.0%
Formal meetings with agency staff in offices affected by the recommendations	69.2%	30.8%	50.0%	15.4%
Raising the issue in testimonies and/or written reports to Congress	56.5%	43.5%	30.4%	13.0%
Raising the issue with the agency's compliance office (if such an office is present in the agency)	53.3%	46.7%	40.0%	13.3%
Informal conversations with relevant congressional staff	39.1%	60.9%	13.0%	17.4%

Source: Electronic survey of the IG community in the fall of 2016 by the co-authors. See Appendix B, this volume, for the questionnaire.
a The sum of these categories may be less than 100% because of missing responses, no opinion, or unclear.

Final passage and presidential approval of new legislation in 2019 requiring that agencies report on open IG recommendations in their annual
budget justifications may influence whether and how agencies respond to
such recommendations. The Senate report urging approval of the legislation prior to its passage highlighted that in 2016 there were 15,222 open
and unimplemented OIG recommendations totaling more than $87 billion
in potential cost savings. The report continues by noting the following:

> To shine a light on agencies' failures to act on GAO and OIG recom-
> mendations, [this bill] requires agencies to include a list of open, unim-
> plemented GAO and OIG recommendations. . . . Agencies must also
> provide explanations for not implementing each recommendation. By
> disclosing open recommendations and being required to explain the
> lack of implementation in an agency's budget request, agencies will be
> held more accountable for unimplemented recommendations.[7]

Auditing and Investigating within the IG's Strategic Environment

The findings of IG work influence thinking about agency performance
within the IG's home agency, as well as among external stakeholders, including Congress. As we have noted, each IG operates within a strategic environment that is distinctive due to the nature, size, and context
of the IG's home agency. Elements of this distinctive environment in
each agency influence IG initiatives and priorities; shape the pursuit of
audits, investigations, and evaluations; and can affect the impact of the
IG work on the home agency. Again, the three key sources of influence
on the operations and performance of the OIG are (1) the stakeholders
interested in and affected by an IG's work, (2) the expectations held by
the IG's stakeholders, and (3) the system stressors creating challenges and
opportunities for an IG.

STAKEHOLDERS

For IGs, the two primary stakeholders with legal authority over them,
and to whom they officially report, are Congress and the leadership in
their home agency. While statutorily independent, IGs must pay atten-

tion to the preferences of and requests from these stakeholders as the IGs plan where to target their work and as they frame their recommendations to fix problems and improve agency operations.

Sometimes Congress or agency leaders call upon an IG to initiate work where the IG had not planned to focus. If the requestor is extremely forceful in voicing his or her preference, the IG is likely to accommodate and incorporate the new focus within his or her plan—as resources allow. However, most of the time, ongoing IG financial and performance auditing work remains below the radar of both Congress and agency leadership. Sometimes Congress or agency leadership intervenes and may push an IG to focus more (or less) on a specific program or problem. The outcome of any such external pressures will vary depending on how significant the focus of the work is to the IG and how the IG interprets the motivations behind such interventions. An IG is unlikely to back down on investigations in any case. Even when agency leaders express opposition to planned audits, it is still unlikely that their OIGs will pull back once public declarations of the work have been made. Similarly, when Congress voices opposition to OIG work that is underway, it is also unlikely to stop the OIG work in progress.

A secondary group of stakeholders that is likely to affect the initiation of and conduct of IG work includes OIG staff; the GAO and the Office of Special Counsel in the DOJ; agency employees whose work IGs review—and upon whom IGs rely for information and for implementation of recommendations; and nongovernmental stakeholders, including clients or consumers of an IG's home agency (for example, contractors hired by the agency) and interest groups dedicated to the home agency (such as professional associations or employee unions associated with the agency). All of these secondary stakeholders affect the work plans and the conduct of the OIG work.

In terms of establishing work plans and conducting audits, OIGs are especially dependent on their ability to work in a cooperative fashion with agency employees whose work they review and upon whom they rely for information and for implementation of recommendations. Similarly, OIGs want to maintain good relationships with nongovernmental stakeholders—including clients or consumers of their home agency—so the OIGs can collect information from these stakeholders when needed as part of IG work.

Maintaining a reputation for independence, fairness, integrity, and accuracy in OIG work is critical to ensuring that IGs can secure the cooperation and support of agency leadership, Congress, and especially the agency employees whose work OIGs review. By law, an IG is expected to keep both agency leadership and Congress fully informed about discoveries of serious problems, actions needed to correct the problems, and progress the home agency has made to implement corrective actions the IG has recommended.

As discussed above, OIGs communicate often, both formally and informally, with their agency leadership and affected program managers to ensure that IG recommendations are feasible and that the implementation of audit recommendations proceeds smoothly. There is considerable interaction between an IG, the home agency, and Congress—especially if the problem to be addressed is highly charged. Principals talk with each other to exchange information before, during, or after a financial or performance audit or investigation. Maintaining positive engagement with secondary stakeholders is also key to ensuring that OIGs can perform their work.

While largely unrestrained as they conduct their work, IGs are accountable for the outcomes of their audits and investigations. As mentioned earlier, cost savings expected to result from implementation of IG recommendations are published—although the reliability and comparability of the figures publicized are questionable, since the cost savings are only estimates, not all of the recommendations are fully implemented, and the years over which the savings are expected to accrue vary, especially across OIGs.

Legislation mandates that OIGs post all individual reports and semiannual reports on the internet. However, the distribution and posting of reports does not guarantee close review of an IG's work by either primary or secondary stakeholders. Nonetheless, the DOJ provides a check on an

IG's investigative activities by deciding whether to prosecute individuals whom OIG investigators accuse of criminal or civil violations; thus, IG investigations are under scrutiny.

Scrutiny of the quality of the auditing work undertaken by OIGs is not as rigorous as it is for investigations. While the Council of the Inspectors General for Integrity and Efficiency (CIGIE) issues quality standards for the work IGs conduct and conformance with these standards is the subject of peer evaluations, the peer review process does not address quality. Interviews with IGs for this research revealed some skepticism within the IG community that the peer review process really does much more than simply assess compliance with the quality standards as a bare threshold. It is difficult to assess the quality of IG audits by keeping track of the proportion of IG recommendations implemented, as the reasons that recommendations are not implemented are often out of the control of the OIG and are not indicative of the quality of the work.

SYSTEM STRESSORS

Since IGs answer to both Congress and their own agency leadership, stress stemming from legislative and executive disagreements can affect the work OIGs undertake. Disagreements between the executive branch and Congress involving IG powers can create stresses on IGs, collectively and individually, which influences their audits and investigations. For example, questions about executive decisions limiting IG access to particular records, documents, and data prompted forty-seven IGs to write to Congress in August 2014 to complain about executive interpretations of the law, which grants access to any executive records needed for their work.[8] Subsequent congressional interest in IG access to agency records eventually led to the passage of the Inspector General Empowerment Act of 2016, which broadened IG powers to access records.

Budgetary resources are also critical to permitting IGs to pursue their work. Congressional efforts to cut federal budgets during the Republican control of Congress under Presidents Obama and Trump have affected IG budgets as well. Even flat budgets, combined with the increasingly complex environments and problems that the federal government faces, present OIGs with resource constraints that especially limit their ability to hire staff with needed expertise, in areas such as information technology.[9]

As noted above, agency leaders sometimes take a personal interest in seeing that IG recommendations are implemented, but sometimes they do not. The personality and priorities of agency leaders, as well as their appreciation for and relationship with their IGs, greatly determine the extent to which agency leaders exert any influence to see IG recommendations implemented. The relationship between the agency leadership and the IG affects the will and the ability of program offices to implement recommendations, since these offices need to have the authority and resources to implement the recommended changes. Additionally, some recommendations may require congressional action in the form of increased funding or changes in authorizing legislation. In these latter circumstances, agency leadership and members of Congress may need to engage and make compromises regarding the shortcomings identified in a report. An IG may face intransigence by agency leadership, inaction by Congress, clashes between executive and congressional branches, or even broadened discussion of the recommendations by various secondary stakeholders interested in the issue.

Political appointees in home agencies or Congress may present particularistic agendas to IGs in terms of desired audits or even investigations. Virtually all IGs are asked to conduct more work than their budgets support, and they must make choices on which suggestions from agency or congressional leaders they can honor. Yet, IGs prefer not to find themselves in the middle of a highly partisan conflict.

Patrick McFarland—the IG at the Office of Personnel Management—had been in his position for more than 20 years and had never sought publicity nor wished to be caught up in partisan conflict. And still, his office's audit of the extensive information technology overhaul undertaken by OPM's CIO was fodder in the highly publicized controversy that led to the forced resignation of OPM's director, Katherine Archuleta. The digital data breach that resulted in the theft of personal information belonging to more than four million current and former federal employees drew attention to weaknesses in the information technology supporting OPM, and OPM's IG had already pointed out flaws. McFarland found himself front and center in the congressional hearings, a position he likely never sought and definitely did not enjoy. Those highly politicized congressional hearings were the last he attended in his long career in the IG community.

Conclusion

Federal inspectors general strive to identify appropriate targets—or problems—and marshal appropriate and adequate resources—both monetary and in terms of budget and skilled staff—to address alleged problems and examine where improvements are needed in their agencies. IGs all work in environments where they must balance the requests and expectations of their primary stakeholders—the leadership in their home agencies and Congress. In addition, to truly make a difference in their agencies, the IGs must continually work to maintain a reputation for fairness and integrity among a variety of agency-specific stakeholders—including, most importantly, the program managers in the offices in which the IGs conduct financial and performance audits, and the clienteles of those programs.

Recommendations are tools that the IGs can use to help fix problems and improve agency operations, and they are very intentional in framing feasible recommendations. The most significant factor affecting IG deliberations as they develop recommendations is to ensure that the recommendations will advance the mission of the agency and of their OIG. Draft recommendations are shared with agency personnel to ensure that they are clear and feasible, and IG staff accept feedback in their effort to offer feasible and well-targeted recommendations.

Not all IG recommendations are implemented, and these open recommendations frustrate IGs and can attract the attention of Congress and other important stakeholders. However, root causes of observed problems are not always easy to uncover and understand, and effective remedies may be challenging to implement due to lack of resources and/or the need for legislative changes. Agency leaders need to possess the will and the clout to see that open IG recommendations are closed, and that will varies across agencies and even across leaders within one agency over time within an administration.

IGs exert influence on the performance of their agencies beyond fixing immediate problems. Getting recommended actions on the table—even if they are controversial or vague—can provoke discussions that enlighten and expand considerations about programs and processes. The impact of IG work tends to be measured in the short run, by counting the number of recommendations offered and the amount of cost savings, but IGs influence thinking about agency performance over a longer term. Our research suggests that IGs are generally persistent and vigilant in attending to their home agency's operations, and view their own success as tied to their ability to improve their agency's performance—but IGs also appreciate it is a long game.

FIVE

Independence and Engagement with Agencies and Congress

MAINTAINING PRINCIPLES AND
BALANCING PRINCIPALS

"It is absolutely critical to maintain confidence of agency leadership and congressional contacts—[this] speaks to the ability to be effective and to make a difference."

—*Comment from confidential interview with IG*
included in the six case studies for this book (2014)

To be effective, an IG must navigate within a sometimes turbulent, and always challenging, strategic environment. The routine workings of an OIG, as described in the previous chapter, are substantially shaped by the office's relationship with two key stakeholders to whom they are statutorily accountable and who receive reports on audits, investigations, and evaluations: (1) leadership of the agency and (2) members of Congress (and their staffs). Unique among federal executive officials, on a daily basis IGs face the challenge of maintaining independence and being accountable, both while being constructive, collaborative, or even cooperative to advance their home agency's mission and to fulfill expectations of the relevant congressional committees. Failing to manage or achieve a balance often leads to trouble for the IG and distress for the office he or she leads.

How and under what circumstances IGs balance expectations of independence and accountability while also being collaboratively engaged are the subject of this chapter. It draws heavily on case studies involving six federal agencies. The case studies included personal interviews with IGs and their staffs, agency leadership, and congressional staff involved in oversight of IGs. Our aim is to describe efforts by IGs, agency leadership, and Congress to forge working relationships. The six case studies reveal the varying approaches that IGs take to build collaborative relationships, and we identify factors that appear to account for variations from one agency to another and from one OIG to another. We also describe practices used by IGs while working with agency leadership and congressional contacts to achieve desired results while maintaining independence.

Independence and Collaborative Engagement

Independence, accountability, and engagement are principles established in law for IGs. The very beginning of the Inspector General Act of 1978 highlights that OIGs were established "In order to create independent and objective units . . . to conduct and supervise audits and investigations . . . [to] promote economy, efficiency, and effectiveness in administration . . . [to] prevent and detect fraud and abuse . . . [and to] keep the head of the agencies and the Congress fully and currently informed about problems and deficiencies."[1] The legislation mandates accountability by requiring that IGs make semiannual reports to the agency head and to Congress concerning their findings and "to recommend corrective action concerning such problems, abuses, and deficiencies and to report on the progress made in implementing such corrective action." Engagement or collaboration with agency and congressional leadership is also addressed in the 1978 legislation by setting expectations that IGs would offer recommendations to remedy shortcomings identified in audits and investigations. IGs are not directed to collaborate or cooperate with agency leadership, per se, and agency leaders were not directed to accept all recommendations. However, the legislation calls for IGs to "provide policy direction," "review existing and proposed legislation and regulations," and "recommend policies for . . . the purpose of promoting economy and efficiency . . . or preventing and detecting fraud and abuse."[2]

Operationally, IGs recognize that their work also involves some measure of collaboration, coordination, or cooperation with officials in their home agency.[3] As discussed in chapter 4, OIGs conduct audits, investigations, and evaluations, working with agency leadership and staff to gather information and records, sharing draft reports for comment, and making recommendations for improvements. A survey of OIGs by Kathryn Newcomer and George Grob found that "having good open lines of communication with department and management" is the top response (48.9 percent) to what IGs perceive to be important for "successful implementation of recommendations."[4] Newcomer and Grob also note that executive branch managers and members of Congress increasingly have involved OIGs in discussions about "top management challenges they believe confront their agencies."[5]

Quality standards developed and adopted by IGs acting officially as the Council of the Inspectors General for Integrity and Efficiency (CIGIE) (and its forerunners before 2008)[6] also address expectations about the relationship between OIGs, their home agencies, Congress, and other stakeholders. As a general matter, these standards indicate that "the IG and OIG staff shall coordinate their activities internally and with other components of government to assure effective and efficient use of available resources."[7] More specifically, CIGIE's quality standards hold that "the OIG should coordinate, where applicable, with agency management to ensure that OIG priorities appropriately consider agency needs. The OIG should take into consideration requests from the Congress, the OMB, other external stakeholders, the CIGIE, complaints from employees and, as appropriate, private citizens."[8] Finally, these standards call on OIGs "to identify the causes of fraud, waste, abuse, and mismanagement in high-risk agency programs, and to help agencies implement a system of management improvements to overcome these problems."[9] Thus, the IGs collectively recognize that an OIG does not work in isolation—coordination with its home agency and with other stakeholders is expected, and some level of collaboration is expected as recommendations for improvements are advanced and implemented.

Expectations of independence and collaborative engagement can produce conflicting pressures for OIGs when independence might be compromised by collaborative engagement. Highly critical OIG reports often make front-page news in national media, and IG findings that become the subject of congressional hearings often place agency leadership on the defensive. Understandably, relations between an OIG and the agency leadership might be adversely affected by such reports and their public airing. And, IGs have been publicly criticized and forced to resign when collaborative engagement appears to have compromised their independence.[10] This perceived lack of independence, in particular, can adversely affect an IG's relationship with Congress, since the IG is expected to make regular reports to Congress that are not filtered by agency leadership and staff.

Accounts by former IGs regarding relationships between their office and their home agency or Congress reveal tensions between IGs, agency leadership, and Congress over issues of independence and expectations of collaborative engagement. For example, Neil Barofsky, the first special inspector general for the Troubled Asset Relief Program (SIGTARP), details day-to-day tensions with Treasury officials (including the inspector general for the Department of the Treasury). He reports that during his tenure conflicts emerged involving how investigations were to be pursued and whether recommendations to improve programs were adopted as prescribed by TARP legislation. Similarly, Clark Ervin, who served as IG in the Department of State and as acting IG in the newly created Department of Homeland Security (DHS), highlights tensions between his office in DHS and the department's leadership. Ervin's book on his service in DHS documents frictions between his OIG and DHS leadership, including the disinclination by the DHS secretary to meet with him or members of his office, presenting significant barriers to their inquiries.[11]

Case Studies of IGs' Independence, Accountability, and Engagement

We conducted interviews with officials in six federal agencies and congressional staff members to collect data about their perceptions, views, and experiences regarding IG independence, accountability, and engagement. Our general approach is described in box 5-1, and our interview guides are presented in appendix A. We acknowledge that our sample of six OIGs cannot be viewed as representative of the entire OIG community, and our findings cannot be viewed as generalizable to all IGs. Nevertheless, our findings are instructive about offices that have received very little scholarly attention. The questions we asked and our findings provide a basis for more case studies of OIGs or surveys of the entire IG community.

OIG INDEPENDENCE AND THE AGENCY

In many respects, we learned that conversations between an IG and officials in the home agency regarding independence are often framed by previous relationships between their respective offices. If independence was a matter of concern for a previous IG, the agency, or Congress, then the issue draws more initial attention than in those agencies were a culture (or norm) of independence seemed to be accepted. In two agencies, our interviewees indicated that experience with one or more previous IGs led to conversations about the expected relationship with the agency. One of those agencies previously experienced friction between the IG and agency leadership, and in the other the IG was perceived as being too close to the leadership. In both instances, OIG respondents to our questions expressed the view that independence was critically important, that the IG would work to keep the agency informed of the OIG's work, and that there would be no "gotcha games." IGs in both agencies reported having conversations with agency leadership about how the OIG would approach various tasks. A history of questions or tensions between a third OIG and its home agency led to development of a written memorandum of understanding regarding the relationship between the OIG and the agency, which seemed to set expectations on such items as the OIG's authority, access, and communications with leadership. In the three agencies with no indications of such issues between the OIG and the agency, conversations were reported as being somewhat informal and even brief or superficial. By mutual agreement, the IGs' independence was understood to be important.

Among the three IGs whose tenure involved a change in agency leadership, each IG undertook initiatives to inform the new leadership about his or her expectations about the OIG's mission, work within the agency, and current understandings about independence. IGs reported that such discussions seem to be well received by agency leadership—an observation confirmed in conversations with agency officials in subsequent interviews.

BOX 5-1

*Research Methods for Six Case Studies of IGs, Agency
Leadership, and Congressional Contacts*

This study provides insight into how IGs work, the challenges they face, and what they do to manage their operations. The basic data come from case studies of six OIGs, for which we conducted in-person interviews with IGs, OIG staff, agency leadership, and congressional contacts. Given the dearth of research on IGs, these interviews aimed to provide basic information on the workings of IGs and to highlight factors that appear to account for their actions.

During the summer of 2014, we conducted structured interviews in six federal agencies with six inspectors general, twenty-one members of their respective staffs, seven representatives from their respective agencies' leadership, and two leading congressional staff contacts. The interviews were conducted with the understanding that the interviewees, their host agencies, and congressional positions would be confidential.* Our aim was to have PAS and DFE IGs represented among the case studies; agencies and OIGs of various sizes; and IGs who had at least one year of experience in their position. A total of ten IGs were contacted sequentially via email, and six agreed to participate in the study. Once IGs agreed to be interviewed, senior members of each OIG and agency leadership were contacted with requests for confidential interviews. Most OIG staff contacted for interviews agreed to participate in the study, as did at least one senior agency official in five of the six agencies.

---

* In agreeing to be interviewed, IGs understood that we would be contacting members of their staffs, agency leadership, and congressional contacts.

RELATIONS WITH AGENCY LEADERSHIP TEAM

The extent to which agency leadership considers an IG to be a member of the agency leadership team varies across the federal agencies. However, the prevailing norm among our interviewees is captured by an IG statement that the "IG is always invited to the party, but [is] never the special

The six IGs included in the study represent a variety of agencies, including cabinet-level departments and smaller federal agencies. Reflecting the size of their host agencies, the size of the OIGs varied substantially, ranging from the largest having several hundred employees to a relatively small OIG with fewer than twenty-five employees. Three of the IGs were appointed by the president and confirmed by the Senate (PAS IGs), and three were appointed by agency heads or governing boards (DFE IGs). The sample included IGs who served previously in other OIGs and IGs with no OIG experience prior to their current IG appointment. The time in their current positions ranged from less than three years to over fifteen years in the office. Thus, the sample of IGs and their host agencies was broadly inclusive of different sizes and types of organizations, and office holders. We must acknowledge that the six agencies and their respective OIGs are not a statistically representative sample of all agencies or their OIGs—something that is perhaps difficult to achieve. Nevertheless, we believe these six agencies allow us to offer informed, empirically based observations about IGs, OIGs, the work they do, and how they relate to significant others in their environment.

Most interviews were sixty to ninety minutes in length. With two exceptions, all interviews were conducted by both authors. Handwritten interview notes were then merged and summarized by a graduate assistant. We reviewed the summaries to confirm and make corrections.

guest." In four of our case-study agencies, IGs did not attend leadership-level staff meetings. Those who did attend leadership meetings reported that they did not participate in policy discussions, but instead gave updates on current initiatives or simply listened to presentations.

In all but one of the agencies, interactions with agency leadership primarily involve regular biweekly or monthly meetings with agency heads and/or deputy heads. In some instances, the agency's general counsel is also involved in these regular meetings. IGs reported that during these meetings, discussions with the agencies' top leadership often involve "hot issues," concerns about open OIG audit recommendations, difficulties regarding access to information, delayed responses for pending draft reports, or requests the OIG had received from Congress. Often such meetings are used to ensure that agency leadership is not caught by surprise by any IG activities; one IG indicated that agency leadership is given a heads-up when there are any "hot seat" items on the horizon. Drafts of pending reports are typically not discussed in staff leadership meetings or in meetings between the IG and agency leaders. Final reports might be discussed in meetings with agency leaders to inform them of a forthcoming release. Again, the norm among the IGs we interviewed is to keep agency leadership informed and to avoid surprises.

For most IGs, collegial relationships between OIGs and the agency are desired. However, our interviews revealed a mutually held wariness regarding how OIG independence and collegiality are perceived by the agency and by Congress. One experienced IG commented, "Independence is a challenge, if you remain too aloof, you may not get needed information or become irrelevant, but the closer you get, the greater the chance you'll be perceived as captured." Addressing the same issue, another IG remarked that the "goal is to improve the agency, not to embarrass the agency; to work in cooperation and [a] collaborative way, [and to] never intentionally sandbag the agency or its leadership." These IGs consider themselves to be both independent and collaborative.

RESOLVING CONFLICTS WITH THE AGENCY

While IGs tend to view having good relations with agency leadership as one of their aims, conflicts or disagreements with agency leaders do emerge in an OIG's day-to-day business. These conflicts involve issues such as delayed or blocked access to information, responses to audit findings critical of the agency, and differing interpretations of IG authority by the OIG's legal counsel and the agency's general counsel. Notably, if a conflict involves the delivery of a critical report or bad news, OIGs appear simply to give agency leadership a heads-up and then release the report. Among IGs and OIG staff we interviewed, there were no indications that final reports are subjects of dispute resolution efforts or procedures.

Across all six case studies, OIG conflicts with agency officials tend to be handled initially at the lower levels of the agency bureaucracy and only emerge as discussion items with agency leadership when attempts to resolve the issue are unsuccessful. If an issue is important, the matter is raised informally and in person by the IG with agency leadership—often during a one-on-one, regular meeting between the IG and the agency's secretary or director. In half of the agencies, conflicts that remain unresolved informally can also move to formal procedures. Designated steps in these procedures involve high-level executives in the agency whose assignment includes resolution of conflicts related to OIG work or recommendations. OIGs rarely leave disputed matters unresolved. Sometimes, however, we learned the matter is simply left open, with points of view being clearly articulated by the OIG and agency leadership; they agree to disagree, and then wait until the issue arises again.

A specific action authorized by the IG Act of 1978 for an IG who encounters resistance involves issuing a seven-day letter, where Congress is informed of the difficulty by the IG and the agency head within seven days if the matter is not resolved.[12] None of the IGs we interviewed had ever used a seven-day letter in the face of agency resistance. One IG reported drafting such a letter but not sending it. In this instance, the agency changed its view in light of informal congressional pressure to do so after the OIG informally consulted with congressional contacts regarding the standoff.

INITIATIVES OR PRACTICES TO ENCOURAGE COLLABORATION

Because cooperation appears to be key to IGs' work, we asked IGs, OIG staff, and agency leadership about initiatives taken by either the OIG or the agency to promote cooperation between these two entities. This question sought to identify long-term policies or systematic initiatives undertaken by the OIG, the agency, or both to encourage collaboration, cooperation, or generally smooth relations. While some responses were particular to specific OIGs or agencies, OIG responses fell into four general categories and agency responses fell into two categories. Table 5-1 lists these categories and examples of responses given in our interviews.

Initiatives discussed by the IG or OIG staff focus primarily on communications regarding what the IG is doing or about to do; encouragement of feedback or suggestions from agency leadership; making contact with an agency's day-to-day operational staff and external agency stakeholders; and making accommodating structural changes to the OIG itself. Several IGs noted that communication efforts at the agency's leadership level are important to avoiding surprises, which they hope builds trust in the OIG. While all OIGs solicit suggestions from agency leadership for areas where audits, evaluations, or investigations should be considered, interviews with OIGs and with agency leadership indicated that suggestions are typically not forthcoming. Notably, however, IGs reported that they are always responsive to ad hoc agency requests and give such requests consideration. Every OIG has some mechanism to receive comments through the congressionally mandated hotlines maintained by their offices.

As a general matter, OIGs serving large agencies or geographically dispersed agencies are likely to undertake special efforts to reach out to geographically distributed mid- and lower-level management. Among OIGs in our study, several were organized along functional lines corresponding to the home agency's organization or maintained regional offices to foster relationships among mid- and lower-levels in their home agency. Facing a challenge of unusually high staff turnover in one of our case study agencies, the OIG regularly communicated with agency staff about what the OIG was, what the office did, and how it could be contacted with relevant concerns. Thus, OIGs generally organize their offices in accord with agency organization and special circumstances.

In addition to communicating with their agency leaders and management, as well as Congress, OIGs maintain lines of communication with customers or stakeholders relevant to their respective agencies. These lines of contact afford OIGs additional insights for audits or investigations, and offer an OIG opportunities to explain audit, investigatory, or

TABLE 5-1

Initiatives or Practices That Promote Cooperation between OIGs and Host Agencies

OIG INITIATIVES TO PROMOTE COOPERATION WITH HOST AGENCIES

I. Communicating Regarding Mission and Actions of OIG
   - Meet with mid-level staff of agency
   - Arrange quarterly meetings between OIG staff and program offices or counterparts in agency to review ongoing projects
   - Ensure that there are no surprises to management, share report with agency before forwarding report to Congress or posting on web
   - Work to assure no surprises to agency leadership from OIG activities
   - Arrange OIG leadership meetings with agency's regional leadership and staff annually

II. Soliciting and Considering Requests from Agency
   - Invite recommendations from agency leadership for annual audit plans
   - Give priority to requests from agency leadership
   - Solicit ideas from agency leadership regarding annual statement of congressionally mandated "Major Challenges" statement

III. Reaching out to Working-Level Agency Staff and Agency Stakeholders
   - Explain mission and processes to working-level agency staff
   - Establish contact with major agency customers and stakeholders
   - Conduct regular meetings around the country with agency staff at the second or third level down, where work gets done

IV. Making Structural Changes in the OIG to Accommodate Agency Functions
   - Organize OIG offices functionally in parallel with agency
   - Establish process and expectations for review and comment on audit reports

AGENCY LEADERSHIP INITIATIVES TO PROMOTE COOPERATION WITH OIGS

I. Assigning of Specific Staff or Offices to Coordinate with OIG
   - Assign lead staff person in agency to work with OIG at beginning of inquiries to facilitate audit or investigation
   - Establish coordination offices within agency to facilitate audits and follow-up on audit recommendations

II. Encouraging Cooperation with OIG Inquiries through Leadership Directives
   - Establish targets by agency leadership for response times and for closing recommendations, including periodic reviews on status of IG reports
   - Issue widely distributed memoranda from agency leadership encouraging contact and cooperation with OIG

evaluation recommendations that might affect the customers' or stake-holders' relationships with the agency.

Many federal agencies, especially the larger ones, appoint specific offices or officials to coordinate with their OIG to facilitate work on IG audits and evaluations. These "bridging" offices are usually used to promote collaborative relationships between IG and agency offices. The offices or individuals usually have titles that include such terms as *audit liaisons* or *compliance*, and are supported by and report to agency leadership.

Our interviews confirmed that agency leadership finds relationships are enhanced when offices or personnel are designated to facilitate work with the OIG on audits or evaluations. Some agency executives are pointedly and visibly involved in systemically following up on OIG reports and recommendations on a weekly or biweekly basis, with the aim of reducing backlogs of open recommendations. Other agency leaders deliver formal and informal messages to their agency to urge cooperation with OIG officials and inquiries. Doubtless, the degree to which those messages flow through the organization varies, but communications from agency leadership reportedly help to facilitate OIG work based on comments from OIG interviewees in corresponding agencies.

OIG INDEPENDENCE AND CONGRESS

The relationship between IGs and Congress differs in many respects from the relationship between IGs and their home agencies. Unlike the reporting relationship between IGs and agency leadership, the IG-Congress relationship involves diverse principals who encompass multiple committees in both houses of Congress that oversee particular agencies or programs; committees that oversee the operations of all OIGs; and appropriations committees or subcommittees that fund OIGs. Additionally, instead of working with a secretary or director (and his or her team), IGs dealing with Congress often work with and respond to individual senators or representatives with episodic, particular, and political interests who turn to IGs for information advancing those interests. Moreover, congressional staff members play critical roles in filtering information from IGs to committee chairs or elected representatives, and from those representatives to IGs. Though the IG-congressional relationship differs from the IG-agency relationship, IGs recognize that Congress represents a significant principal because the institution offers critical political and fiscal support for maintaining OIG independence relative to their agencies.

OIG INTERACTIONS WITH CONGRESS

The frequency of interactions involving the six OIGs in this study and Congress varies greatly. As one might expect, presidentially appointed and Senate confirmed (PAS) IGs hold initial meetings with congressional contacts—usually staff members. Such meetings do not generally occur for DFE IGs since their appointment by agency leaders does not require Senate confirmation and these agencies' visibility is lower than that of agencies with PAS IGs. However, DFE IGs reported varying frequencies of contacts with Congress after assuming IG responsibilities, with the OIG for the largest DFE in our study reporting having more frequent contacts than other DFE OIGs. Just as experiences of previous IGs tend to frame IG-agency relations for newly appointed IGs, relationships between Congress and former IGs also appeared to affect congressional expectations of newly appointed IGs across the six case-study OIGs. Congressional contacts reported that if an agency's previous IG appeared to be too close to agency management, the message delivered to the incoming IG is that he or she needs to be more independent of the home agency. If the previous IG was viewed very positively, and the office was well regarded on the Hill, then congressional staff members communicate that they hope the positive relationship they enjoyed continues under the new leadership.

Across all of our OIG interviews, it is clear that IGs and their staff are highly attuned to requests from Congress. Perceptions about congressional motivations include views that some requests are politically driven and sometimes vengeful; in other instances, congressional contacts are passing along constituency inquiries, and sometimes the IGs are being asked to provide cover for decisions affecting particular constituencies or districts. Interviewees reported that the number of requests to OIGs from Congress ranged from several hundred annually to just a few dozen, depending on the size of the agency and the scope of an agency's responsibilities. Also, our OIG interviewees reported that when they learn of legislative mandates that are being considered, the OIG staff members usually attempt to shape congressional thinking so as to create a mandate to which the OIGs can reasonably respond. Given Congress's control of the budget, OIGs are very aware that the institution can punish or reward OIGs based on congressional views of an office's work and relations with Congress. Our interviews revealed that in some cases congressional contacts seem to view IGs as being agents of Congress. But in all instances, IGs and their staff indicated they are always wary of serving an agent-like role to advance the political interests of individual representatives.

Our interviews with IGs and their staff showed that OIGs are typically quite attentive to requests from Congress and tend to respond quickly to requests for information or inquiries from congressional contacts. As with prospective legislative mandates, OIG staff members talk regularly with congressional contacts to understand the context of the request and map out a plan and timetable for what actions are needed to be responsive. In any case, as with requests from agency leadership, OIGs find ways to respond positively to almost every request from Congress and make efforts to keep congressional contacts informed of progress on their requests.

While responding to congressional requests, all six OIGs in this study try to keep lines of communication open with contacts in Congress. Supplementing the congressionally mandated semiannual reporting, OIGs offer periodic, semiannual, or annual briefings to relevant appropriations, authorizing, or oversight committees. Beyond formal appearances for annual appropriations, the larger OIGs proactively engage congressional contacts—walking the halls of Congress—offering to brief committees or testify on areas in which members of Congress are interested.

Keeping Congress "currently informed" as is required by the IG Act of 1978 is a challenge for OIGs in terms of when to share information and what information to share. Some OIGs in our study regularly give congressional contacts timetables or monthly updates on the status of OIG activities. None of the six OIGs in this study share reports with Congress prior to the reports being shared with their respective agencies, although sometimes findings may be shared prior to the development of final recommendations. In the normal course of audits and evaluations, this information is also shared preliminarily with the agency.

Just like OIGs, agency leadership also maintains regular contact with Congress. Our interviewees in OIGs and interviews with agency leaders, however, revealed that formal coordination between an OIG and its home agency leadership rarely occurs. However, OIG interviewees reported that they usually inform agency leadership of congressional interest in a topic. Clearly, however, all of the OIGs and agencies in this study communicate with Congress on two parallel pathways.

RESOLVING CONFLICTS WITH CONGRESS

As with IG-agency relationships, there is no routine pattern in OIG responses regarding resolution of conflicts, except that IGs work to avoid conflicts with Congress. When conflicts emerge, the OIG officials we interviewed reported that they devote much energy to resolving disagreements. When members of Congress are publicly unhappy with a particular IG office, our OIG interviewees reported working with a member's or committee's staff to obtain guidance about how best to resolve the conflict. The OIG's legal counsel was also likely to be brought in to help resolve the issue. But a minority of interviewed IGs indicated that on occasions when conflict continued to be unresolved, their strategy is to simply and carefully outline what the OIG could do legally and responsibly. Congress may or may not accept this strategy, and may use public hearings or budget reviews to continue pressing the issue.

CONGRESSIONAL VIEWS OF IGS

Our interviews with congressional staff indicated that Congress is likely to be more concerned about independence and collaboration involving OIG-agency relationships than OIG-Congress relationships. As a general matter, a strategically located congressional staff member we interviewed doubted whether members of Congress or their staffs fully understand the mission and authority of IGs. Certainly, the staff member asserted, that is not the case in oversight committees. Among oversight committee members, a prevailing view is that IGs are " 'partners' with the committee"—and from this perspective, IGs are accountable to the committee beyond the semiannual reports mandated by the IG Act of 1978.

Congressional staff also indicated to us that a "major concern of the committee is reaching out to gauge whether the IG is independent [of the agency]." According to these staff members, congressional committees are aware that IGs vary in independence and that actions have been taken in the past, such as holding committee hearings, if an IG appeared to be obstructed in his or her work by agency leadership. If an IG appears to Congress to be "captured" by agency leadership, or is viewed as too close to agency leadership, then actions may well include holding committee hearings to raise this issue and press the IG about his or her independence. Individual members of Congress may also issue statements expressing doubts about an IG's independence or quality of work.[13]

Echoing comments from IGs, a congressional staff member that we interviewed also mentioned the current issue of when IGs should tell Congress what they are investigating and what is being done. This staff member also acknowledged the difficulty of finding the right balance between not having the OIG report daily and waiting until a report is completed, especially if the matter involves a major issue. The staff member opined that "if the committee is finding out about a major issue or matter when it receives a written report, then there has been a mistake or miscommunication." When asking IGs for information about an ongoing investigation, one of our congressional respondents indicated that IGs sometimes request a written letter from a committee chair asking for particular documents or data that are the subject of conflict.

PROMOTING COOPERATION BETWEEN OIGS AND CONGRESS

Just as we asked about initiatives to encourage collaboration between IGs and agency leadership, we asked similar questions of IGs, OIG staff, and congressional contacts. OIG responses fell into three general categories and congressional responses fell into two categories. Table 5-2 lists these categories and gives examples of responses from our interviews.

Our OIG interviewees reported taking great pains to be responsive to Congress. But OIGs aim to be more than merely responsive—they appear to make every effort to communicate with congressional contacts, and especially seek to inform staff about what the OIG is doing, what projects it is pursuing, and the status of specifically requested inquiries. Proactive contacting and briefing activities are routinely undertaken by some OIGs. Upon learning about requests (or prospective requests) coming from Congress, OIGs are likely to work to reshape requests that are overly broad or too narrow. And, OIGs handle overtly political requests by seeking to understand the political context, sensitizing staff to that context, and occasionally outlining what an IG could (and could not) do relative to the particular request.

Relationships with Congress are institutionalized differently across the IG community. Among the six OIGs in this study, larger OIGs have one or more staff members responsible for congressional relations, and they serve as a liaison between the OIG and congressional contacts. Two of the OIGs in this study had OIG staff members temporarily assigned to congressional committees at the committees' request. Reportedly these assignments help take OIG perspectives to the committee and bring committee views back to the OIG.

Congressional staff interviewees argued that their committees are supportive of OIGs by encouraging agencies to be responsive to IG recommendations—leverage that several OIG interviewees acknowledged in conversations about following through on recommended changes. Congressional staff also reported efforts every one or two years to engage IGs or OIG staff from twenty or so of the larger OIGs in conversations about what their specific offices are doing and whether they encounter obstacles in their work. An interesting initiative by one committee involved developing prospective lists of IG candidates for open positions that were forwarded to CIGIE for its consideration. The expressed motivation for this initiative was to identify highly qualified candidates who might optimally fulfill the role of IGs—which, of course, included awareness of the special relationship with Congress that OIGs enjoy.

Balancing Relationships with Executive Agencies and with Congress

Maintaining independence and engaging collaboratively is complicated by the imperative that IGs must balance relationships with their two

---

TABLE 5-2
Initiatives or Practices That Promote Cooperation between OIGs and Congress

OIG INITIATIVES OR PRACTICES TO PROMOTE COOPERATION WITH CONGRESS

I. Proactive Briefing and Communicating about OIG Activities
    • Meet with appropriations and oversight committee leadership semiannually
    • Express willingness to meet informally with congressional contacts and to be available for hearings
    • Respond to requests with timely reports or updates
    • Meet frequently with congressional contacts when responding to specific requests
    • Solicit suggestions for areas in which congressional representatives or staff are interested
    • Have senior OIG staff regularly brief congressional staff on authorizing and appropriations committees
    • Share lists of current projects periodically with agency and congressional contacts
    • Produce good work and communicate that work to congressional contacts

II. Working with Congress to Shape Requests or Mandates for OIG Inquiries
    • Outline authority and resources the OIG has to respond to congressional requests
    • Work to broaden congressional requests that are viewed as too narrow, too broad, or too partisan
    • Avoid exercising political filter in responding to congressional requests
    • Work with congressional contact to understand basis and context of request
    • Work with OIG staff members to assure they understand the political context of a request if applicable

---

principals—the agency and Congress. To gain insights about IG relations with their respective agencies and with Congress, we asked IGs and OIG staff how the OIG "managed reporting expectations by the agency and Congress"; what actions the respondents' OIGs took "to maintain independence"; whether the respondents "encountered questions about leaning too much toward the agency or Congress"; and whether the OIG had undertaken "any particular initiatives to maintain the confidence of key agency leadership and congressional contacts." We also asked whether the OIG had internal discussions about relationships with the agency

- Request formal letter outlining request for OIG to inquire into a matter—may assist in drafting letter

III. Dedicating OIG Staff Members to Work with Congressional Contacts
- Funnel most contacts with Congress through office dedicated to external relations
- Encourage and support temporary assignment of OIG staff member to congressional office
- Assign deputy IG or assistant IG responsibility for contacts with Congress

CONGRESSIONAL INITIATIVES OR PRACTICES TO PROMOTE COOPERATION WITH OIGS

I. Following up on OIG Reports Regarding Open or Unimplemented Recommendations
- Collect, publicize, and (possibly) hold hearings about open recommendations with an agency
- Ask agency for information about responses to OIG reports and recommendations

II. Maintaining Contact with OIG Offices
- Invite IGs from large OIGs for discussions with congressional committee staff regarding topics being worked on and any obstructions to inquiries
- Invite individual IG (and possibly staff) from large OIGs to join congressional staff every two years for informal, relaxed conversations regarding major projects or ongoing difficulties
- Offer suggestions regarding IG appointments

and Congress and whether and how agency or congressional actions influenced audits, investigations, or inspections/evaluations. Responses to these questions showed that the dynamic between their offices, their agencies, and Congress is very much at the forefront of our interviewees' thinking. Additionally, it appeared that managing this dynamic challenges even the most creative and professional OIGs.

All of the IGs interviewed for this project recognize the importance of achieving the right balance with an OIG's home agency and with Congress. "Straddling the barbed wire fence" separating the executive branch and Congress is one metaphor often used to describe the predicament facing IGs who are legally responsible to two principals. In addition, our interviewees offered other metaphors—dancing on a tight rope, walking the line, and walking through a mine field—which convey the crosscutting pressures of reporting to an agency head and to Congress. Creating positive relationships in this environment is deemed essential, as one IG commented that "we think about this [agency/congressional relations] all the time." The challenge of having two principals is, as one OIG staff member reported, "tricky and not well understood." In managing this challenge, none of our interviewees or documents we reviewed suggest that IGs handle crosscutting pressures by playing one principal against the other. To do so would threaten positive relationships with both agency management and Congress.

RESPONDING TO CHALLENGES AND MAINTAINING BALANCE AMONG PRINCIPALS

There are several different kinds of challenges to OIG independence and collaboration. Some OIG interviewees reported facing questions about their legitimate role relative to the agency and to Congress, such as whether the IG is being too aggressive, too expansive, or stepping outside the bounds of an IG's statutory authority. For example, as discussed in previous chapters, IGs have experienced difficulties regarding their access to information. These differences, our interviews revealed, often involve conflicting interpretations of statutes by an agency's general counsel and the OIG's counsel. Congress resolved much of the issue surrounding access through passage of 2016 legislation confirming IGs' general authority to broad access to agency personnel and information.

Communications with an IG's agency and with Congress pose delicate challenges: When should an IG inform Congress that an inquiry has been initiated or is nearly closed? What information can be shared with Congress and when? How much time (if any) should elapse between informing the agency and informing Congress? And, should communications with one principal be shared with the other principal? In addition, interviewees in OIGs reported they sometimes receive requests from

Congress that are too narrow, overly broad, or motivated by political considerations. Another challenge is requests that the OIGs consider outside the scope of OIG authority or difficult to accomplish because sufficient resources for the project are not available.

IGs and OIG staff reported pursuing several strategies to address these aforementioned challenges. Those initiatives and practices are summarized in table 5-3, which lists responses of IGs and OIG staff to questions regarding the balance between the agency and Congress. Two strategies highlighted by IGs and their staff reference reputational attributes of their offices—aiming for fairness and honesty in dealing with the agency and Congress, and producing quality work that is well received (if not always accepted) by the agency and Congress. Relatedly, our respondents emphasized that they provide information to their agency and to Congress, but they do not become part of the policymaking process. IGs attending their respective agency's executive leadership meetings indicated that they do not participate in policy discussions, and IGs not attending such meetings cited the desire to avoid policy decisions as a reason for avoiding leadership meetings.

All of the OIGs in this study hold orientation programs for new staff members regarding the work of inspectors general. These programs emphasize IG independence and stress the need to maintain an independent stance relative to the agency and to Congress. Some OIGs regularly have discussions at staff meetings about independence and the IG's stance relative to the agency and Congress.

IGs and OIG staff reported using a variety of strategies to handle requests from Congress that are viewed as "out of bounds." Smaller questions may be consolidated by the OIG into larger questions that subsume the original narrow request. Another strategy is that OIG staff look into the problem raised by Congress to see if there are ways to address the issue within the OIG's authority and resources. OIGs also work with the requesting congressional contact to set expectations about the resources and time needed to fulfill the request, and to help the congressional contact make a manageable request in a formal letter.

On some occasions IGs face challenges from one principal or the other, but usually not from both on the same issue. When a request is viewed

TABLE 5-3
OIG Initiatives, Practices, and Strategies Aimed at
Balancing Agency and Congressional Relations

I. Aiming for Fairness and Honesty in All Relations
    - Aim to drive right down the middle on reports
    - Work hard to speak truth on what needs to be done and how
    - Be an honest broker
    - Deal with problematic issues, not personalities
    - Be fair, but firm
    - Be comforted when it seems you are being criticized from both sides

II. Producing Quality Work
    - Focus on what the job is—fraud, waste, and abuse—and do it in a timely manner
    - Look at important programs administered by the agency and prepare a report that the agency can use
    - Rush a report if needed by the agency, but maintain quality
    - Document reports, as they are especially critical for acceptance of audits and investigations
    - Detail scope and methods used in reports; why topic is being audited, reviewed, investigated, etc.

III. Avoid Engaging in Policy Discussions and Decisions
    - Just report outcomes of inquiries, not recommend policies
    - Shut down political discussions in OIG meetings with staff
    - Do not participate in drafting policy when the OIG participates in agency working groups
    - Defer to policymakers, give facts and audit recommendations, but not policy

IV. Maintaining Internal Vigilance Related to Issues of Independence
    - Emphasize OIG independence in new employee training and in-service training
    - Address matters of independence in the department from the bottom up

as inappropriate or when an IG's authority is challenged, one strategy is to respond forthrightly that pursuing such a request "would put us at risk." Another strategy is to ask that a formal letter be sent including the signatures of several interested committee members, thus demonstrating broad support for the request. Before passage of the 2016 IG Empower-

- Ensure that everyone knows that skepticism is important
- Be alert to conflicts of interest
- Be clear that OIG is a different kind of government agency since it does not have program responsibilities
- Safeguard independence by acting carefully
- Encourage discussions in the OIG about walking the line between Congress and agency

V.   Responding Creatively to Requests That Uncomfortably Stretch Legal Authority and Available Resources
- Help the requester to reframe the question or request
- Help write the letter to focus request and avoid too broad a question
- Add item to OIG's agenda if requested by agency director, if at all possible
- Work proactively to create a reservoir of good will with Congress to be able to work through difficult requests

VI.   Pushing Back on Inappropriate Requests or Challenges to Authority
- Go to the agency head or to Congress to complain about slowness of agency response
- Perform the work if the law says to do it; if not, then do not do it
- Protect the process; do not overly rush the process
- Use authority under the 2008 law giving IGs the authority to tell Congress that funding is insufficient to support OIG work
- Use and reference GAO's Federal Yellow Book as a strong basis for independence
- Require more signatures on letters of request in sensitive matters if the letters do not come from chair or ranking member
- Plan what you want to do and use supportive Congress members to help get resources to execute your plan

ment Act, denials of access to agency documents or lack of follow-up to IG reports occasionally resulted in OIGs making complaints to an agency's senior leadership or to Congress. When either principal presses for a quick study or report, OIG staff reported that they respond by indicating that weighing the processes and time required for a proper study is a critical aspect of independence. That is, except in instances where a requested study is mandated in legislation that becomes law, OIGs have, by virtue of their independence, the authority to decline a congressional or agency request. IGs or OIG staff also indicated that they may use the authority in the 2008 amendment to the IG Act to press for budget increases when they are needed to accomplish their mission or particular projects. When issues emerge with either principal, the IG or OIG staff may stress the need for independence by referencing standards for conducting audits as outlined in the GAO's Yellow Book, or federal rules covering investigations.

Factors Associated with Collaboration of OIGs with Agencies and Congress

Each of the IGs in this study expressly indicated a strong sense of independence, and interviews with agency leadership in their corresponding agencies confirmed that sense. In two agencies, however, disagreements about independence between the OIG and agency leadership resulted in higher levels of tension and lower levels of collaboration between the OIG and the agency compared with the four other agencies in our study.[14]

In one of the two agencies evidencing higher levels of tension, the IG indicated that participating as a member of the leadership team was a matter that "currently remains unresolved—[it is] a difficult area." The IG commented that there is "lots of discussion, [but] unresolved issues" regarding independence of the IG in the agency. An OIG staffer in the same agency expressed the view that agency leadership wants the "OIG to be more accommodating with agency desires" and that agency leadership probably views the OIG as a "necessary evil" mandated by legislation. An interview with a member of this agency's leadership confirmed difficulties with the comment that "IG is a dirty word everywhere in the agency." And, this interviewee's response to the question of whether the IG is a member of the agency's leadership team was simply "doesn't feel like it."

In the second of these two agencies, the IG responded to our questions about independence by commenting that the agency's "general counsel has challenged the IG's authority regularly." Differences over OIG authority prompted this IG to consider sending a seven-day letter to Congress, but this action was forestalled by a compromise over the immediate issue under discussion with the general counsel. This IG reported that there are continuing tensions about access to information that the OIG deems important to its work, but that the agency's leadership feels it is not obligated to provide.

Tensions in these two agencies contrasted with comments (and the lack of reports in public documents) in the study's other four agencies. Interviewees in these agencies expressly characterized OIG-agency relations as collegial, even when disagreements arise. IGs reported positive working relationships with agency leadership generally, and OIG staff reported similarly collegial relationships with counterparts within the agency. Agency leadership acknowledged there are occasional disagreements with their respective OIGs regarding accessing information held by the agency or implementing OIG recommendations; however, such occasions are usually addressed amicably or left unresolved for further discussion as necessary. Additionally, leadership in these four agencies viewed OIGs as positive forces producing useful findings and providing information that strengthens the agency. In these agencies, engagements seem to be more collaborative than in the two agencies with higher levels of strain and tension.

Strain between OIGs and Congress was reported by two OIGs—one of whom also reported OIG-agency conflicts. In one instance, a member of Congress publicly disagreed with a particular action of an IG. In the other instance, the OIG was specifically criticized by a different member of Congress for not identifying what this congressperson believed was a serious slip-up by the agency. Interviewees in both of these OIGs mentioned these criticisms during interviews and characterized the disagreements as exceptions to generally smooth relations with Congress. Nevertheless, interviewees in these two OIGs indicated that their respective offices are still devoting considerable attention to addressing concerns raised by these two members of Congress. To maintain the confidentiality of the agencies involved in our research, we did not raise these specific instances in conversations with the congressional staff that we interviewed. As noted previously, congressional staff interviewees expressly indicated that their (and presumably Congress's) major concern involves instances where IGs are not sufficiently independent or aggressive, where agencies ignore requests for information, or where agencies consistently do not implement OIG recommendations. Accordingly, relations with Congress are collaborative for OIGs who are viewed as strongly independent of their home agencies, keep their congressional contacts informed, and are responsive to congressional requests.

Key Factors Associated with Maintaining Independence,
Assuring Accountability, and Engaging in Collaboration

Several factors account for differing levels of collaborative engagement between OIGs and their respective agencies and/or Congress. IGs' individual styles and personality traits are clearly important in setting the tone for OIG relations with both agency leadership and with Congress. The IGs, OIG staff, executive officials, and congressional staff we interviewed are seasoned professional leaders who are dedicated to serving the public good and work to minimize personality-based conflicts in that service. Though OIGs are well meaning and well intentioned, differences do occur between IGs, agency leaders, and Congress. In addition to attributes distinctive to individuals, our interviews and publicly available information suggest that at least four key organizational factors are associated with an IG maintaining independence and successfully engaging in collaboration with his or her agency and Congress:

- Mutually shared views of the inspector general role by the IG, agency leadership, and Congress

- Confidence and trust in the IG by agency leadership and Congress

- Reciprocal responsiveness by the IG, the agency, and Congress

- Substantial investments in building and maintaining collaborative relationships by the OIG and the agency

ROLE OF THE INSPECTORS GENERAL

The role of inspectors general in the federal government is quite distinctive. The offices of an IG differ from most federal offices in several ways: (a) IGs report to an executive office and to Congress; (b) IGs perform a watchdog role while residing in the agency they oversee; (c) IGs are expected to be independent of managerial pressures or political influences from the agency, Congress, or other outside forces; (d) IGs have independent administrative resources and legal authority to pursue auditing, law enforcement, and evaluation responsibilities; and (e) IGs have open-ended appointments, and their dismissal requires notice be given to Congress by the president or agency head.

While the IG Act of 1978 and subsequent amendments establish IG authority and responsibilities, views about the role of inspectors general vary across federal agencies. Agreement on the role of the IG appears to be a critical factor in establishing productive relationships between an IG, his or her agency, and Congress. If the IG and the agency or Congress view the role of the OIG differently and these views are in conflict, then stresses are almost inevitable. These strains, in turn, reduce collaborative engagements between the OIG and its two principals. The two key areas where IGs and agencies or Congress may hold different views about the role of IGs relate to (1) the relationship of the IG to the agency or to Congress, and (2) the authority of the IG to carry out his or her responsibilities.

Our interviews confirm that IGs and their staff never consider themselves to be fully members of their home agency's leadership team, even if the IG attends agency leadership meetings. This view is not shared by leadership in some agencies or by members of Congress. Tensions between the agency and the OIG may arise when the agency's leadership expects the OIG to have greater loyalty to or closer engagement with the agency than the IG believes is appropriate. For example, when discussing his service as acting IG for DHS, Clark Ervin details a meeting he had with Tom Ridge, secretary of Homeland Security. Ridge met with Ervin after a difficult congressional hearing in which, Ridge stated, "'[I] got my head handed to me over this new report of yours.'" Ridge then asked the pointed question: "'Look, Clark. Are you *my* [emphasis original] Inspector General? When I was Governor of Pennsylvania, I had an Inspector General, but he wasn't out there like you constantly criticizing and embarrassing us.'" Clark's response was, "'Well, sir, you've put your finger on the problem we're having here.'"[15]

Similar views were expressed by an official in one of the agencies included in this study, in which the agency's leadership expected the OIG to have greater loyalty to or closer engagement with the agency than the IG believed is appropriate. The agency's leadership also appeared to be uncomfortable with the OIG's efforts to expand its role by conducting performance evaluations and other reviews not performed by previous IGs for that agency. The agency's IG, correspondingly, indicated that the OIG relationship with agency leadership remains a matter of discussion, as does the degree to which the IG should be a member of the leadership team. A member of this agency's leadership expressed the view during an interview that the IG should be "validating" that the agency was performing well and should be helping the agency relative to various stakeholders, including Congress.

Another source of strain for IGs that emerged in our interviews involves occasions when agency leadership views IGs through a private sector lens. This is especially likely if the agency head, deputy head, or general counsel comes from the private sector or if that is the leadership's orientation. Since private sector organizations have nothing comparable to federal inspectors general, agency leaders with primarily private sector experience appear to have difficulty understanding that while the IGs report to agency heads, they are largely independent actors and the IGs also report directly to Congress.

Our interviews also highlighted different expectations about the role of IGs arising from interpretations of federal law about IG authority. In two of the agencies in this study, we found higher levels of tension between the OIG and agency leadership, and also found that the OIG has been denied access (or has had delayed access) to information and data. In the view of OIG interviewees in these two agencies, limited access to information held by the agency violates the IG Act of 1978 and limits their role as inspectors general.[16] At the time we conducted interviews, the matter was a source of tension that appears to have adversely affected collaborative engagement with the agency. On the other hand, interviewees in the other four agencies with lower levels of tension about access revealed that informal discussions and remedies resolve access issues at least temporarily.

CONFIDENCE AND TRUST IN THE IG

Maintaining confidence and trust in the IG by the agency and by Congress is critically important for OIGs to be effective. As one OIG staff member told us, the "key is to devote time and energy to developing positive, functional relationships to build confidence and trust, and to lay critical groundwork for collaborative engagements with their agency and with Congress." The degree to which OIGs are successful in building confidence and trust correlates positively with the extent of collaborative engagement of an OIG with its agency and Congress.

Relations between the IG and Congress have overarching influence on establishing levels of confidence and trust. As one congressional staff member indicated, a successful IG "(a) has good relations with the agency to know what efficiencies might be obtained and (b) maintains good relations with Congress to get changes made to address problems." Another congressional staff member remarked that a committee "watches for 'capture' of an OIG by the agency" and commented that it is "hard to distinguish between capture and incompetence." An agency leadership interviewee underscored the importance of congressional confidence and trust by commenting that "IGs are in a precarious position because Congress can go after IGs easily." Indeed, as reported in chapter 3, pressures from Congress appear to be the most frequent reason for involuntary IG resignations. As mentioned earlier, two IGs and their staffs in our study reported devoting a great deal of time to assuaging concerns by vocal and potentially powerful members of Congress who had raised questions about the IGs' decisions and performance.

OIGs are quite diligent in communicating with and responding to Congress. These communications in all OIGs are most often direct and not coordinated with agency leadership. That is, communications from the agency and the OIG to Congress are on separate tracks. Perceptions of OIG responsiveness and separate communications with Congress can, however, lower an agency's confidence and trust in the OIG. When agency leadership and the OIG are not communicating well, the agency's communications office may not fully share pertinent information with the OIG's communications staff, and conversely, requests made of the OIG by Congress may not be revealed to the agency as quickly as agency leaders would prefer.

We found consistently that perceived OIG receptiveness and responsiveness to communications from the agency also affects the confidence and trust agency leaders have in the OIG, and in turn, has implications for collaborative engagements involving the OIG. When the OIG enjoys higher levels of confidence and trust, agency officials and staff are more willing to approach the OIG and to cooperate more fully on OIG audits and evaluations. For example, in three OIGs evidencing higher levels of mutual confidence and trust, agency officials reported being quite willing to approach the OIG. In one of those agencies, the current IG was lauded for making visits to field operations, in contrast to the previous IG, who rarely ventured outside of Washington. This new approach, an OIG interviewee noted, resulted in a reputational shift for the OIG and "others now come to OIG to talk about stuff because they know that we will treat the issue fairly." In another agency, a leadership interviewee expressed confidence in the OIG and said that the IG is seen "as a useful, trustworthy tool to help leadership by looking into complaints against the agency." Relative to Congress, an OIG interviewee in another agency remarked that the IG appears to be trusted by committees, and that congressional requests made to that OIG "reflect their [the committees'] confidence in the independence and integrity of their [the OIG's] work." By contrast, we did not hear similar comments from the two agencies that evidenced higher levels of strained relationships. In one of these agencies, an administrative leadership interviewee characterized local agency staff as having an "us-versus-them" view of the relationship with OIG representatives. In the other agency, lower levels of confidence and trust appear to be partly the result of considerable turnover in the agency's offices and lower levels of understanding of the OIG's role by agency staff and field personnel. The two latter OIGs and agencies have lower levels of collaborative engagement with their agency than the other four OIGs.

RECIPROCAL RESPONSIVENESS

Establishing communication routines and taking actions that respond to needs, requests, or inquiries from OIGs to the agency or to Congress—and vice versa—can advance collaborative engagement between these parties. However, a lack of responsiveness—perceived or real—may result in tensions or strains that dissuade collaboration. While levels of reciprocal responsiveness can be difficult to assess precisely, there are variations in levels of reciprocity across the OIGs, and these differing levels correspond roughly to differing levels of collaborative engagements. Reciprocal responsiveness between OIGs and Congress appears mostly to involve heightened attentiveness by OIGs to congressional requests and inquiries. Congressional committees also vary in how responsive or reactive they are to occasional requests by OIGs for support in negotiations with their agencies, but a positive relationship between an OIG and Congress is viewed as highly beneficial.

Among the OIGs in this study, IGs tend to be open to altering OIG working agendas to respond to agency requests for inquiries. The OIGs also actively seek to inform Congress about relevant activities and quickly respond to congressional requests, short of sharing reports and information before they are shared with agency leadership. When planning future audits or evaluations, each OIG office solicits suggestions from both Congress and its agency leadership for areas that need examination. However, OIGs and their respective agency leadership report that such requests for input often do not generate many responses from either the agency leadership team or congressional contacts.

Interviews with OIG officials suggest that they may not always receive timely replies to OIG requests for information, responses to OIG audit reports prior to their final release, follow-through on OIG recommendations, and actions to close OIG recommendations that are open. A lack of timely response is a source of consternation for OIGs and increases the potential for strain or conflict between an OIG and its agency. One agency leadership interviewee in an agency evidencing high levels of collaboration acknowledged concern that the "agency needs to be more responsive to IG requests." This official went on to say that such responsiveness is "simply part of good leadership and high-level management."

A recurring issue in our interviews concerned OIG requests for information that were met with assertions from agency leadership that the information could be withheld under interpretations of other federal statutes or policies. OIG interviewees and agency leaders indicated that such matters are usually handled at the lower levels of the OIG and the agency, but that on occasion the IG goes directly to the agency head and, in doing so, usually gets a response from the agency. However, such occasions raise tensions between the OIG and the agency, and lower the potential for collaborative engagements.

Seeking congressional assistance in addressing the slowness of agency responses to OIG requests can be tricky. Interviewees pointed to occasions when reaching out to congressional contacts successfully reversed slow agency response to OIG requests. Congressional staff, for example, helped one OIG in our study by including language in an appropriations bill encouraging agencies to be responsive to OIG requests. In another instance, the agency became responsive when attentive members of Congress halted legislative actions for the agency until it was more responsive to the OIG. However, the costs of securing congressional help are that such efforts are time consuming, requiring multiple meetings with congressional representatives over an extended period, and may result in alienating agency leadership, thus lowering levels of mutual collaboration in the future.

INVESTMENTS IN BUILDING AND MAINTAINING COLLABORATIVE RELATIONSHIPS

OIGs, agencies, and congressional offices invest resources—time, energy, and money—in developing ongoing mechanisms to maintain collaborative relationships. Some of these initiatives are listed in tables 5-1, 5-2, and 5-3. Here we discuss specific programmatic efforts or organizational units that have fostered engagement between OIGs and agency representatives, or between OIGs and congressional contacts.

For the most part, OIGs rely on personal relationships at the leadership and operational levels to foster collaboration. These relationships are institutionalized through weekly, biweekly, or monthly meetings between the IG and the agency head. These are usually one-on-one meetings attended only by the IG and the agency head, although some meetings include either the agency's deputy head or general counsel. These regularly scheduled meetings provide opportunities for exchanges of information, although in some cases the meetings may be more one-way conversations, with the agency head saying very little. Corresponding meetings between officials at lower levels of the OIG and the agency are typically held in larger agencies, especially when the OIG is structured functionally or regionally to mirror the agency's organization.

On the critical issue of following up on recommendations, most OIGs in this study have monitoring mechanisms to periodically trigger the OIG to inquire whether the agency has made changes consistent with audit recommendations. These triggers are usually generated from databases that contain recommendations, dates, and timed messages. Responsibility for follow-ups varies across the OIGs—for example, ranging from a deputy or assistant IG in smaller OIGs to a dedicated office in larger agencies, where the office maintains the database and contacts agency officials about implementation of open recommendations.

Three agencies in our study, including the two with lower levels of collaborative engagement, reported that they have formal dispute resolution mechanisms, such as a written policy or designated process, to resolve open recommendations or access questions. Interviewees in the OIGs and their home agencies reported that these mechanisms are rarely used or are viewed as largely ineffective. Where positive personal relationships are in place, OIGs and agency leadership prefer to work through issues informally or to decide that the matter can be set aside until a later time.

At the time of interviews for this study, each of the six agencies devoted time and resources to follow up on OIG recommendations.[17] In the smaller agencies, program-level officials have responsibility for following up on recommendations. For the larger agencies, compliance or internal control offices are charged with facilitating and assuring acceptance and closure of recommendations by agency leadership. These offices work with (a) auditing teams in the OIGs who are usually responsible for determining that a recommendation has been implemented, and (b) agency program officers charged with implementing the recommendations. Joining these offices, many agencies employ individuals specifically designated as audit liaisons with whom the auditing team in an OIG works, often throughout the auditing process. OIGs rely on audit liaisons to explain audit processes to agency personnel; assist auditors in obtaining information needed for the audits; explain to agency personnel any findings and recommendations to be reported in the audit; and assist agency personnel in responding to audit recommendations, including any continuing open recommendations stemming from an audit. Audit liaisons in the agency may, according to a senior OIG interviewee, "put pressure on program managers" to facilitate audits and implement recommendations.

Agency leadership in four of the agencies evidencing higher levels of collaborative engagement reported holding weekly, biweekly, or periodic meetings with agency officials—not including OIG officers—to assess the status of open recommendations. These meetings are initiated by the current office holders, often in response to what they characterize as large numbers of open recommendations. Such meetings were infrequent in the remaining two agencies with lower levels of collaboration and higher levels of stress. Thus, we conclude that personal, frequent, and visible involvement by agency leadership within the agency management team increases the responsiveness of agency offices to OIG recommendations.

As reported earlier, OIGs pay particular attention to Congress. Correspondingly, some members of Congress or their staff pay attention to IGs. Ongoing routinized communication with congressional staff is useful in bringing an OIG's message to Congress, and messages from Congress back to the OIG. Congressional staff members reported initiating meetings with larger OIGs to discuss what they are doing, hear about any problems, and ask whether Congress could help with issues such as access or open recommendations. Meetings held with OIG staff are helpful for the congressional staff as a means of fostering communications and gaining a sense of what is happening in the IG community.

An IG's Strategic Environment

Our interviews and review of public documents underscore how important it is to take cognizance of an IG's strategic environment to understand the actions of IGs. As presented in chapter 1 and discussed in subsequent chapters, this environment is composed of at least three major elements: (a) stakeholders interested in and affected by an IG's work; (b) expectations held by the IG's stakeholders; and (c) system stressors that create challenges and opportunities for an IG. This closing section discusses briefly these three elements and elaborates on how they influence the actions of U.S. inspectors general.

STAKEHOLDERS OF IGS

Interviews reported in this chapter confirm that Congress and leadership in the home agencies—the two stakeholders with legal authority over IGs and to whom the IGs officially report—are critically important to the operation of IGs. While statutorily independent, IGs clearly pay attention to the preferences of and requests from these stakeholders. By and large, IGs respond to virtually every request from agency or congressional leadership. Similarly, IGs seek to avoid public disputes with these stakeholders and to smooth private differences to the greatest extent possible. Nearly every individual we interviewed indicated that high levels of attentiveness and nurtured collegial relationships are essential to an IG's long-term success.

IGs we interviewed are also aware of secondary groups of stakeholders, which to some degree are distinctive for each agency. Nearly all of the IGs in this study indicated that his or her OIG staff is a critical constituency. In large OIGs, the staff members have considerable influence because of their expertise and links to operational levels of the home agency. In at least one agency, staff members clearly serve as gatekeepers and agenda setters; in another OIG, the allegiance of the IG to the staff serves as a constraint on what that IG considers possible. Similarly, the size of the staff and its level of expertise influence what the IG can reasonably do given those resources.

The Council of the Inspectors General for Integrity and Efficiency (CIGIE) has the potential to serve as an important secondary stakeholder. This statutorily created council composed of all IGs creates a venue for conversations among IGs and OIG staff; however, the council has only a small administrative staff and no authority over the IGs per se. Committees composed of IGs and OIG staff set professional standards for

IG activities; and they assist in appointment processes, recruit staff, and guide training opportunities for IGs and their staff. Views of CIGIE and its operations varied among our interviewees; some thought the organization provided important services, but others raised questions about the organization's efficacy and impact. CIGIE's chair, a fellow IG elected by the council, appears before congressional committees to speak on behalf of the IG community. The current chair as of June 2019, Michael Horowitz, DOJ IG, played a critical role in testifying for components of the 2016 IG Empowerment Act.[18]

IGs in our study were also asked about other potential stakeholders or collaborators, such as the GAO or the DOJ's Offices of Special Counsel. Most respondents reported they have virtually no contact with these agencies and their work rarely overlaps with that of these other agencies, though there are occasions when the GAO and an OIG coordinate an evaluation or inquiry to avoid overlapping activities. Occasionally the DOJ or a U.S. Attorney becomes a critical stakeholder in carrying out recommended prosecutions resulting from OIG investigations. When investigations are a major portion of an OIG's operation, these stakeholders are critical to the OIG's success because DOJ officials have the final determination on whether to prosecute an individual or corporation investigated by an OIG. Relations with another potentially important stakeholder, the media, have led some OIGs to create offices to handle media-related matters, to explain reports and actions as clearly as possible. While the media often cover IG testimony and IG reports, none of our interviewees indicated that they engage the media to pursue their OIG's mission or interests.

EXPECTATIONS OF IGS

If the two principal stakeholders in an IG's environment are an agency's leadership and Congress, then meeting expectations of these two principals is critically important to an IG's success. As discussed extensively in chapter 2, Congress set a number of expectations in the IG Act regarding OIGs' operation and their relationships with home agencies as well as with Congress. Interviewees regularly referred to the IG Act as setting expectations about independence, accountability, and engagement. Understanding those expectations clearly shapes the way IGs approach their work.

Independence   Virtually all of our interviewees mentioned independence as a key expectation of inspectors general. The Inspector General Act underscores an IG's independence by providing that he or she is free to initiate and pursue audits, investigations, or evaluations. Agencies are directed to cooperate with an IG and to provide information as needed for audits, investigations, or evaluations. An IG largely organizes his or her office and hires staff; and an IG may officially complain to Congress that the budget recommended by agency management, OMB, or the president is insufficient to carry out the OIG's responsibilities. Given these statutory protections, the IGs and their staff we interviewed underscored that they have considerable latitude in pursuing audits, investigations, and evaluations. That view was not, however, universally held by agency leadership. Differences in views about what independence actually means was a source of considerable friction between the IG and the agency in at least two organizations involved in this study. While IGs voiced strong views about their independence in our interviews, they also acknowledged that they are discreet in asserting independence—seeking to engage agency leadership in identifying areas for audits or evaluations, keeping agency officials informed of forthcoming reports, and working with liaison personnel throughout the auditing process. Similarly, IGs respond to congressional demands by attempting to shape, or reshape, inquiries from Congress and, on occasion, gently pushing back on requests they view as plainly partisan or outside the IG's authority.

Accountability   The IGs we interviewed acknowledged that they are accountable for outcomes in their activities, management of the office, and relationships with stakeholders. Interviewees initially framed accountability in terms of the reports IGs are required to file under the IG Act—semiannual reports to Congress (SARCs) and, more recently, posting of all reports on individual OIG websites. Among our interviewees, there were doubts about the degree to which the SARCs are read by congressional representatives or their staffs. Congressional staff interviewees indicated that SARCs were usually read by staff working for relevant committees, but there is no systematic review by congressional oversight committees. Nevertheless, the six OIGs in our study invested considerable time and effort in producing lengthy reports with high-quality graphics in magazine formats. To the extent that accountability is an issue for Congress, nearly all of our interviewees suggested that congressional interest is often greater in agency reactions to and implementation of IG audits, investigations, or evaluations. In fact, one congressional interviewee indicated that holding hearings on agency actions or inactions on an IG's report often occurs to fill committee time or highlight a committee's interest in a particular matter.

Accountability to agency management occurs in several forms. Comments by OIG and agency officials indicated that agency management reviews SARCs very closely—probably more closely than congressional offices. Agency leaders often provide reactions, comments, or clarifications in attached letters, which become part of SARCs before they are sent to Congress. Interviewees also indicated that individual audit reports are often reviewed closely by agency management as part of auditing and reporting processes. For example, agency offices that are the subject of an audit or evaluation usually receive draft statements of findings and recommendations, and the OIG may alter its report in light of the agency's reactions to the draft. OIG interviewees maintained that final reports and SARCs are not, however, subject to negotiation. Agency management, on the other hand, is not legally obligated to accept recommendations and may choose to pursue a different approach to the problem identified by an IG.

On the investigative side, the DOJ provides a check on an IG's investigative activities by deciding whether to prosecute individuals or companies accused of criminal or civil violations by the OIG. Our interviews suggested the OIGs develop a sense of what DOJ and various U.S. Attorney offices across the country are willing to accept as a prosecutable violation. For example, some U.S. Attorneys have high thresholds for the amount of money involved in cases of fraud and will not prosecute cases under those thresholds. But interviewees familiar with investigations also indicated a willingness to seek out state or local prosecutors if they feel that federal prosecution is unlikely and state-level prosecution might be possible. SARCs also report the number of criminal prosecutions and recovered funds, but it is unclear whether reports of these figures are ever used to hold OIGs accountable.

Accountability can also be enforced by dismissal of the IG by either the president or the agency head, depending on which one is the appointing authority. None of our interviewees, however, seem concerned about the possibility of dismissal as a form of enforced accountability. But IGs did indicate considerable caution and sensitivity to criticism from Congress. In these cases, Congress's mechanisms for enforcing accountability include hearings focusing on an IG's activities and performance, or congressional action on an OIG's budget—highlighting shortcomings or cutting the budget of an OIG falling short of congressional expectations. As reported earlier, at least two IGs we interviewed admitted that they are carefully responding to criticisms by one or more members of Congress regarding OIG activities. Another IG indicated that the OIG had received increased budget allocations, which the IG viewed as an indication of congressional satisfaction with the office's work.

Finally, we asked IGs about the statutorily mandated peer review process organized by CIGIE. This process, which involves a committee composed of members from the IG community, focuses on whether quality standards issued by the IG community are being met by an individual OIG. Basically, the peer review asks whether an OIG's audits, investigations, and evaluations are conducted in accord with CIGIE's published standards. Peer reports are shared with the OIG, agency leadership, and Congress. Most IGs and staff we interviewed commented that the peer reviews are of questionable value as accountability mechanisms, since the reviews do not address the effectiveness of the OIG in terms of focusing on critically important topics, making significant recommendations, and having an impact on agency performance. Another CIGIE responsibility is evaluating allegations of misconduct by IGs and senior OIG staff. Interviewees indicated that such investigations are viewed as serious but acknowledged that delays in such evaluations often undercut the process.[19]

Engagement   The Inspector General Act clearly sets expectations for engagement by an IG with leadership in the home agency. An IG is expected, for example, to keep agency leadership and Congress fully informed about discoveries of serious problems, actions needed to correct the problems, and the progress being made to resolve those problems.

While interviewees generally agreed that IGs can identify problem areas in audits or evaluations, there is less consensus about what the OIG can recommend to resolve an issue and how much can be done to design solutions to the problems identified. Most of our interviewees indicated that their reports or investigations point to problems, but it is the agency's responsibility to develop solutions to those problems. In particular, several interviewees pointed out that the OIG might be asked to assess the eventual solution to a problem the OIG has identified, and the OIG is placed in a compromising position if asked to evaluate a program that he or she helped to design or create. Thus, while IGs may frame recommendations as standards to be met, our interviewees indicated a disinclination to become involved in policy discussions or programs designed to solve the problems the IGs identified or to meet the standards they recommend.[20]

Sometimes, engagement is initiated by an IG's two primary stakeholders. Agency leaders we interviewed reported that they bring issues to their IG for evaluation or investigation—sometimes to provide an independent review involving a politically hot issue and sometimes to simply buy time while seeking a solution to a problem. Similarly, IGs frequently pointed to congressional mandates that an IG review an issue, and individual members of Congress may request that an IG inquire into a matter of interest. Wanting to be responsive, the IGs in this study reported that they always respond to these requests, but in doing so they seek to clarify the boundaries of what is being asked, the resources available to conduct the inquiry, and the authority the IGs have to explore the issue.

SYSTEM STRESSORS

Our interviews suggested two systematic stressors that have influenced offices of inspector general since their creation in 1978: (1) shared powers in the U.S. government, which require joint actions by Congress, the president, and/or the judiciary to effectuate government actions; and (2) partisan and personal agendas of public office holders, which impinge on government officials as they pursue their official responsibilities.

Shared Powers   Within the constitutional framework of the United States, Congress, the president, and often the judiciary must come to an agreement on legislation, policies, or fiscal matters to undertake government actions. Sometimes agreements are only partial, sometimes they are the result of serious conflicts, and sometimes they are only temporary.

Stresses stemming from shared powers may emerge even before an IG is appointed to his or her office. For example, appointments of IGs that require Senate confirmation may be hastened or held up for a variety of reasons by either the president or Congress.[21] The IGs we interviewed indicated that their appointment processes were lengthy, especially for PAS appointments, but not particularly stressful.[22]

Once appointed, IGs reported facing questions that led to controversies about their authority and responsibilities in particular areas such as access to records, documents, or data. Significantly, our interviews documented that Congress serves as a critically important ally for pressing agencies to accommodate IG requests and ultimately passing legislation clarifying IG authority to obtain information held by an agency.[23] Interviewees also cited congressional support in the budget process, pointing to the 2008 legislation giving IGs the authority to publicly inform Congress that a budget recommended by the agency, OMB, or the president was insufficient to conduct their work. One of our IG interviewees and corresponding agency leader interviewee reported that funds were added to the OIG budget after the IG reported to Congress that the OIG's budget request was reduced in the executive budget process. Another IG with friendly congressional relations reported an increase in that OIG's budget after informal conversations with Congress.

Partisan and Personal Agendas   One of the IGs we interviewed reported being targeted for intense scrutiny because a powerful congressional representative believed the IG failed to be sufficiently critical of an agency's actions. Another IG raised the ire of a key member of Congress because of a series of recommendations regarding the agency's policy options. In both instances, OIG staff were concerned about whether the IG would survive the substantial pressures brought to bear by members of Congress. These two IGs in our study were undertaking extraordinary efforts to meet with congressional staff and representatives to smooth ruffled feathers and improve relations. More generally, IGs we interviewed clearly play very close attention to demands and requests from Congress, and they develop strategies to accommodate, avoid, or gently push back such requests.

Conclusion

Interviews with officials reported in this chapter draw varied pictures of how IGs pursue their responsibilities. Without a doubt, individual attitudes, capabilities, and preferences among our interviewees account in some measure for their decisions and actions. But our conversations with IGs, OIG staff, agency leadership, and congressional contacts suggest that there is a common basis for much that U.S. inspectors general do and how they do it. As such, IGs operate in what we term a strategic environment that places them between Congress and executive officials who occasionally hold conflicting views about IG activities. Moreover, IGs in this strategic environment operate independently with broad authority and yet depend on cooperation and resources from the executive and legislative branches. Variations over time from one administration to another, from one session of Congress to another, and from historically significant events inevitably alter features of the IGs' strategic environment. Our interviews suggest that IGs who survive and thrive clearly are attentive and responsive to those changes.

SIX

Making a Difference

Perhaps the OIGs' greatest opportunity to contribute to government operations is to force a conversation among the principals on the terms of accountability. Their success in this role depends on the way that they manage their engagement with political overseers in Congress, the press, and elsewhere and with program managers who must carry out or adjust their proposals.[1]

—*Mark Moore and Margaret J. Gates, authors of* Inspectors General: Junkyard Dogs or Man's Best Friend?, *commenting on how IGs could make a difference in the federal government*

When we interviewed inspectors general as part of this research, we heard one singular aspiration voiced by all IGs from across the federal government. When asked how they would measure their own success, they all replied they would want to see that their office's efforts had improved their agency's operations. Not one IG told us that monetary savings for the agency was his or her personal goal, despite the very public nature of that performance measure.[2] But achieving success by improving agency operations is not a straightforward or easy process.

As we noted earlier, the federal IGs were originally established by law to both improve financial management and accountability for federal government operations, and elevate congressional engagement with executive activities through legislative oversight. Over the last four decades, IGs have worked to detect and prevent fraud, waste, and abuse by recommending actions to improve agency systems and operations. How and when do the IGs make a difference to improve the work and impact of their agencies?

In this chapter we first discuss how and when IG work makes a difference. Second, we discuss operational challenges that IGs face in making a difference. Third, we describe the magnitude of the monetary impact that IG offices have made through their investigations and audits in recent years. Fourth, we investigate how agency-specific factors affect the performance of the IG offices in making a difference. And finally, we discuss how the impact of IG work is affected by and may affect the IGs' stakeholders, the expectations held by those stakeholders, and system stressors in the IGs' strategic environment.

How and When IG Work Makes a Difference

The intended impact of IG work might be viewed along a continuum, from the more immediate process fixes to the more elusive and time-consuming improvements in laws and regulations that IGs deem are needed to allow agency operations to be more effective in achieving mission-driven goals. As figure 6-1 depicts, there is a degree of difficulty that IGs face in working to achieve impact. At the lowest level of difficulty, IGs employ financial audits and investigations to identify where agencies may control costs more effectively. The IGs may identify waste due to inefficiencies or lax controls that permit questionable, or even fraudulent, use of agency resources.

Through successful investigations, IGs can hold both agency employees and contractors accountable, and through successful prosecutions and personnel actions, the agencies may save money and improve internal risk assessment processes. Ideally, once IG audits and investigations identify risks and insufficiently effective internal controls, the IGs develop feasible and targeted recommendations that, if implemented, lead to strengthened internal controls within their agencies.

Improving agency processes and policies is frequently challenging, since achieving the desired impact is not under the control of the IG and bureaucratic inertia is likely to work against change in most agencies.

FIGURE 6-1

Degree of Difficulty for IGs to Improve Agency Performance

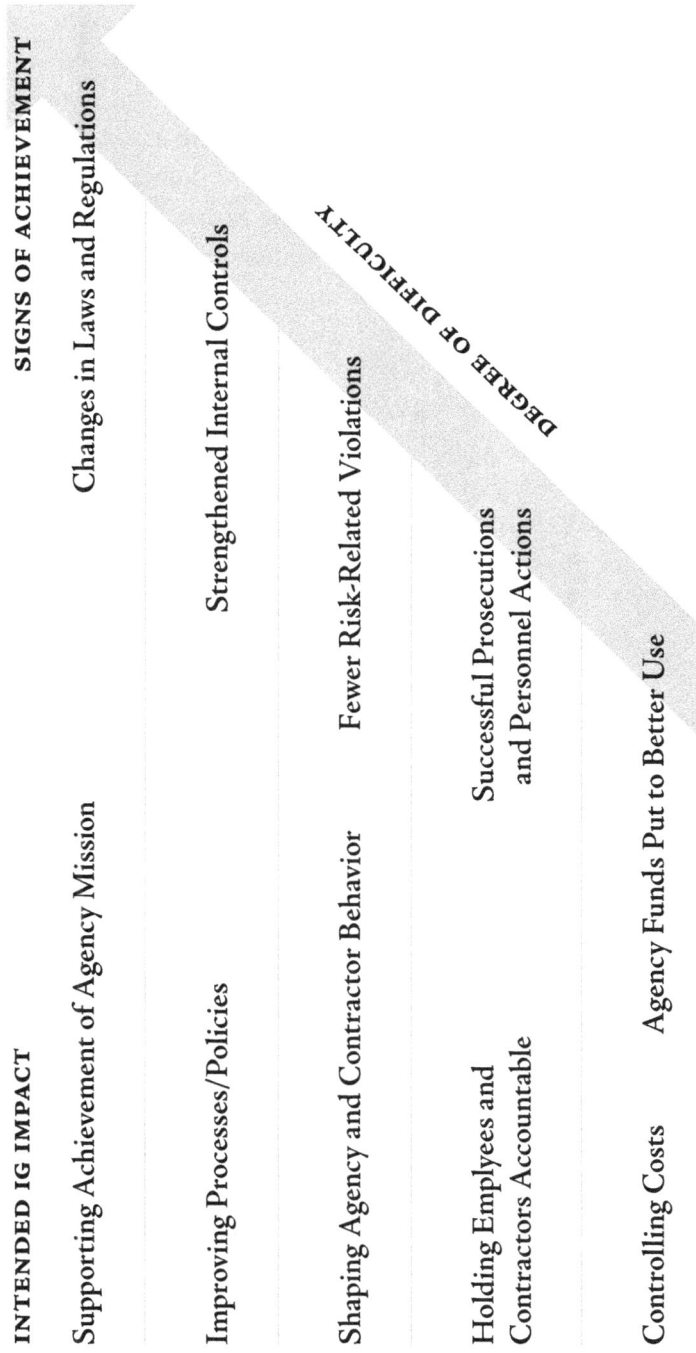

SIGNS OF ACHIEVEMENT

DEGREE OF DIFFICULTY

INTENDED IG IMPACT

Supporting Achievement of Agency Mission

Changes in Laws and Regulations

Improving Processes/Policies

Strengthened Internal Controls

Shaping Agency and Contractor Behavior

Fewer Risk-Related Violations

Holding Emplyees and
Contractors Accountable

Successful Prosecutions
and Personnel Actions

Controlling Costs

Agency Funds Put to Better Use

Even if IG recommendations are crystal clear and sufficiently identify root causes of problems, the actions recommended are up to the agency leadership to take—or not. Frequently, inadequate resources, competing leadership priorities, changes in leadership at or near the top of the agency, and/or existing laws or regulations may inhibit even what may seem to be reasonable enhancements—such as hiring more and better trained contract managers, purchasing additional equipment, or modernizing current technologies—from being implemented. The prevention impact of IG work is especially difficult to measure. That is, IG work may urge managers or contractors not to make foolish decisions or take fraudulent actions; however, which actions are not taken is hard to measure. And even though IGs track how many of their recommendations are implemented, they are not always aware of the extent to which internal controls are strengthened or efficiencies achieved—unless they later encounter the same problems when conducting work in the same arena.

TIMING AND PERSISTENCE MATTER

Identifying potential cost savings, developing actionable recommendations to fix problems or improve agency operations, and then seeing them implemented constitutes "instrumental use" of IG findings. This term was coined by Carol Weiss, a pioneer in evaluating government programs, who distinguished among ways in which to use the findings from government program evaluations—a concept that is pertinent to OIG work.[3] She noted that instrumental use occurs when evaluation findings directly inform decisions about a specific program or a policy, such as when specific IG recommendations are implemented as the IG envisioned in a fairly short time frame.

Of equal importance, Weiss noted that "conceptual or enlightenment use" occurs when research or evaluation findings generate new ideas and concepts, and promote and foster learning about the program under study. She explained that program managers and leaders may gain new insights or perspectives that may influence how they view and manage their programs, even if a specific recommendation is not immediately implemented. Of particular relevance to IG work, Weiss noted that managers sometimes may have already assessed what the root cause of a problem is but lacked the evidence to support moving in a particular direction. Evaluation and audit findings may provide the evidence needed to mobilize advocates and garner support around a specific issue or strategy, even if change is not immediate. Consequently, evaluation (or auditing) may become an instrument of persuasion for subsequent actions.[4]

Drawing from research in the social and behavioral sciences, Gary Henry and Mel Mark expanded on the use of evaluation and research findings, which are also quite pertinent to IG work. They explored the pathways and theory of change involved in evaluation use, specifically "evaluation processes or findings that directly cause some change in the thoughts or actions of one or more individuals."[5] Henry and Mark distinguished among three levels of evaluation influence: individual influence, which refers to changing an individual's thoughts, perceptions, or beliefs due to evaluation findings; interpersonal influence, which results from interactions between and with others; and collective influence, in which there is direct or indirect influence on a public or private entity or organization's decisionmaking process and/or practices.[6]

Taking a narrow view on the impact of IG work—that is, focusing only on the identification of cost savings, prosecution of crimes, and implementation of audit recommendations—underestimates the impact that IG studies may have on shaping the perceptions of agency leaders and other key stakeholders, and the interactions among agency leaders and among other stakeholders, including Congress. IG financial and performance audits, as well as investigations, bring issues to light that may not be immediately solvable but may offer evidence that supports pre-existing views among managers about weaknesses in internal controls or program operations. Putting recommendations on the table—even if they are controversial or vague—will likely provoke discussion that enlightens and expands considerations about how to improve programs and processes.

IG work can influence thinking about agency performance, even when specific recommended actions do not fix problems in the short run. Sometimes the influence eventually emerges in action outside of the agency—for example, when Congress pressures the agency to change or when interest groups pressure both the agency and Congress to make a change. The

Office of Personnel Management (OPM) data breach provides an example of the former, where a highly public event sparked immediate congressional interest. There are many instances where a series of IG reports influenced subsequent congressional action. For example, the 2006 and 2009 Department of Homeland Security (DHS) IG reports on the U.S. Coast Guard's Deepwater modernization program sparked prolonged congressional interest in the role of contractors in overhauling Coast Guard assets.[7]

While there are many instances where IGs produced a series of reports on one topic that influenced action taken by a variety of stakeholders, one especially compelling example is that of the Health and Human Services (HHS) IG's work focused on the Medicare home health program. Based on a series of studies that the HHS IG performance and financial auditors and investigators conducted, Congress passed a law to reform the Medicare home health program, which the Congressional Budget Office (CBO) scored as saving more than $40 billion over a five-year period. The reforms also established a structure for making payments that was much more conducive to planning and delivering home health services for individuals based on the severity of their needs, and to protecting them from unqualified providers.[8] See exhibit 6-1 at the end of this chapter for a description of the process through which a series of twenty IG studies were undertaken over six years and presented well-supported findings that influenced the actions of many—including Congress—and eventually resulted in changes to pertinent law and regulations.

Implementation of recommendations offered in multiple reports issued by smaller IG offices, such as that at the Smithsonian Institution, also may result in significant operational improvements that support achievement of mission for their agencies. See exhibit 6-2 at the end of this chapter for two examples of such improvements at the Smithsonian. On many occasions, IGs address problematic programs or policies with a few targeted reports to direct attention to complicated intergovernmental issues and inform relevant stakeholders over the course of a few years. The Department of Energy (DOE) IG did just that with the weatherization program during the time of the federal stimulus package, a large influx of federal funding spent to jumpstart a failing economy during the Great Recession. See exhibit 6-3 at the end of this chapter for that story.

The Operational Challenges IGs Face in Making
a Difference in Their Agencies

In chapter 4 we described the thoughtful process through which IGs develop actionable recommendations, and in chapter 5 we discussed the importance for IGs to maintain independence, be accountable, and engage collaboratively with agency leadership and Congress to operate effectively. Here we examine additional obstacles that arise from challenges to IG organizational capacity and may hinder IGs from enhancing the operations of their agencies.

For IG offices to operate in an effective manner, at a minimum, organizational capacity entails effective leadership, adequately trained staff, clear communications, clear operational procedures, sufficient resources for travel, and completion of work plans that adhere to all relevant statutory and regulatory guidelines. However, making a difference to improve agency performance typically entails more than adequate resources and work plans. A more aspirational definition of organizational capacity is "the ability of an organization to fulfill its mission through a blend of sound management, strong governance, and a persistent rededication to assessing and achieving results."[9] Given the multiple sources of guidance that govern the work of the IG offices— including the IG statutes, the *Government Auditing Standards*, and quality standards issued by the Council of the Inspectors General for Integrity and Efficiency (CIGIE)—agency-specific organizational cultures, and the high level of scrutiny given their work by key stakeholders, such a heightened level of capacity may affect how well IGs make lasting improvements in their agencies.

One way to trace concerns with IG capacity over time is through analyzing the foci of the studies that the Government Accountability Office (GAO) has conducted to examine specific IG offices, sets of IG offices, or the IG community. GAO is an instrument of the U.S. Congress and conducts studies upon request of the Congress, typically in response to inquiries transmitted to GAO by committee chairs. Thus, the foci of the GAO reports reflect congressional concerns about IGs.

Between 1978 and 2017 the GAO issued 103 reports focused on IGs and the IG community. Of those reports, 40 were issued between the IG Act of 1978 and 1989. Another 33 reports were issued between 1990 and 1999, 19 between 2000 and 2009, and only 11 between 2010 and 2017. It is noteworthy that about half of the reports provided no recommendations, thus indicating that GAO did not find sufficient evidence to support their offering changes in IG operations. Only two IG offices have been the focus of multiple GAO inquiries—eight in the Department of Defense (DOD) and four in the Department of State (DOS). Very few IG offices have been extensively criticized in recent GAO reports—for example, the Denali Commission[10] and Department of State (DOS)[11]—but there were more critical reports offering multiple recommendations to improve IG work in the earlier years, including the DOS,[12] Department of Commerce (DOC),[13] Department of Transportation (DOT),[14] and General Services Administration (GSA).[15]

The vast majority (at least 82 percent) of the GAO reports have addressed internal IG capacity issues. The reports focused on IG capacity have examined the effectiveness of OIG operations, resources, and independence. The capacity issues addressed include concerns with IG work not sufficiently adhering to standards, inadequate work planning based on risk analyses, insufficient staffing, and too narrow coverage of the IG work within the agencies. Only a very few of the GAO reports have targeted the behavior of specific IGs, upon the request of Congress—for example, with the IG for NASA (National Aeronautics and Space Administration).[16]

Over the years, GAO has offered a number of recommendations that are related to raising the quality of work in smaller (DFE) IG offices and that have addressed management and capacity issues. For example, in its 1993 report on the DFE agencies, the GAO offered the following recommendation: "To improve the effectiveness of the OIG at the designated federal entities, the Inspectors General at those entities should develop strategic plans which assess their respective entities' risks and problems, describe the strategies for resolving the risks and problems, detail the OIG resources required and available to implement their strategies, and provide performance measures to evaluate their progress."[17] Concerns regarding sufficient resources for IGs in the DFE agencies have been noted across the years, as in the GAO report on the U.S. International Trade Commission (USITC) IG, when the GAO recommended that

"The USITC IG should prepare a staffing analysis to determine the level of budget and staff resources needed to conduct the audits identified in audit plans, including audits required by statutes; audits of management challenges identified by the IG; and performance audits of economy, efficiency, and effectiveness of USITC's programs, offices, and activities."[18]

Capacity—in terms of effective and talented leadership, strategic and risk-based audit planning, resources, and well-trained staff—might well be viewed as necessary yet not always sufficient elements that enable IGs to undertake impactful work in their agencies. And measuring how well the IGs do in terms of making an impact, either across time or compared with one another, is extremely challenging.

Measuring Impact in Actions, Money Recovered, and Questioned Costs

As mandated by Congress, quantitative data are collected on the work of IG offices that provide an indication of the magnitude of the OIGs' combined and individual achievements. We include some of the IG data that have been collected and vetted by CIGIE in this section. First, we examine the footprint of the entire IG community in terms of investigative and auditing work. Table 6-1 shows the aggregate data for all OIGs for fiscal years 2010, 2012, 2014, and 2016.[19] Second, we display the breakdown of criminal actions and monetary savings resulting from investigative and auditing work for ten agencies in fiscal year 2016, the most recent year for which data are available at the time of this publication. Table 6-2 shows these data for the six large agencies with sizable budgets and large civilian workforces, the two median-sized agencies, and two small agencies.

Typically, work involved in investigations or audits spans across fiscal years, and it may take years for prosecutions to be completed. For example, the data in table 6-1 for cases and dollars recovered during one fiscal year reflect work undertaken over multiple years. Thus, work initiated during fiscal year 2010 not completed in that year may be reported in subsequent years, and work initiated in 2014 or 2016 may not be fully reported for those years. Nevertheless, with a few exceptions noted below, these annually reported data paint a reasonably complete picture about the magnitude of the work done by OIGs that may be quantified and give an indication of trends in that work.

As we report in table 6-1, the total number of criminal actions for all OIGs across these four fiscal years does not show great variance in ranging from nearly 5,000 actions to 5,900 actions, but the number of civil actions reported for fiscal years 2014 and 2016 shows a marked increase over the previous two years reported (2010 and 2012). Suspensions and indictments show greater variation during these four fiscal years, and they show no particular trend. Similarly, the widest range of variation is shown for monetary recoveries, which range from nearly $7 billion in fiscal year 2010 to nearly $32.7 billion in fiscal 2014. The general trend has been upward since fiscal year 2010, but the climb has not increased steadily. It is worth noting that not all estimated monetary savings actually occur. Sometimes settlements are the result of legal or administrative actions, and the actual settlement amount is likely lower than initial estimates. And sometimes the actors prosecuted for fraud no longer have the money to return. Notably, there are virtually no analyses or studies that compare reported monetary savings and the monetary savings actually realized by agencies.

When the outcomes of investigative work across individual IG offices are examined in table 6-2, there are some striking differences in the number of criminal actions and monetary savings linked to investigations. The type of work performed by the different agencies also can explain the quite disparate numbers across agencies. For example, the high numbers of criminal actions taken by HHS reflect the large numbers of vendors and contractors involved in Medicare and Medicaid. And the extremely high levels of monetary savings claimed by the DOD IG reflect the extremely expensive systems and assets purchased by the military; there is simply more money involved in contracts at stake. Notably, the number of investigatory actions and the amount of monetary recoveries drop substantially for median- and small-sized agencies, which have significantly fewer contracts, less capital-intensive purchases, and fewer clients than larger agencies. While these OIGs conduct occasional investigations, their numbers are vastly different from the number of actions undertaken by the larger federal agencies.

The monetary impact of financial and performance audits undertaken by IGs is reported by the IG offices to CIGIE and in their semiannual re-

TABLE 6-1

IG Investigations and Audits: Outcomes for Actions and Projected Monetary Values
Reported by CIGIE for Fiscal Years 2010, 2012, 2014, and 2016

	FY10	FY12	FY14	FY16
Investigative Actions				
Criminal Actions	5,593	5,374	5,895	4,894
Civil Actions	973	1,069	1,827	1,580
Suspension/Debarment	5,114	5,805	5,195	6,448
Monetary Recoveries	$6,971,759,873	$10,431,592,390	$32,713,019,025	$19,905,661,607
Indictments/Information	5,610	6,669	5,521	5,120
Audits with Questioned Costs				
Value of recommendations that had no management decisions at the beginning of the fiscal year	$10,895,969,850	$11,501,754,919	$13,548,637,713	$21,312,757,767
Value of recommendations for the fiscal year	$62,173,747,225	$12,810,083,550	$14,212,459,131	$17,717,970,098
Agreed to by management	$56,577,408,559	$10,475,824,965	$4,289,324,798	$9,214,046,309
Not agreed to by management	$8,098,739,751	$2,128,670,804	$6,576,050,942	$6,750,791,909
No management decision at the end of the fiscal year	$8,496,158,683	$11,547,683,339	$13,466,303,450	$22,806,821,650
Audits with recommendations for better use of funds				
Value of recommendations that had no management decisions at the beginning of the fiscal year	$29,282,932,681	$33,667,488,581	$30,266,938,515	$46,002,468,012
Value of recommendations for the fiscal year	$42,014,062,365	$61,956,640,547	$51,783,786,767	$22,652,457,701
Agreed to by management	$23,654,925,334	$25,466,666,873	$9,514,990,528	$15,997,994,770
Not agreed to by management	$8,881,583,857	$27,524,796,938	$15,638,556,139	$4,745,644,202
No management decision at the end of the fiscal year	$38,753,531,869	$42,639,205,547	$56,831,294,382	$47,780,984,321

Source: CIGIE on Investigative Statistics and Management Decisions. Tables presented on FOIA Reading Room of CIGIE website (https://www.ignet.gov/content/foia-reading-room-1).

TABLE 6-2

Reported Outcomes of OIG Investigations and Audits for Large-, Median-, and Small-Sized Agencies in Fiscal Year 2016

	Large-Sized Agencies						Median-Sized Agencies		Small-Sized Agencies	
	DOD	DOJ	DOS	HHS	IRS	USDA	NSF	NRC	CFTC	FCA
Investigative Actions[a]										
Criminal Actions	237	100	19	935	103	584	12	46[b]	0[c]	0
Civil Actions	120	5	0	722	30	7	4	3[b]	0[c]	0
Suspension/Debarment	304	14	25	3654	0	666	26	0[b]	0[c]	0
Monetary Recoveries	$1,105,371,061	$7,589,598	$2,975,859	$3,597,534,714	$26,904,035	$153,306,129	$9,212,861	$0[b]	$0[c]	$0
Indictments/Informations	299	90	6	918	106	714	25	4[b]	0[c]	0
Audits with Questioned Costs										
Value of recommendations that had no management decisions at the beginning of the fiscal year	$12,015,815,000	$0	$91,058,000	$944,267,000	$45,167,000	$188,016,188	$0	$1,647,715	$0	$0
Value of recommendations for the fiscal year	$6,385,076,000	$25,546,342	$139,994,000	$673,775,000	$375,671	$52,325,854	$0	$0	$0	$0
Agreed to by management	$876,045,000	$25,546,342	$25,662,000	$1,173,864,000	$375,671	$228,104,789	$0	$0	$0	$0
Not agreed to by management	$3,381,372,000	$0	$3,210,000	$81,458,000	$0	$0	$0	$0	$0	$0
No management decision at the end of the fiscal year	$14,143,474,000	$0	$202,180,000	$362,720,000	$45,543,000	$12,237,253	$0	$1,647,715	$0	$0

Audits with recommendations for better use of funds

Value of recommendations that had no management decisions at the beginning of the fiscal year	$17,314,458,000	$0	$267,113,000	$15,094,517,000	$0	$0	$0	$0	$0
Value of recommendations for the fiscal year	$6,503,278,000	$2,055,383	$18,247,000	$83,149,000	$40,394,080	$161,623,180	$0	$0	$143,200
Agreed to by management	$6,763,689,000	$1,793,281	$76,953,000	$121,237,000	$40,394,080	$46,033,953	$0	$0	$143,200
Not agreed to by management	$1,931,473,000	$262,102	$192,444,000	$5,561,000	$0	$0	$0	$0	$0
No management decision at the end of the fiscal year	$15,122,574,000	$0	$15,963,000	$15,050,868,000	$0	$115,589,227	$0	$0	$0

a Investigative Actions for each agency includes actions by the OIG of the agency and joint actions with OIGs in other agencies.

b NRC data not presented on CIGIE documents; these data are drawn from NRC SARCs for FY16 (October 1, 2015–March 31, 2016, and April 1, 2016–September 30, 2016).

c CFTC data not presented on CIGIE documents; these data are drawn from CFTC SARCS for FY16 (October 1, 2015–March 31, 2016, and April 1, 2016–September 30, 2016).

Source: Nomination and confirmation data from Congress.gov; resignation and vacancy dates from CIGIE Inspector General Historical Data tables, agency press releases, leader biographical data, and newspaper archives. CIGIE on Investigative Statistics and Management Decisions. Tables presented on FOIA Reading Room of CIGIE website (https://www.ignet.gov/content/foia-reading-room-1).

Note: This table counts IGs formally nominated to PAS positions by the president that were successfully approved by the Senate and those that did not receive Senate confirmation (failed) or were withdrawn before a final vote by the Senate. Five IG appointments are excluded from this table: three Special Inspectors General for Afghanistan (SIGAR) and Iraq (SIGIR) who were appointed by the president, but did not require Senate confirmation; and Clark Ervin's recess appointment as the DHS IG, which was not voted on by the Senate and is counted as "failed" (see, Ervin, 2006). Also not included in the table is an unknown DFE appointment (if one was made) for the Community Development Financial Institutions Fund (CDFIF) in the U.S. Department of the Treasury.

ports to Congress (SARCs) as "questioned costs" or "better use of funds." In general, questioned costs refer to issues that IGs identify with the money agencies paid to contractors where an OIG believes that an agency may have expended funds (a) in violation of federal laws, policies, or contractual agreements governing the expenditures; (b) where expenditures were unsupported by documentation; or (c) where expenditures for the intended purpose were unnecessary or unreasonable.[20] Questioned costs identified by an OIG may lead the agency to seek reimbursement of the expenditures from the contracting organization or individual. Additionally, questioned costs may lead to changes in management practices to avoid future instances of questioned costs.

IG recommendations "that funds be put to better use" (or better use of funds) refer to possible efficiencies or savings that the agency could achieve "if management . . . took actions to implement and complete the [OIG's] recommendations."[21] These actions could include (a) reduced outlays; (b) de-obligation of funds from programs; (c) withdrawal of subsidies; (d) avoiding costs not incurred by implementing recommended improvements; (e) avoiding unnecessary expenditures noted prior to awarding a contract or agreement; or (f) any other specified savings.[22] In fact, what could qualify as better use of funds was interpreted for the IG community in 1998 as follows:

> Neither the text nor the legislative history of the IG Act offers clear evidence of how broadly Congress intended to define "recommendation that funds be put to better use." Nevertheless, we conclude that, on balance, the better interpretation of that term is that it not be limited to only those audit recommendations that achieve identifiable monetary savings.[23]

In effect, this open-ended interpretation largely makes it easier for OIGs to count monetary savings in nearly any way they deem appropriate. Since OIGs can decide themselves what constitutes better use of funds, the open-ended standard also means that what counts as monetary savings is likely to vary from one IG office to another, thus making comparisons difficult and uncertain.

We also present aggregate and agency-specific data on questioned costs and better use of funds in tables 6-1 and 6-2. The data in table 6-1 for all OIGs generally show that the value of recommendations for better use of funds exceeds the value for audit findings of questioned costs. A notable exception occurred in fiscal year 2010, where the questioned costs of $62.2 billion exceeded the better use of funds total by more than $20 billion. This exception shows the impact of a single OIG's finding. In this case, the U.S. Postal Service OIG reported a questioned cost valuation of $57.3 billion owing to its analysis of how the postal service was allocating funds to remedy an employee retirement fund shortfall. Notwithstanding this exception, because questioned cost judgments usually involve analysis of fiscal payments and contracts—that is, documented fiscal transactions and legal obligations—agency management is much more likely to agree to recommendations of this type. Recommendations for better use of funds, on the other hand, may involve judgments about whether expenditures were appropriate or effective. The agency may judge these decisions differently and, thus, the agency's management may not as readily agree with the recommendation.

The other trend revealed by the aggregate numbers for questioned costs and better use of funds is a steady increase in the values reported for "no management decision." The valuation for pending decisions on questioned costs increased from $8.5 billion in fiscal year 2010 to $22.8 billion in fiscal year 2016; and for better use of funds the increase was from $38.8 billion to $47.8 billion for the same two respective years. The lack of agency management decisions is also revealed in the values reported as carryovers at the beginning of each fiscal year: questioned costs increased from $10.9 billion in fiscal year 2010 to $21.3 billion in fiscal year 2016; figures for better use of funds increased from $29.3 billion to $46.0 billion for the same years, respectively.

The valuation of questioned costs with better use of funds in fiscal year 2016 reported in table 6-2 for select agencies shows considerable variation from one agency to another. Agencies such as the Department of Justice (DOJ), DOS, and the Internal Revenue Service (IRS)—with smaller budgets, fewer contractual obligations, and fewer payments to individuals—have smaller totals for questioned costs involving no management decisions at the beginning of the fiscal year as well as fewer recommendations for fiscal year 2016. By contrast, agencies such as DOD, USDA, and HHS—with larger budgets and more substantial contractual obligations or payments to individuals—have larger amounts of questioned costs at the beginning of fiscal year 2016 as well as more new questioned costs at the end of fiscal year 2016. The same observation generally applies to better use of funds.

Data reported in table 6-1 for all agencies show that better use of funds valuations generally exceeded questioned costs. Looking at what individual agencies reported in table 6-2, however, shows that this was true for only the OIGs of three large agencies—DOD, IRS, and USDA. Including carryover valuations from previous years reveals shifts by three agencies, with DOJ and DOS reporting greater dollar figures for questioned costs and with the IRS reporting greater better use of funds valuations. These individual differences across agencies demonstrate that observations based on aggregate data for all OIGs cannot reliably apply to individual OIGs. Moreover, careful examination of individual OIG reports over time reveals year-to-year differences and occasional high-dollar recommendations that make generalizations about the work of individual OIGs problematic.

Table 6-2 also presents data on agency management responses to OIG findings of questioned costs and better use of funds in selected agencies. These management responses are reported to Congress in SARCs and in summary reports to CIGIE. OIGs give annual totals for three categories of agency management decisions: (a) agreed to the OIG recommendations and dollar amount, (b) did not agree to the OIG recommendations and dollar amount, and (c) no decision or decision remaining on OIG recommendations and dollar amount. For fiscal year 2016, table 6-2 reports that the DOJ, IRS, and USDA accepted all or most of the questioned cost recommendations, although a large carryover figure remained for the IRS. On the other hand, faced with $6.4 billion of questioned costs in fiscal year 2016 and $12.0 billion in carryover questioned costs in the beginning of fiscal year 2016, DOD accepted only $0.8 billion, rejected $3.4 billion, and made no decision on $14.1 billion in questioned costs. Agency acceptance of recommendations for better use of funds among the six large agencies showed greater acceptance rates by DOD, DOJ, HHS, IRS, and USDA, although DOD and HHS had billions of dollars that were not decided upon by management at the close of fiscal year 2016.

It is important to remember that OIG findings of questioned costs and better use of funds are recommendations for the agency's consideration. Agency management is not obligated to accept the recommendations, but it is expected to reply to the findings and indicate whether the agency accepts, partially accepts, or rejects the OIG's findings and any recommendations. Agency responses are reported in SARCs and are occasionally the subject of congressional hearings or follow-up inquiries from congressional staff. As mentioned earlier, the increasing number of recommendations about which the agency has taken no action is the subject of a law in 2019 mandating that agencies report on the status of open recommendations in their budget requests.[24]

LIMITATIONS OF OIG REPORTS ON QUESTIONED COSTS AND BETTER USE OF FUNDS

Our discussions with IGs, OIG staff, and CIGIE officials suggest that the numbers reported in tables 6-1 and 6-2 are problematic. First, our conversations with IGs and OIG staff suggest that the dollar figures IGs give in original audit reports and totaled for a single year may in subsequent years be revised upward or downward as the OIG works with agency management on review of the report and recommendations. One assumes (or hopes) that the reported annual totals reflect these adjustments. Examining CIGIE reports and individual SARCs, we found that specific figures change from one year's report to another and that totals for carryover amounts and current year figures do not always equal the sum of the figures for agency agreement, no agreement, and no decision for the fiscal year. In some instances these differences are several million dollars, which raises questions about how much adjustment in the numbers actually occurs on a year-to-year basis. Additionally, figures posted on the CIGIE website may include typographical errors, which may or may not be corrected in other documents.

Second, distinctive events, agency-specific problems, or critical one-time audits of high-cost programs can exaggerate the dollar amounts for questioned costs or better use of funds. For example, and as mentioned previously, between 2007 and 2012 the U.S. Postal Service (USPS) faced a financial crisis due, in part, to a new requirement established in 2006 to prefund its retirement health care liability. During this period, several of the USPS OIG reports focused on alternative solutions to address funding of this large liability. Because the size of the USPS employee and retiree population is large, this liability is substantial. Thus, reports in this area included significant dollar amounts for questioned costs and for better use of funds. Similarly, audits concerning big-ticket items in DOD, DOT, and DHS may variously contribute to wide variation in year-to-year reported agency totals.

Third, agency treatments of OIG recommendations may vary between agencies and over time because of vacancies and temporary appointments in agency leadership or the presence of an acting IG. Also, an agency may change its general rules about the acceptance of OIG recommendations. Contrary to most agencies, for example, the Veterans Administration (VA) reportedly accepts all OIG recommendations, but actual implementation of recommendations may be imperfect or ignore the thrust of the OIG's questioned costs or recommended better use of funds.[25]

And, finally, as previously mentioned in this chapter, where some agencies have smaller budgets and very few contractual obligations and where the agencies' mission is primarily regulatory, there are simply fewer targets for critical audits concerning finances or that result in recommendations that can be quantified. As a result, many of these agencies do not lend themselves to audits that lead to significant dollar amounts for questionable costs or better use of funds. In fact, twenty-nine OIGs reported zero dollars for fiscal year 2016 for questioned costs and forty OIGs reported zero dollars for better use of funds. Review of SARCs from these OIGs indicates that their activities primarily involve audits for compliance with federal laws and policy and the agency's internal operations.

Because of these limitations, a focus on dollar amounts reported by OIGs for questioned costs or better use of funds presents an incomplete and possibly inaccurate accounting of OIGs' work and their impact on their respective agencies. Indeed, as reported earlier, the IGs we interviewed raised questions about the value and accuracy of the required reporting of such dollar amounts in SARCs. Yet, many IGs and their staff also point out that such reporting was mandated by Congress in the

IG Act of 1978 and acknowledge the political value to highlighting cost savings in reports to Congress and the public, even if the numbers are "fuzzy" and ignore other areas of IG work to which a dollar value cannot be attributed.[26]

Making a Difference within the IG's Strategic Environment

As we have noted, each IG operates within a strategic environment that is distinctive due to the nature, size, and context of its home agency. Elements of this distinctive environment for each agency influence IG initiatives and priorities; shape the pursuit of audits, investigations, and evaluations; and can affect the impact of the IG work on the home agency. Again, the three key sources of influence on the operations and performance of the OIG are stakeholders interested in and affected by an IG's work; expectations held by the IG's stakeholders; and system stressors that create challenges and opportunities for an IG.

STAKEHOLDERS

Much of the time, ongoing IG financial and performance auditing work remains below the radar of the IG's primary stakeholders—the agency leadership and Congress. Sometimes agency leadership or congressional committees may be enticed to pay attention, but it may take repeated IG audits—as was the case with the home health program at HHS and the weatherization program at DOE. Or, an opportunity may arise and congressional leaders may be looking for issues, in which case an IG can provide support to spark and maintain the interest to make a more lasting change in an agency.

A secondary group of stakeholders that is available to help an IG make more lasting improvements consists of senior civil servants in the agency and nongovernmental stakeholders, including clients or consumers of an IG's home agency (such as contractors hired by the agency) and interest groups dedicated to the home agency (such as professional associations or employee unions associated with the agency). Stakeholders who have a long-term vested interest in the agency's mission are those who are likely to join conversations about the terms of accountability that are needed to make a difference in agency operations and policies.

EXPECTATIONS

Maintaining positive engagement with both primary and secondary stakeholders is key to ensuring that the OIGs can recruit allies to work over a longer term to make lasting improvements. While IGs post all individual reports and semiannual reports on the internet, simply posting reports does not guarantee close review of an IG's work by either primary or secondary stakeholders. Persistent communication and maintenance of personal contacts with key agency executives and congressional staffers is key to prolonging important conversations. Yet balancing engagement with both agency leadership and Congress while ensuring independence is challenging.

SYSTEM STRESSORS

The priorities of agency leaders, as well as their appreciation for and relationship with their IG, greatly determine the extent to which agency leaders will work with their IG over a long term to address important issues regarding agency performance. The relationship between the agency leadership and the IG affects the will and ability of program offices to make significant changes in operations. When congressional action is needed in the form of increased funding or changes in authorizing legislation, well-publicized scandals—such as with the Deepwater capitalization project at the Coast Guard—often provide an incentive to action.

Conclusion

The intended impact of IG work is best viewed along a continuum, from the more immediate process fixes to the more elusive and time-consuming improvements in laws and regulations that IGs deem are needed to allow agency operations to be more effective in achieving mission-driven goals. There is a degree of difficulty that IGs face in working to achieve impact.

At the lowest level of difficulty, IGs can fix things in the short term. They employ financial audits and investigations to identify where agencies may control costs more effectively. Through successful investigations, IGs can hold both agency employees and contractors accountable; through successful prosecutions and personnel actions, the agencies may save money and improve internal risk assessment processes.

However, to make improvements in agency processes and policies, long-term engagement with both primary and secondary stakeholders is needed to keep conversations alive. Frequently, inadequate resources, competing leadership priorities, or existing laws or regulations may inhibit implementation of what seem to be reasonable enhancements. Timing and persistence matter in terms of any IG making lasting improvements in agency operations.

Adequate organizational capacity—in terms of effective leadership, adequately trained staff, clear communications, clear operational procedures, sufficient resources for travel, and completion of work plans that adhere to all relevant statutory and regulatory guidelines—is necessary, but it may not be sufficient for IGs to make lasting improvements in their agencies. A persistent dedication to both assessing weaknesses and searching for solutions and allies in their efforts is needed for IGs to make important differences.

The quantitative data available on the number of criminal actions undertaken, money recovered, and questioned costs and better use of funds identified by IGs are impressive, even though they are simply estimates at best. The monetary impact of IG audits and investigations appears to be large, but it varies across the federal agencies due to the work undertaken by the agencies, agency size, and IG capacity. Not surprisingly, IGs face very different barriers and facilitators in terms of their agency-specific environments.

EXHIBIT 6-1
HHS OIG: The Home Health Story

In the early 1990's the Office of Inspector General (OIG) of the Department of Health and Human Services noticed a rapid increase in spending for Medicare covered home health services. The $18 billion of expenditures in 1997 was five times the $3.5 billion spent in 1990. By then, home health expenditures accounted for 9 percent of total Medicare spending compared to 3.5 percent in 1990. At the same time, OIG investigators and auditors were uncovering mammoth fraud, waste, and abuse in Medicare payments for home health. They found that 40 percent of payments, more than $7 billion, was being improperly paid. Without intervention, total payments would surpass $20 billion within another year. Not only were the payments improper, but the quality of care was subpar. No one knew how to plug the leak and get the quality of care up to what it should be.

Simultaneously, our evaluators (a separate component of the OIG) had started a series of studies to determine the nature, extent, and causes of the problem, how private insurers were addressing it, what kind of quality control could be expected, what supplier associations and beneficiary groups knew about it, and what their concerns were. Altogether we conducted about 20 studies over six years. In addition to our own auditors and investigators, we teamed up with the Government Accountability Office (GAO) who, independently of us, had also noticed and were analyzing the problem.

Gradually, we got a handle on it and began developing countermeasures. We finally broke through to senior congressional staff. Eventually, in July 1997, a GAO representative and I were asked to testify jointly before the Senate Aging Committee. The hearing, which also heard testimony from a private sector insurance company, the head of the Louisiana Department of Health and Hospitals, and an incarcerated witness, turned out to be a game changer. Committee members were appalled by what we told them. Some of us were asked to testify several additional times.

The head of the Center for Medicare and Medicaid services joined us. Secretary Donna Shalala backed us. We called for an immediate halt (moratorium) to enrolling new home health care providers into the program until the payment and oversight methods were straightened out. Certain senior Medicare officials said they had no authority to do it. The industry representatives objected. Secretary Shalala and the head of Medicare intervened and called the moratorium.

We submitted legislative options to the Congress to change the method Medicare used to reimburse for home health. The Congress picked our main proposal—do not pay by the visit, but pay for incidents of care. The law was enacted quickly. Payments dropped by $8.5 billion in one year (coincidentally equal to 40 percent of previous payment levels—the auditors were right on!). These lower payment levels continued for several years. Ten-year saving surpassed $50 billion. At the same time, quality control standards were improved, and disreputable billers fled the scene.

Meanwhile, the Secretary became worried that we had gone too far, that people needing home health care could not get it. At her request, we conducted several very quick studies showing that home health agencies were having no problem placing patients.

There is a huge back story here—our work with reputable members of the home health industry and home health medical equipment providers, dramatic confrontations at congressional hearings with the industry claiming that all our studies were flawed, coverage in national newspapers and the industry magazines. Our staff worked long hours against impossible deadlines to prepare the reports and testimonies; some staff members were reluctant to join us because they thought we could never win. However, recognition of the value of our work resulted in our being invited into other problem areas, and eventually winning a Presidential award.

We tell this story now to illustrate the value of (indeed, even the need for) creating a body of work rather than relying on one study and the importance of working with other stakeholders and collaborators to understand complex issues, call attention to them, and develop practical options to address them.

Source: George S. Grob, Former Deputy Inspector General for Evaluation and Inspections, U.S. Department of Health and Human Services.

EXHIBIT 6-2

Audit Reports on the Workers' Compensation Program

In 2007, the Smithsonian Institution (Smithsonian) Office of Inspector General (OIG) began work reviewing the administration of the Workers' Compensation Program that resulted in two audit reports.

In the first report, OIG determined that management did not effectively administer Continuation of Pay (COP) benefits, resulting in both overpayments and improper payments to employees.[a] The Smithsonian generally did not ensure the accuracy of COP benefit payments. For fiscal years 2004 through 2007, the Smithsonian paid over $400,000 in COP benefits for the 97 COP cases that OIG reviewed. The Smithsonian made overpayments or improper payments, totaling over $189,000, in 68 of the 97 cases. The Smithsonian did not ensure that supervisors and timekeepers were adequately trained in COP policies and procedures. Additionally, the Smithsonian did not maintain complete and accurate workers' compensation files and had no system in place to properly track COP benefit payments. The Office of Human Resources did not provide sufficient oversight of the COP program and did not adequately support Smithsonian units, which manage individual claims. Likewise, unit supervisors and timekeepers did not effectively administer employee COP cases; for example, they did not consistently track COP usage and obtain required medical documentation.

In the second report, OIG found that the Smithsonian generally did not manage the workers' compensation program because it failed to verify the accuracy of the chargeback reports, conduct periodic reviews of workers' compensation cases, or develop and implement a return-to-work program.[b] The Smithsonian did not aggressively manage its periodic roll (PR) cases. OIG identified potential problems such as outdated or incomplete medical reports, possible overpayments, lack of cooperation with vocational rehabilitation specialists or refusal of job offers, and possible fraud. OIG identified eight claimants who if removed from the workers' compensation rolls, the Smithsonian could avoid up to $7.3 million in costs over their projected lifetimes. Given the magnitude and escalation of the Smithsonian's workers' compensation costs, OIG believed that management needed to invest in a comprehensive return-to-work program.

IMPACT

Smithsonian management concurred with the two reports' 12 recommendations to strengthen the workers' compensation program and reduce the Smithsonian's costs with this program. As a result, management (1) revised policies and procedures pertaining to the workers' compensation program, (2) sought corrective action from OWCP [Office of Workers' Compensation Programs], (3) hired a contractor to conduct periodic reviews of case files, and (4) developed and implemented a pan-institutional approach for returning employees to work. Management's efforts to aggressively monitor workers' compensation cases and return claimants to work resulted in avoiding the payout of almost $6.2 million of workers' compensation expenses over the life of multiple claimants. Management's continuance of this program has led to additional claimants' being removed from the workers' compensation rolls and returned to the work force.

Collections Stewardship of the National Collections at the National Museum of American History (NMAH)—Preservation and Physical Security

(This report was one of a series of audits that reviewed collections stewardship, which is essential for safeguarding the collections for public and scholarly use and reducing the risk of loss or theft, at the Smithsonian. It was the second report on the collections at the NMAH. The collections drive the mission and the work of the Smithsonian. Failure to adequately secure and care for the collections affects the Smithsonian's ability to fulfill its mission as well as its credibility with the American public and donors.)

OBJECTIVE

The audit objectives were to determine whether (1) physical security is adequate to safeguard the collections, (2) inventory controls are in place and working adequately to ensure that the collections are properly accounted for, and (3) collections are properly preserved at the National Museum of American History (NMAH).ᶜ

WHAT OIG FOUND

NMAH dedicates its collections and scholarship to inspiring a broader understanding of our nation and its many peoples. The museum holds in trust approximately 3.2 million objects that encompass all aspects of the history of the United States. A wide variety of these artifacts, approximately 5,000, are on display at the museum. The remaining collections are stored at NMAH on the Mall, the Smithsonian Institution Services Center in Landover, MD, and the Museum Support Center and the Paul E. Garber Facility in Suitland, MD.

OIG found that many of NMAH's collections were stored in substandard conditions. The majority of storage areas that OIG tested were not conducive to the long-term preservation of the collections. For example, nearly all storage rooms at the museum had exposed pipes and conduits, resulting in frequent leaks that threaten collection items. Some storage buildings were contaminated with asbestos or lead-containing dust. Overcrowding in storage rooms and cabinets damaged some objects.

Although NMAH has used internal Smithsonian funding to improve conditions for certain collections, OIG found that the Smithsonian did not have a comprehensive preservation program to mitigate the deterioration of objects so that they are available for exhibitions, education, and research purposes.

To ensure the long-term preservation of collections, we made recommendations to management to develop a prioritized, Smithsonian-wide plan for addressing collections storage needs; establish and implement a preservation program and explore opportunities to maximize storage space; replace substandard storage equipment; and acquire appropriate housing materials for the collections.

IMPACT

The impact of this audit was that Smithsonian management acknowledged the need for a Smithsonian-wide approach to collection storage concerns and developed the *Smithsonian Collections Space Framework Plan*. This plan allowed for a cross-disciplinary approach to collections-related challenges. Based on our audit work, the plan used NMAH as a pilot site for the "existing building prototype." NMAH began to renovate storage rooms with state of the art equipment. Our audit helped establish the foundation for the changes that are now underway here.

Source: Cathy Helm, Inspector General, The Smithsonian.

a Smithsonian OIG, *Administration of Continuation of Pay Program* (A-07-09-1, July 18, 2008).
b Smithsonian OIG, *Report on the Administration of the Workers' Compensation Program* (A-07-09-2, March 24, 2009).
c Smithsonian OIG, *Collections Stewardship of the National Collections at the National Museum of American History—Preservation and Physical Security* (A-10-03-2, September 30, 2011).

EXHIBIT 6-3
The Weatherization Assistance Program Story

For 40 years, under the statute enacted at the time and as amended over the past four decades, the Department of Energy (DOE) has operated the Weatherization Assistance Program. The Weatherization Program reduces energy costs for low-income households by increasing the energy efficiency of their homes, while ensuring health and safety. Based on a national study of the history of the Program, DOE claims that it has provided weatherization services to about 35,000 homes every year using agency funds. Through its Weatherization website DOE asserts that through the home improvements and upgrades, these households save on average $283 or more every year. Further, the Program has the potential to enhance the "livability" of the housing stock for low-income individuals, reduce the demand for energy for these residences, and result in the employment of over 8,000 contractors who perform the actual housing remediation work.

In brief, the Weatherization Assistance Program relies on Federal Financial Assistance awards made by the Department of Energy to the individual states. The states contract with local agencies (often non-profits) which essentially manage the operation of the program—all following Federal guidelines and state implementing regulations and procedures. In general, these agencies enter into agreements with local firms that evaluate the needs of the assistance applicants and with contractors responsible for the work.

The Department of Energy's Office of Inspector General (OIG) has a long track record of audit, inspection, and investigation related to the Weatherization Program. The OIG's emphasis on the Program was largely driven by its level of funding. Between 1977 and 2008, congressional appropriations totaled nearly $8.7 billion. However, the Program received a huge boost in funding as part of the FY 2009 American Recovery and Reinvestment Act, which included $5 billion for the Weatherization Program, or an amount equal to nearly 60 percent of the funds spent in the prior eleven years. Through a series of about ten audit reports and numerous successful investigations, the OIG had concluded that the Program was vulnerable to fraud, waste and abuse. The huge influx of additional funding associated with the Recovery Act only exacerbated this concern.

Based on past experiences documented in its body of work, the OIG took the following actions:

First, it issued a preliminary report alerting Department officials to the historic problems in the operation of the Program. This report, in the form of an official "heads-up," was designed to sensitize the Department to the Program's history so that preventative actions could be taken to ensure that the $5 billion in Recovery Act funds were spent efficiently and effectively, and to ensure that the intended beneficiaries of the Program, the low-income population, received the maximum benefits possible.

Second, the OIG, faced with many priorities as a result of the significant increase in supplemental funding under the Recovery Act, decided to devote substantial resources to help the Department achieve this goal.

The results, captured in over a dozen audit reports and the initiation of nearly 100 criminal investigations, were disturbing. The IG reported that, despite its relatively uncomplicated nature, the Weatherization Program was not being well managed and that the Recovery Act's $5 billion investment was at risk. The IG found that: 1) Neither the Federal government nor state government had the infrastructure in place to properly manage the greatly expanded Program; 2) State funding issues, many of which were recession-related, had led to staffing shortfalls—often in the very offices designated to manage the state functions of the Weatherization Program; 3) The Davis-Bacon Act requirements, mandated for the Weatherization Program for the first time under the Recovery Act, had a pernicious impact on Program timeliness and effectiveness; Davis-Bacon requires certain wage rate floors for workers working on select federally funded projects—it had not previously been applied to the Weatherization Program; 4) In some locales, there were not enough qualified weatherization contractors to meet the demand; 5)

The Recovery Act's emphasis on "shovel ready" projects to prime the economic pump, caused some officials to bypass regulations and procedures designed to safeguard the system. There was intense pressure to distribute the Program funds as quickly as possible—this was understandable given the purpose of the Recovery Act, but clearly was counterproductive in many instances; and 6) There were significant operational problems at the state, local, and agency levels—this included ineligible applicants; poor quality workmanship; poor funds control; inadequate inspections and oversight; and payment for work that had never been completed, in fact, had never been initiated even though funding for the projects had been disbursed. In some cases, the OIG reported that the quality of the work was so poor that it resulted in "health and safety risks."

The IG's work culminated in numerous public reports, successful criminal prosecutions and several congressional hearings on this subject. The substantive body of work is well exemplified by a June 2013 audit report on the State of Michigan's operation of the DOE's Weatherization Assistance Program Funded under the American Recovery and Reinvestment Act (Report OAS-M-13-25).

In the long run, the impact of the OIG work is the most important part of this story. In short, the Department, including its most senior management levels, initiated corrective actions in response to the recommendations of the OIG. The Department assigned additional personnel to carry out management responsibilities of the Program. Given the devolved nature of the Program's actual operations, the Department took steps to enhance its oversight of the actions of the state offices involved in the Program. The DOE also issued a comprehensive set of new guidelines to assist primary grant recipients (generally state governments) and sub-recipients (local governments and agencies) in enhancing Program integrity and ensuring outcomes consistent with its mission.

The OIG concluded that the "buy in" by Department officials, as well as the positive attitude expressed by responsible state officials, suggested that the identified Program weaknesses and deficiencies were being addressed, or that actions were in process to achieve the intended results.

The Weatherization Program, if properly operated, benefits low-income citizens by reducing energy costs and providing them with more comfortable surroundings. Through the potential of reducing the demand for energy, the Program also benefits the Nation. Operational and reputational challenges to the Program, as outlined in the OIG work, could, if not resolved, threaten the continuation of the Program. Thus, the constructive work and positive outcomes of the OIG work in the Weatherization Program had important consequences for the public good.

Sources: The Department of Energy Office of Inspector General; the department's Weatherization Assistance Program website; and the Congressional Budget Office.

SEVEN

Looking Forward

ONGOING AND EMERGING CHALLENGES

I want to mention several other issues on which we are focused in the IG community that impact our work. First, it is
critical that vacant IG positions be filled promptly. There are
currently 12 IG positions that are vacant—9 for Presidentially-
appointed, Senate-confirmed IG positions; 2 for agency appointed IG positions; and one for the Architect of the Capitol,
who is appointed by Congress. During the period of an IG vacancy, acting Inspectors General and career staff carry on the
work of their offices, and they do it with the utmost of professionalism. However, a sustained absence of permanent leadership is not healthy for any office, particularly one entrusted
with the important and challenging mission of an IG.

—Statement of Michael E. Horowitz, Chair, CIGIE, and
IG, U.S. DOJ, before the U.S. House of Representatives
Committee on Oversight and Government Reform concerning
"Empowering the Inspectors General" on February 1, 2017

Inspectors general possess great institutional knowledge about the systems and operations of their home agencies, and they view their own
success as tied to their ability to improve their respective agency's performance. Over the past four decades, IGs have made a difference by recommending ways to improve efficiency and effectiveness within their home
agencies.

However, the capacity that the IGs have to act on the knowledge they
have accumulated to fix weaknesses and strengthen systems is vulnerable.
Each IG operates within a strategic environment that is distinctive due to

the nature, size, and context of his or her home agency, and elements of this distinctive environment in each agency influence the capacity of the IG to improve the home agency. In addition, there are some government-wide challenges and opportunities facing the IG community.

In this last chapter we discuss what we view as the most significant challenges to the federal inspectors general and to the IG community. We organize the challenges in accordance with the primary topics we have covered in this book: appointments, doing the work, and making a difference. We relate the challenges to the influence on agency operations and performance that the IGs may have. We also align the challenges to the key elements of IGs' strategic environment: stakeholders interested in and affected by an IG's work; expectations held by the IG's stakeholders; and system stressors that create challenges and opportunities for IGs. We conclude with a discussion of how to elevate the IG community moving forward and a set of recommendations.

Appointments

Challenge 1: Attracting qualified and high-quality candidates to seek IG positions, especially the presidentially appointed and senate confirmed (PAS) positions, is increasingly difficult, and making timely permanent IG appointments is increasingly problematic.

It is essential that highly skilled and effective leaders are recruited to serve as federal IGs. A professional track for IGs is currently in place, and the Council of the Inspectors General on Integrity and Efficiency (CIGIE) has a vetting committee. The challenge is convincing the president and agency heads to use the IG community (and the broader auditing community) to recruit highly qualified nominees (PAS) and designate federal entity (DFE) appointees for timely appointments, and to secure timely consideration by Congress on review and confirmation. There is an urgent need to decrease the time that acting appointments serve while permanent appointees are recruited, nominated, and confirmed.

The long delays for candidates to get vetted and nominated by the White House, added to delays in getting Senate confirmation hearings scheduled and completed, can easily deter outstanding candidates who do not want to wait years to secure a position. Our research suggests that the long and intimidating nomination and confirmation process can have a chilling effect on whoever is willing to stand for nomination as a PAS IG.

There have been long delays by successive presidents (G. W. Bush, Obama, and Trump) in vetting and nominating quality candidates for PAS IG positions. As Michael Horowitz, chair of CIGIE and IG of the U.S. Department of Justice (DOJ), explained to Congress in his statement cited above, when the executive office staff either does not understand the IG's role or is suspicious of the IGs, extended vacancies can hurt the IG offices and their agencies, as has been the case for over a decade.

To assure that IG appointment processes are initiated and move forward in a timely way, specific positions or officials in the White House personnel office for PAS IGs and in the Office of Personnel Management (OPM) could be designated to work with CIGIE staff to facilitate recruitment, review, and appointment processes for vacant IG positions. We understand that agency leaders themselves are often advocates for appointments of senior officials for the operational side of their respective agencies. However, the priority that agency leaders give to filling vacant IG positions is an unknown. Assigning responsibility and accountability for timely handling of filling those vacancies to designated White House and OPM officials may accelerate the appointment processes for IGs, by giving specific officials the authority to champion appointments to vacant IG positions.

Doing the Work

Intelligence, persistence, and, perhaps, a bit of luck are required to do the work of IGs: conducting investigations, audits, and evaluations; pursuing waste, fraud, and abuse; and identifying efficiencies and economy in government operations. But that is not all. Our interviews with IGs and stories told by OIG staff we visited have convinced us that challenges for the IG community include lack of a broad understanding about what IGs actually do and the importance of relationships with others in the IGs' strategic environments. And, success requires resources that support and extend the capability of OIGs to pursue their work with technological tools and skills that are at the forefront of modern government and business operations. Accordingly, we see three notable challenges (2–4 below) related to doing the work.

Challenge 2: Ensuring that agency leadership and Congress understand the appropriate role of the IG is difficult, especially across leadership changes.

Agency leadership needs to understand the role of the IG on the leadership team and agree with the IG regarding the role he or she should play in the agency's leadership team. Agency leaders will not understand how they can use the IG office without a full understanding of how an IG can help. And, especially in the DFE agencies, agency leadership needs to understand how the IG should operate so that the leadership has the will and capacity to identify and vet quality candidates.

IGs themselves must be willing and eager to have conversations with agency leadership about their role and the expectations of principal stakeholders, including agency officials, Congress, and the IG community. An agency's leadership and the IG for that agency should make every effort to work collaboratively to produce working relationships between their offices and those of other agency leaders, as well as at operational levels within the agency and the OIG.

Challenge 3: Maintaining trust from the various stakeholders, especially agency leadership, Congress, and the program managers within the agency with whom the IGs work, is a continuing challenge for all IGs we surveyed.

IGs continually struggle to find the right balance of independence and collaboration/engagement with agency leadership to solve problems facing their home agency. Trust is always fragile and can easily be eroded by one misunderstanding. Trust helps to ensure that the IGs have access to other agency personnel and to agency data the IGs may need to conduct their work. When there is a lack of mutual respect and trust, there is a risk that the IG will not enjoy timely access to information or receive timely responses from agency management, and not be able to forge useful noncrisis processes for handling disputes regarding OIG requests.

Challenge 4: IGs' capability to conduct their work is dependent on their capacity to actually do their work.

IGs are vulnerable to unreasonable budget cuts from both the president and Congress. While the 2008 amendments to the IG Act of 1978 gave some insulation to IG budgets, there are still opportunities for both the Office of Management and Budget (OMB) and Congress to make budget cuts that are unwarranted and not supported by data on IG performance. In fact even with flat budgets, the real budgetary capacity of IG offices goes down due to the increasing costs per full-time equivalent (FTE), which means OIGs have less capacity to conduct their work. Congressional mandates for IG work have increased over the last three decades as well. Furthermore, IG offices, like most of the federal government, continue to be challenged to keep up with technological changes. The increasing rapidity of societal and technological changes, accompanied by the slowness of governmental processes and resources to adapt accordingly, places the IGs at risk of being consistently one step behind external agents who can take advantage of lapses in security. There will continue to be new sources of risk to agencies posed by changes in technologies such as the internet. The types of staff that OIGs need to bring on board to address emerging risks, such as cybersecurity, are more expensive to hire and retain, and this staffing challenge has been on the IG community's agenda for over a decade.[1]

The resources and capacity of small IG offices in DFE agencies render them especially vulnerable. Small IG offices, especially in DFEs that operate with very few staff members, are at risk of not possessing adequate budget, appropriate skills, and/or staff to conduct needed audits. The Government Accountability Office (GAO) has reported on the OIGs' capacity issues in DFE agencies on several occasions.[2] CIGIE may be in a position to provide or facilitate the acquisition of common resources to enhance the capacity of smaller OIGs. Or alternatively, CIGIE may be able to coordinate discussions of strategies among these offices to address the challenge of adequate resources, including the possible consolidation of smaller OIGs.

Making a Difference

Over the past four decades, IGs have made a difference by recommending ways to improve effectiveness, efficiency, and responsiveness of their respective home agencies. However, the capacity that the IGs have to act on the knowledge they have accumulated to fix weaknesses and strengthen systems is vulnerable. Each IG operates within a strategic environment that is distinctive due to the nature, size, and context of his or her home agency, and elements of this distinctive environment in each agency influence the capacity of the IG to improve the home agency.

Challenge 5: Current measures of IG productivity and level of success are widely but quietly acknowledged to be neither valid, reliable, nor broadly accepted as means to assess the impact of IG offices on their respective agencies.

As we discussed earlier, there are many ways that IGs can affect their agencies. Through IG audits and investigations, they can recommend actions to improve efficiency in operations; hold employees and contractors accountable for criminal behavior; shape agency and contractor behavior to be more effective; improve internal controls processes; and recommend changes to help their home agencies better achieve mission-driven goals. The IG Act requires IGs to report estimated dollar figures regarding questionable costs and funds that could be put to better use, as well as the number of successful convictions and recommendations offered and implemented. These dollar figures have become the usual, and nearly only, measure of IG work and success.

Virtually every IG and OIG staff member we talked with acknowledges that these measures inadequately capture the impact that OIGs have on their respective agencies or that the IG community as a whole has on federal programs. There are numerous success stories about IG work and at least a few stories that reveal instances where IGs were wrong or not successful in meeting their mission. We readily acknowledge that it is difficult to accurately assess the impact of IG work across time or across the IG community, but we believe that broader efforts should be pursued to refine existing measures of dollar impact (such as standardizing how estimates are made) and to assess the impact of IG recommendations that do not involve agency finances. Such efforts should involve the obvious stakeholders—agency managers and staff as well as Congressional representatives and staff. In the forty years since passage of the IG Act, the act's reporting requirements have focused too much attention on a narrow slice of what IGs do and neglected to fully reflect the impact of their work. Developing systematic, broader, and consensus-driven measures of impact is likely to improve the work IGs do and heighten receptivity to their recommendations.

Challenge 6: There is no adequate means to evaluate the performance of individual IGs.

No one provides an annual performance appraisal to an IG, and there are no systematic processes for feedback from agency management, Congress, or anyone in an IG's workplace. Moreover, IGs are not subject to reviews during appointment renewals, since they continue to serve through changes in executive officials or presidential administrations. IGs may be fired by the president (for PAS) or the hiring authority (for DFEs), and forced resignations are also possible and have reportedly occurred, especially after a review of allegations of misconduct in office. However, regular performance evaluations are typically not part of dismissals or forced resignations.

In assessing IG performance, it is difficult to select which actions (or outputs) to count or to determine how they should count. Prior to passage of the 2008 amendments to the IG Act, there was extensive discussion about setting seven-year term limits and/or establishing that IGs could only be fired "for cause" to address the issue of IG poor performance.[3] However, the preponderance of views espoused by previous IGs, senior agency leaders, and other critical stakeholders was that term limits might jeopardize independence as IGs looked to secure second terms and could make the position less attractive to potential candidates. In addition, listing the specific reasons an IG could be fired "for cause" could not really entail an overly subjective category of poor performance. Finding a way to rid agencies of low-performing IGs is virtually impossible, thus raising the importance of recruiting and vetting high-quality candidates for the job.

Our analysis of the data from the IGs' semiannual reports suggests that the data are neither reliable enough nor presented in sufficiently consistent format to gauge the performance of IGs or provide a sense of comparable OIG performance. Fully documenting the impact of IG work in a more reliable fashion will require reasonable allocations of time and resources to provide demonstrative, convincing evidence regarding an IG's level of performance. Peer review processes currently in place essentially only confirm that IG work meets minimum standards as stated in the Yellow Book governing audit processes and the Blue Book setting expectations for government evaluators. These standards do not, however, evaluate whether an IG is having an impact in his or her home agency by, for example, (a) selecting important or helpful areas for inquiry; (b) making responsible, realistic, and actionable recommendations; and (c) following up on recommendations to assess their implementation and impact. Simply stated, there are no community-wide standards for acceptable levels of achievement or review procedures to evaluate processes that IGs use to work with agency management, Congress, and others in their strategic environment. Nor are there systematic efforts to assess the impact of recommendations individual IGs make each year.

In addition to making a difference in their own agencies, IGs work together to address crosscutting issues that affect multiple agencies. There have been some notable successes with such joint actions, including the previously mentioned Recovery Accountability and Transparency (RAT) Board that oversaw the federal investments made as part of the American Recovery and Reinvestment Act. Developing and supporting means for IGs to work together in allied agencies or on common issues as they arise—through self-organized councils, CIGIE committees, or legislatively authorized councils with charters specifying responsibilities and authorities—is another facet of successful IG work. Assessment and feedback tools are also needed for such activities within the IG community, as well as instances involving cooperation among IGs, agencies, and Congress to set agendas for interagency and inter-IG audits and evaluations.

Elevating the IG Community

The CIGIE, the IGs' umbrella organization, provides needed connective tissue for a network of otherwise disparate units. Our research, as well as that of other observers, suggests that it is important for the IG community to maintain an institution, such as CIGIE, with enough capacity to help in recruiting and training personnel with the skill sets needed for IGs and IG offices; to provide forums for IGs to learn from one another; and as needed, to act in concert effectively when, for example, a major natural disaster or major federal actions require interagency cooperation. Sustaining a vital and effective CIGIE is imperative to supporting the IG community going forward.

Challenge 7: There is still no separate funding approved by OMB and Congress to support CIGIE, and CIGIE's budget is modest.

Despite some efforts on the part of the IG community during the last decade to secure direct funding for its activities, CIGIE relies on funding obtained through taxing IG offices and fees paid by OIGs for the training services CIGIE provides. CIGIE funding is not impressive, and thus far expectations from the community tend to be in line with CIGIE's capacity to meet them. Our research suggests that CIGIE's capacity for supporting the IG community needs to be increased and increasing that capacity would likely yield positive results for how OIGs operate and for enhancing the independence, accountability, and engagement of IGs.

The executive branch should recommend, and Congress should authorize, an annual budget to support CIGIE's programs that enhance the capacity of the IG community to recruit, train, and retain skilled OIG staff. Currently, programs for professional development are largely supported by annual taxes paid by each OIG or by fees paid to the CIGIE Training Institute by OIGs that send individuals to training sessions. The tight budgets under which OIGs operate serve as a significant constraint on the creation and presentation of training programs for IGs and OIG staff. Should Congress provide funding for this training, then CIGIE could provide more extensive training to the IG community, creating a cadre of auditors, investigators, evaluation specialists, and policy specialists needed to successfully conduct IG work. Additional funding would also allow CIGIE to proactively organize sessions to inform the IG community about critical issues and share promising practices. Relatedly, issue-specific or crisis-related networks (or councils) of relevant IGs could be formed and facilitated in working together to address particular issues involving multiple IG offices.

An adequately funded CIGIE could also assist or take the lead in addressing several of the aforementioned challenges. CIGIE could, for example, institutionalize a clear process that involves CIGIE staff and the White House personnel office to normalize the PAS IG nominations process, and a clear process for CIGIE and OPM to facilitate DFE IG appointments. CIGIE could help to monitor appointment processes and encourage timely actions by the appropriate decisionmakers in the appointment process. As discussed under Challenge 1, CIGIE's collaboration with designated White House and OPM officials could raise the transparency and urgency of recruiting and vetting high-quality candidates for vacant IG positions.

An adequately funded CIGIE could also play a positive role in addressing previously discussed challenges associated with doing the work. For example, addressing Challenge 2, programs offered by CIGIE could afford newly appointed IGs and senior OIG staff the opportunities to learn from more experienced IGs how to clarify expectations and establish trust with their agency leadership and congressional contacts. Suitable and consistent support for formal mentors is critical, as is dedicated support for sustaining mentoring programs,[4] and CIGIE is in the most appropriate position to accomplish both—given sufficient resources.

In like manner, CIGIE could also assist with Challenge 3, which involves building and maintaining relationships with various stakeholders. For example, CIGIE programs that offer briefings on the role of IGs to congressional staff, newly elected members of Congress, and newly appointed executive officials would efficiently provide base-level information that would apply to all OIGs, allowing individual OIGs to build on this information as they work with their specific stakeholders in agency management and Congress. Similarly, CIGIE could provide core materials on IGs (as it currently does in publications and its website) to inform the media and the public about who the IGs are and what they do.

Representing the IG community, CIGIE has overseen the development of quality standards for the operation of OIGs and the conduct of investigations, audits, and evaluations. A CIGIE committee is also responsible for assessing whether OIGs are meeting these standards through peer evaluations. And, a committee operating under CIGIE investigates allegations of IG misconduct. Missing from this set of activities is the development and implementation of processes evaluating the degree to which IGs are making a difference—a matter discussed previously in Challenges 5 and 6.

Working with other stakeholders, CIGIE is the obvious organization to lead in the development of standards and processes for evaluating IG performance. Additional funding would allow CIGIE to work with the IG community to develop a process for standardizing evaluation of IG impact, as well as an implementation manual that delineates a process for OIG to use in assessing the outcomes of recommendations they have made in their respective agencies. Representing the IG community, CIGIE is in the best position to give a broad and comprehensive view of the full range of OIG activities. Working with executive and congressional officials, CIGIE could facilitate development of standards and measures of performance that go beyond the current legislative requirements for reporting dollar amounts associated with questioned costs, funds that could be put to better use, and agency responses to those recommendations.

Similarly, CIGIE could take the lead in developing and facilitating implementation of standardized evaluation processes across the community for IGs and senior OIG staff. We suggest that CIGIE, whose membership consists of all sitting IGs, develop a process for evaluating the performance of individual IGs in a way that is not threatening to IG independence. Development of the process is likely to involve conversations with agency leadership and congressional staff, as well as associated federal agencies (such as GAO) and external groups with an interest in the success of government evaluations.

Conclusion

Since passage of the Inspector General Act of 1978, the number of Offices of Inspector General has increased from thirteen to seventy-four as of 2019.[5] Since 1978, the federal government has increasingly focused on fiscal accountability and the degree to which federal programs are operating efficiently and economically. U.S. IGs have been and remain central to executive and congressional efforts to rein in wasteful financial practices and identify inefficiencies and mismanagement in government offices and programs.

This final chapter outlined challenges facing IGs and their staff as they move beyond the fortieth anniversary of the IG Act of 1978. Some of these challenges, such as appointment processes, have been under discussion since passage of the 1978 legislation. Other challenges, such as setting expectations and standards for performance, emerged in the 1990s and the twenty-first century. Despite budgetary constraints, we believe that IGs and their offices will likely continue their focus on identifying waste, fraud, and abuse. If political bipartisanship remains strong, this too will create political challenges for IGs as they manage relationships between themselves, executive offices, and corresponding congressional oversight committees—especially if different political parties control these two major stakeholders in the IGs' strategic environment.

Despite the potential consequences of these system stressors, we also believe that IGs will continue to exercise vigilance and oversight of federal offices and programs as expected by various stakeholders. The ability of OIGs to meet those expectations and to pursue impactful oversight will be substantially enhanced by addressing and resolving the challenges discussed in this chapter.

APPENDIX A

Discussion Guides for Interviews
in Six Case Studies

Discussion Guide for Inspectors General

We are interested in engagement with officials in the agency:

When you were appointed or when there is a leadership change in the agency, how would you summarize your initial meetings with agency leadership?

Were there conversations or understandings about OIG responsibilities? Expectations relative to the agency? Relative to Congress?

Any discussion of whether and to what degree the IG was a member of the leadership team?

Any discussion about OIG independence?

How are (potential) conflicts with agency officials handled?

Who do you think are the most important internal audiences within the agency for the IG's office?

Have you or the OIG undertaken any initiatives promoting cooperation with agency officials? What is your assessment of how the initiatives worked?

Turning for the moment to engagement with congressional contacts:

Similarly, when you were appointed or when there is a leadership change on one of the relevant congressional committees, how would you characterize your initial meetings with these congressional contacts?

Were there conversations or understandings about OIG responsibilities? Expectations relative to Congress? Relative to the agency?

Any discussion of whether and to what degree the IG reported to Congress?

Any discussion about OIG independence?

How are (potential) conflicts handled?

How would you characterize ongoing relations with congressional contacts?

Have you or the office undertaken any initiatives promoting cooperation with congressional contacts? What is your assessment of how the initiatives worked?

Other important or helpful contacts?

GAO, OMB, other federal offices?

Media or other groups?

Let's talk for a moment about the balance that OIGs manage with the agency and with Congress:

How is your office managing reporting expectations by the agency and Congress?

What actions do you take to maintain independence as you pursue the OIG responsibilities?

Have you encountered questions about leaning too much toward the agency or Congress? How do you respond?

Any particular initiatives to maintain the confidence of key agency leadership and congressional contacts?

Have you discussed matters of independence, balancing expectations, and engagement with agency and congressional contacts within the OIG's office? How often? To what effect?

OIGs' responsibilities are often discussed in terms of audits, investigations, and inspections/evaluations:

What factors do you consider in allocating staff and other resources to these areas and to other activities?

What considerations have influenced your setting priorities for audits, investigations, inspections, or other activities?

Agency influence or requests?

Congressional influence or requests?

Any particular initiatives seeking out fraud, waste, and abuse or promoting economy, efficiency, and effectiveness of agency programs?

Is timing an issue with some of your activities or requests? Seven-day letters? Does the OIG see inspections for faster turnaround?

When an OIG report or action is complete or nearly so, what sort of processes do you follow?

Discussions with agency leadership and/or program level directors? With congressional contacts?

In addition to circulating the report to agency leadership and to Congress, are there other activities you typically do? For example, briefings within agency, with congressional contacts, with media?

A couple of general questions about the reports you issue:

Are there any reports or initiatives in the last couple of years about which you are especially proud? Why? Changes were made? Issues were settled?

How has your office approached the semiannual reports required by congressional mandate?

We are interested in how you follow up on reports and recommendations made by your office:

> What processes do you use for follow-ups? Designated agency contact? Designated person in the OIG? Frequency?

> Are there particular strategies that you have found effective in bringing about changes or implementing recommendations?

> What do you do if there has been no action on your recommendations?

A few final questions:

> How do you define success for your IG's office? Return on investment? Changes in policy or behavior in agency? Congressional legislation? Other outcomes?

> What do you see as the biggest challenge facing your OIG in the coming three to five years?

> What about the entire IG community?

Discussion Guide for Congressional Contacts

Let's talk about your engagement with officials in the Office of Inspector General:

> When you joined the congressional staff or when a new IG was appointed, were there conversations or understandings about OIG responsibilities? Expectations relative to the agency? Relative to Congress?

> Any discussion of whether and to what degree the IG reported to Congress?

> Any discussion about OIG independence?

> How are (potential) conflicts with OIG officials handled?

> Who do you think are the most important audiences for the IG's office?

Have relevant congressional committees or their staff undertaken any initiatives promoting cooperation with the OIG? What is your assessment of how the initiatives worked? Do you recall initiatives by the OIG to promote cooperation? Assessment?

Turning for the moment to OIG's engagement with the agency to which it reports:

When you joined the congressional staff or when a new IG was appointed, were there conversations with leadership in the agency about OIG responsibilities? Expectations relative to Congress? Relative to the agency?

Any discussion of whether and to what degree the OIG was a part of the agency leadership team?

Any discussion about OIG independence relative to the agency?

Let's talk for a moment about the balance that OIGs manage regarding relations with the agency and with Congress:

What is your sense of your current OIG practices relative to reporting expectations to both the agency and Congress? Has the appropriate balance been maintained?

What sorts of actions have been taken to assure a reasonable balance of OIG responsibilities and expectations relative to the agency and to Congress?

By the OIG?

By the agency?

By congressional contacts?

Have you been concerned about OIG leaning too much toward the agency or Congress? How do you respond to such concerns?

Any particular actions that you recall being taken to assure that congressional contacts have confidence in the OIG? By the IG? By the congressional contacts?

Have congressional leadership and staff leadership discussed among themselves or with the OIG matters of independence, balancing expectations, and engagement with agency and congressional contacts? How often? To what effect?

OIGs' responsibilities are often discussed in terms of audits, investigations, and inspections/evaluations:

Have you sought to influence priorities for audits, investigations, inspections, or other activities?

Do agency interests or activities play a role in your efforts to influence OIG activities?

Any particular initiatives by the agency or the OIG that you recall aimed at seeking out fraud, waste, and abuse or promoting economy, efficiency, and effectiveness of agency programs? With what effect?

When an OIG report or action is complete or nearly so, what sort of processes are generally followed leading to release of the report?

Discussions between the IG, others in the OIG, agency leadership and/or program level directors, and congressional contacts?

In addition to circulating the report relevant to congressional offices, are there other activities that typically happen? For example, briefings with congressional contacts?

A couple of general questions about the OIG reports:

Are there any OIG reports or initiatives in the last couple of years that you thought were especially helpful? Any that were not helpful? Why?

The OIG issues semiannual reports as required by congressional mandate. How are these semiannual reports reviewed? How are they helpful for congressional contacts? How have you responded to the listing of major challenges facing the agency and other elements of their report—for example, unresolved recommendations?

We are interested in how the agency and Congress follow up on reports and recommendations made by the OIG:

> What processes do you use to follow up on OIG reports? Frequency?
>
> What do you do if you learn that there has been no action on OIG recommendations?

A few final questions:

> How do you define success for the IG's office? Return on investment? Changes in policy or behavior in agency? Congressional legislation? Other outcomes?
>
> What do you see as the biggest challenge facing the agency's OIG in the coming three to five years?
>
> What about the entire IG community?

Discussion Guide for Agency Leadership

Let's talk about your engagement with officials in the Office of Inspector General:

> When you were appointed or when a new IG was appointed, were there conversations or understandings about OIG responsibilities? Expectations relative to the agency? Relative to Congress?
>
> Any discussion of whether and to what degree the IG was a member of the agency leadership team?
>
> Any discussion about OIG independence?
>
> How are (potential) conflicts with OIG officials handled?
>
> Who do you think are the most important internal audiences within the agency for the IG's office?
>
> Has the agency's leadership undertaken any initiatives promoting cooperation with agency officials? What is your assessment of how the initiatives worked? Do you recall initiatives by the OIG to promote cooperation? Assessment?

Turning for the moment to OIG's engagement with Congressional contacts:

> When you were appointed to your leadership role or when a new IG was appointed, were there conversations with congressional contacts about OIG responsibilities? Expectations relative to Congress? Relative to the agency?

> Any discussion of whether and to what degree the OIG reported to Congress?

> Any discussion about OIG independence?

Let's talk for a moment about the balance that OIGs manage regarding relations with the agency and with Congress:

> What is your sense of your current OIG's practices relative to reporting expectations to both the agency and Congress? Has the appropriate balance been maintained?

> What sorts of actions have been taken to assure a reasonable balance of OIG responsibilities and expectations relative to the agency and to Congress?

> By the OIG?

> By the agency?

> By congressional contacts?

> Have you been concerned about the OIG leaning too much toward the agency or Congress? How do you respond to such concerns?

> Any particular actions that you recall being taken to assure that agency leadership has confidence in the OIG? Actions by the IG? Actions by the agency?

> Has agency leadership discussed among themselves or with the OIG matters of independence, balancing expectations, and engagement with agency and congressional contacts? How often? To what effect?

OIGs' responsibilities are often discussed in terms of audits, investigations, and inspections/evaluations:

Have you sought to influence priorities for audits, investigations, inspections, or other activities?

Do congressional interests come into play for you or for the OIG?

Any particular initiatives by the agency or the OIG that you recall aimed at seeking out fraud, waste, and abuse or promoting economy, efficiency, and effectiveness of agency programs? With what effect?

When an OIG report or action is complete or nearly so, what sort of processes are generally followed leading to release of the report?

Discussions between the IG, others in the OIG, agency leadership, and/or program level directors? With congressional contacts?

In addition to circulating the report to agency leadership and to Congress, are there other activities that typically happen? For example, briefings within agency, with congressional contacts, with media?

A couple of general questions about the OIG reports:

Are there any OIG reports or initiatives in the last couple of years that you thought were especially helpful? Any that were not helpful? Why?

The OIG issues semiannual reports as required by congressional mandate. Is agency leadership involved in their development? How have you responded to the listing of major challenges facing the agency and other elements of their report—for example, unresolved recommendations?

We are interested in how the agency follows up on reports and recommendations made by the OIG:

What processes do you use to follow up on OIG reports? Designated agency contact? Frequency?

What do you do if you learn that there has been no action on OIG recommendations?

A few final questions:

> How do you define success for the IG's office? Return on investment? Changes in policy or behavior in agency? Congressional legislation? Other outcomes?

> What do you see as the biggest challenge facing the agency's OIG in the coming three to five years?

> What about the entire IG community?

Discussion Guide for OIG Staff

Let's talk about your engagement with officials in the Office of Inspector General:

> When you were appointed or when a new IG was appointed, were there conversations or understandings about OIG responsibilities? Expectations relative to the agency? Relative to Congress?

> Any discussion of whether and to what degree the IG was a member of the agency leadership team?

> Any discussion about OIG independence?

> How are (potential) conflicts with agency officials handled?

> Who do you think are the most important internal audiences within the agency for the IG's office?

> Have you or the office undertaken any initiatives promoting cooperation with agency officials? What is your assessment of how the initiatives worked?

Turning for the moment to engagement with congressional contacts:

> Similarly, when you were appointed or when a new IG was appointed, were there conversations or understandings about OIG responsibilities? Expectations relative to Congress? Relative to the agency?

> Any discussion of whether and to what degree the OIG reported to Congress?

Any discussion about OIG independence?

How are (potential) conflicts handled?

How would you characterize ongoing relations with congressional contacts?

Have you or the office undertaken any initiatives promoting cooperation with congressional contacts? What is your assessment of how the initiatives worked?

As you pursue responsibilities, do you have occasional or routine contact with others outside the OIG and the agency?

GAO, OMB, other federal offices?

Media or other groups?

Let's talk for a moment about the balance that OIGs manage with the agency and with Congress:

How is your office managing reporting expectations by the agency and Congress?

What actions do you take to maintain independence as you pursue the OIG responsibilities?

Have you encountered questions about leaning too much toward the agency or Congress? How do you respond?

Any particular initiatives to maintain the confidence of key agency leadership and congressional contacts?

Do you recall discussions within the OIG regarding matters of independence, balancing expectations, and engagement with agency and congressional contacts? Do you have discussions about such matters with your direct reports?

OIGs' responsibilities are often discussed in terms of audits, investigations, and inspections/evaluations:

What considerations have influenced your setting priorities for audits, investigations, inspections, or other activities?

Agency influence or requests?

Congressional influence or requests?

IG priorities?

Any particular initiatives seeking out fraud, waste, and abuse or promoting economy, efficiency, and effectiveness of agency programs?

When an OIG report or action is complete or nearly so, what sort of processes do you follow?

Discussions with the IG, others in the OIG, agency leadership, and/or program level directors? With congressional contacts?

In addition to circulating the report to the IG, agency leadership, and to Congress, are there other activities you typically do? For example, briefings within agency, with congressional contacts, with media?

A couple of general questions about the reports you issue:

Are there any reports or initiatives in the last couple of years about which you are especially proud? Why? Changes were made? Issues were settled?

How has your office approached the semiannual reports required by congressional mandate?

We are interested in how you follow up on reports and recommendations made by your office:

What processes do you use for follow-ups? Designated agency contact? Designated person in the OIG? Frequency?

Are there particular strategies that you have found effective in bringing about changes or implementing recommendations?

What do you do if there has been no action on your recommendations?

A few final questions:

How do you define success for your part of the IG's office? Return on investment? Changes in policy or behavior in agency? Congressional legislation? Other outcomes?

What do you see as the biggest challenge facing your component of the OIG in the coming three to five years?

What about your OIG overall?

What about the entire IG community?

APPENDIX B

Survey for Inspectors General and Officials in the Offices of Inspectors General

Introduction

I am Kathryn Newcomer, a professor and School Director at the Trachtenberg School of Public Policy and Public Administration at the George Washington University. I am conducting research on the ability of Offices of Inspectors General in the U.S. federal government to get their recommendations implemented as part of a larger study of the operations and outcomes of Offices of Inspectors General.

Introduction to Project, Purpose, and Procedures: You were selected to participate in this project because you have been identified as an individual knowledgeable about the operations within Offices of Inspectors General in the U.S. federal government.

My research project focuses on understanding the factors that affect the ability of Offices of Inspectors General to improve federal agency operations. This survey builds upon previous research I have undertaken within Offices of Inspectors General through interviews within six IG offices during 2014–2015.

Participation in this survey is voluntary and responding to the questions should take no longer than 20 minutes. You are under no obligation to participate and may decline to answer any of the questions or end participation at any time. Your employment status will not be affected by your decision about whether to participate in this research study.

Records: Your name and the name of your agency are not requested, so no names will be connected with responses, and your responses are confidential. Only aggregate information and data will be released for this study. Data will be maintained on the George Washington University computer network and can only be accessed with a password.

Risks, Benefit, and Consent: There are minimal risks associated with this survey. The greatest risk for participants in the study is breach of this confidentiality commitment. There is no direct benefit to you from participation in this survey. Taking part in this survey is your agreement to participate. We will be happy to email to you the aggregate responses to the survey upon request to newcomer@gwu.edu.

If you would like a copy of this statement for your records, please let me know and I will email you a copy now. If you have any questions regarding the research, you may contact me, Kathryn Newcomer, in GWU's Trachtenberg School at newcomer@gwu.edu. If you have any questions regarding your rights as a research subject, please contact the IRB Administrator of GWU's Institutional Review Board at 202-994-2715.

Instructions

For each of the questions below, please place an "X" in the appropriate response. If for any reason you cannot answer a question or you are uncertain about an answer, please mark "Hard to Say." Thank you!

We are interested in learning about your processes for developing and vetting recommendations to increase the likelihood that your work will improve your agency's processes and mission-achievement.

Using the scale listed below, what percentage of the time are the following factors important considerations when you are developing draft recommendations?

	Never, 0% of the time	About 25% of the time	About 50% of the time	About 75% of the time	Always, 100% of the time	Hard to Say
Priorities or goals of IG or OIG						
Views of IG regarding what the agency should be doing to achieve its mission						
Administrative feasibility of the recommendation						
Statutory changes or authorization will be required						
Significant budgetary increases or additional funding will be required						
Projected cost/benefit ratio						
How the recommendation will advance the agency's objectives						
How the recommendation will provide efficiencies in agency operations						
Bringing the agency's actions into compliance with federal laws and policies						
Bringing the agency's financial practices into alignment with general accounting standards						
Anticipated congressional perspectives on the reasonableness, cost, importance and/or challenges in implementation						
Anticipated agency clienteles' perspectives on the reasonableness, cost, importance and/or challenges in implementation						
Anticipated agency leadership's perspectives on the reasonableness, cost, importance and/or challenges in implementation						
Anticipated reactions of affected agency managers on the reasonableness, cost, importance and/or challenges in implementation						
The OIG's assessment that the recommendation will not be fully implemented						
Other considerations (please specify):						

Using the scale listed below, what percentage of the time are the following factors important considerations when you are finalizing recommendations?

	Never, 0% of the time	About 25% of the time	About 50% of the time	About 75% of the time	Always, 100% of the time	Hard to Say
Priorities or goals of IG or OIG						
Views of IG regarding what the agency should be doing to achieve its mission						
Comments from agency officials that the report does not identify the root causes sufficiently or correctly to offer a reasonable recommendation						
Comments from agency officials about the appropriateness and reasonableness of recommendation						
Comments from agency officials regarding a recommendation's vagueness or poor writing						
Conclusion by the OIG that a recommendation will not be accepted by agency management						
Conclusion by the OIG that the recommendation will not be fully implemented for any number of reasons						
Other considerations (please specify):						

In the last three years has your office utilized any of the following approaches or tools to improve your audit planning processes:

Risk-based audit planning? Yes_ No_

Data analytics, e.g., searching for statistical anomalies? Yes_ No_

Systematic analysis of hotline tips? Yes_ No_

Other (please specify): Yes_ No_

We are interested in how your office follows up on your reports and recommendations.

Who in your OIG is typically assigned responsibility for following up on reports and recommendations to determine whether recommendations have been implemented?

The lead staff member who prepared the report or recommendations

The component head in the division producing the report or
    recommendations (e.g., Assistant IG for Audit)

A senior member of OIG leadership (e.g., Deputy IG)

A designated office in the OIG dedicated to follow-up reports and
    recommendations

Other (please specify):

Does your host agency have a designated official or office responsible for following up on OIG reports and recommendations?

Yes_   No_

Is closure of recommendations an element included in senior executives' performance appraisals in your IG office?

Yes_   No_   Don't Know_

How frequently does your office use activities listed below to follow up on recommendations that have been open for over 12 months, and have these activities resulted in recommended changes?

	Happens frequently	Does not happen frequently	Has resulted in recommendation being implemented	Has *not* resulted in recommendation being implemented
Informal conversations with agency staff in offices affected by the recommendations				
Having target deadlines for a response from the affected program office				
Formal meetings with agency staff in offices affected by the recommendations				
Raising the issue with the agency's compliance office (if such an office is present in the agency)				
Raising the issue with agency leadership				
Raising the issue in testimonies and/or written reports to Congress				
Informal conversations with relevant congressional staff				
Other considerations (please specify):				

For recommendations initially accepted by agency management, we are interested in learning what constraints are likely to be present when recommendations are not subsequently implemented for over two years after the report was issued and your office classifies the matter as an "open recommendation" in the OIG's Semiannual Report to Congress.

When draft recommendations are rejected by the agency in a written response to a draft OIG report, what factors most frequently contribute to the rejections?

We are interested in learning about factors that influence your OIG office's decisions to inform the Department of Justice that your office has "reasonable grounds to believe that there has been a violation of federal criminal law." Please note that if you have insufficient experience with investigations, please check here ___ and skip this question.

Using the scale listed below, what percentage of the time do the following factors account for recommendations not being implemented by agency management?

	Never, 0% of the time	About 25% of the time	About 50% of the time	About 75% of the time	Always, 100% of the time	Hard to Say
The affected agency office requires additional resources to take recommended actions						
The affected agency office requires additional authority to take recommended actions due to legislative or regulatory constraints						
Lack of clarity in the recommendations as written						
Managers in the affected agency office do not agree that the recommendations will enhance operations						
Insufficient support from agency leadership to implement the recommended actions						
The recommended change requires longer to accomplish than two years due to the need to coordinate with external entities						
Insufficient vetting of the feasibility (political, administrative, or financial) of implementing the recommendation by the IG team who conducted the audit or inspection						
Congressional interest or intervention that works against implementation of the recommendation						
Current negative relationships between your IG office and agency management						
Other challenges (please specify):						

Using the scale listed below, what percentage of the time are the following factors important considerations when draft recommendations are rejected by the agency in a written response to a draft OIG report?

	Never, 0% of the time	About 25% of the time	About 50% of the time	About 75% of the time	Always, 100% of the time	Hard to Say
The audit/inspection team did not understand adequately the root cause or the importance (or lack thereof) of the issue						
Agency management does not understand what the OIG wants						
Agency management disagrees with the methodology used in the report						
Agency management disagrees with the findings leading to the recommendations						
Agency management does not like the recommendations, even if they acknowledge the findings						
Other considerations (please specify):						

Using the scale listed below, what percentage of the time are the following factors important considerations when your office recommends federal prosecution?

	Never, 0% of the time	About 25% of the time	About 50% of the time	About 75% of the time	Always, 100% of the time	Hard to Say
Priorities of the inspector general						
Priorities of agency management						
Priorities of congressional contacts						
Level of financial fraud involved in the case						
Strength of the evidence in the case						
Perceived priorities of the Department of Justice						
Perceived priorities of U.S. Attorney's Office that would handle the case						
Media interest in the case or issue area						
Alternative civil settlement is available						
Alternative prosecution at the state or local level is available						
Other actions such as suspensions, debarment, or personnel actions are available						
Other considerations (please specify):						

In our research in the IG community we have learned of a number of factors that seem to influence an OIG's effectiveness. Based on your OIG experience, please identify the top three factors that you have found to be the most important factors affecting your work.

Yes, a top
three factor

1. Mutually shared views on the role of the Inspector General held by the agency leadership and the IG   _____

2. Mutually shared views on the role of the Inspector General held by the relevant congressional leaders and the IG   _____

3. Confidence and trust in the Inspector General held by the agency leadership   _____

4. Confidence and trust in the Inspector General held by the relevant congressional leaders   _____

5. Clear communications between the IG and the agency regarding appropriate requests and expectations relative to IG law and resources   _____

6. Ongoing communications between staff at lower levels of the OIG with corresponding agency staff   _____

7. The IG keeping the agency leadership informed to avoid surprises with OIG findings and reports   _____

8. The IG keeping relevant congressional leaders informed to avoid surprises with OIG findings and reports   _____

9. The IG setting clear expectations and timing for comments and suggestions by agency officials on OIG draft and final reports   _____

10. The OIG working to resolve conflicts over access to data or implementing recommendations at the lowest levels possible in the OIG and the agency   _____

11. The OIG dedicating time and resources for IG and OIG staff visits with mid-level agency officials   _____

12. Regular communications with all OIG staff regarding expectations about the role of the OIG vis-à-vis the agency and Congress   _____

13. Other especially important factors (please specify):   _____

We are interested in learning about your experience in requesting information from agency management for OIG audits, evaluations, and investigations.

Filter Question: In the past five years, has your office been denied timely access to any records, reports, audits or documents needed to conduct your work?

Yes_   No_

If yes, using the scale listed below, in the previous five years how frequently has agency management denied your office timely access to the following categories of information?

	Never, 0% of the time	About 25% of the time	About 50% of the time	About 75% of the time	Always, 100% of the time	Hard to Say
Printed materials in agency files						
Electronic information housed on agency servers						
Email housed on agency servers						
Data downloaded from agency databases, e.g., travel card date, financial data						
Use of agency information technology programs to access agency databases						
Information in personnel or agency files that may relate to national security						
Information in personnel files that may relate to individual health matters or other protected data						
Information in files that may relate to agency investigations of agency personnel						
Information in files that may relate to investigations of non-agency personnel, e.g., contractors						
Other considerations (please specify):						

(Again, if yes to #8) When agency management delays or declines to give the OIG timely access to information, which of the following activities has your office pursued and with what result?

	Frequency of Activity		Effectiveness of Activity	
	Happens frequently	Does *not* happen frequently	Has led to OIG having access to requested material	Has *not* led to OIG having access to requested material
Meeting with officials responsible for the office(s) holding the data				
Meeting with the agency's general counsel				
Raising the issue with agency leadership				
Raising the issue in reports or testimony to Congress				
Other considerations (please specify):				

To what extent have limitations on your OIG's authority to issue subpoenas hindered your office's ability to conduct your work?

Not at all __

Occasionally __

Quite frequently __

Within the last two years has your office drafted a seven-day letter, even if the letter was not formally sent?

Yes __   No __

To what extent, if any, has the increasingly polarized politics within Congress, and between Congress and the executive branch, affected the operations of your office regarding?

	Not at all	Occasionally	Quite frequently	Hard to say
Decisions regarding the foci of your audits, inspections, or investigations				
Dedication of more OIG resources to external communications				
Increased OIG staff time allocated to congressional relationships				
Increased resources from Congress				
Higher visibility of your office's work and reports				
Other considerations (please specify):				

We are not asking for your name nor your agency identification, but please give us some information about yourself to help us when we analyze our survey results:

What role do you currently play?

IG _

Deputy or Assistant IG _

Counsel to the IG _

Other _

Who appoints your agency's Inspector General?

Presidential appointment with Senate confirmation _

Agency management appointment (Senate confirmation NOT required by statute) _

Governing board or oversight board appointment (Senate confirmation *not* required by statute) _

What is the approximate size of your OIG in (authorized) FTEs?

100 FTEs or fewer _

101–1,000 FTEs _

1,001–5,000 FTEs _

5,001 or more FTEs _

How many years have you worked in the U.S. Executive Branch in any capacity?

    Less than 3 years _
    3–6 years _
    6–10 years _
    More than 10 years _

How many years have you worked in your current Office of the Inspector General?

    Less than 3 years _
    3–6 years _
    6–10 years _
    More than 10 years _

If you worked in the private sector or nonprofit sector prior to your current position, how many years did you work in that sector?

    Less than 3 years _
    3–6 years _
    6–10 years _
    More than 10 years _

How would you characterize your professional background?

    Primarily law enforcement, investigation, or prosecution _
    Primarily auditing or financial management in public or private
        organization _
    Primarily government management and administration _
    Primarily private non-financial business manager or non-
        governmental organization _
    Administration _
    Private law practice _
    Other _

Thank you very much for sharing your valuable insights. Please offer any other comments that you feel may help us better understand the relationship between agency managers and inspectors general.

Works Cited

Aberbach, Joel D. 1990. *Keeping a Watchful Eye: The Politics of Congressional Oversight.* Washington, DC: Brookings Institution.

———. 2001. *Keeping a Watchful Eye: The Politics of Congressional Oversight.* 2nd ed. Washington, DC: Brookings Institution.

Adair, John J., and Rex Simmons. 1988. "From Voucher Auditing to Junkyard Dogs: The Evolution of Federal Inspectors General." *Public Budgeting & Finance* 8 (2): 91–100.

Anderson, Martin. 1988. *Revolution: The Reagan Legacy.* Stanford, CA: Hoover Institution Press.

Barofsky, Neil. 2012. *Bailout: An Inside Account of How Washington Abandoned Main Street While Rescuing Wall Street.* New York, NY: Simon and Schuster.

Brandon, Paul R., Nick L. Smith, and George F. Grob. 2012. "Five Years of HHS Home Health Care Evaluations: Using Evaluation to Change National Policy." *American Journal of Evaluation* 33 (2): 251–262.

Burrows, Vanessa K. 2009. "The Special Inspector General for the Troubled Asset Relief Program (SIGTARP)." Washington, DC: Congressional Research Service.

Burrows, Vanessa K., and Frederick M. Kaiser. 2007. "Statutory Inspectors General: Legislative Developments and Legal Issues." Washington, DC: Congressional Research Service.

Council of the Inspectors General on Integrity and Efficiency. 2012a. "Progress Report to the President: Fiscal Year 2012." Washington, DC: CIGIE.

Council of the Inspectors General on Integrity and Efficiency. 2012b. "Quality Standards for Federal Offices of Inspectors General." Washington, DC: CIGIE.

Council of the Inspectors General on Integrity and Efficiency. 2014. "The Inspectors General." Washington, DC: CIGIE.

Crosby, Barbara C., and John B. Bryson. 2005. *Leadership for the Common Good: Tackling Public Problems in a Shared-Power World*. San Francisco, CA: Jossey-Bass.

Davis, Christopher M., and Michael Greene. 2017. "Presidential Appointee Positions Requiring Senate Confirmation and Committees Handling Nominations." Washington, DC: Congressional Research Service.

Department of Justice. 2019. "Annual Report to Congress on Outstanding Government Accountability Office and Inspector General Recommendations," February 2019.

Eisenstein, James. 1978. *Counsel for the United States: U.S. Attorneys in the Political and Legal Systems*. Baltimore, MD: The Johns Hopkins University Press.

Epstein, David, and Sharyn O'Halloran. 1999. *Delegating Powers: A Transaction Cost Politics Approach to Policy Making under Separate Powers*. Cambridge, UK: Cambridge University Press.

Ervin, Clark Kent. 2006. *Open Target: Where America Is Vulnerable to Attack*. New York, NY: Macmillan.

Fisher, Louis. 1998. *The Politics of Shared Power: Congress and the Executive*. 4th ed. College Station, TX: Texas A&M University Press.

Fong, Phyllis K. 2008. "The IG Reform Act and the New IG Council: Dawn of a New Era." *Journal of Public Inquiry* (Fall/Winter): 1–6.

Francis, Kathryn A. 2019a. "Statuatory Inspectors General in the Federal Government: A Primer." Updated January 3, 2019. Available at https://crsreports.congress.gov/product/pdf/R/R45450.

Francis, Kathryn A. 2019b. "New Law Requires Agencies to Report on Outstanding IG Recommendations," *CRS Insight*, updated January 28, 2019 (IN11026), available at https://fas.org/sgp/crs/misc/IN11026.pdf.

Fountain, Joselynn, and Kathryn E. Newcomer. 2016. "Developing and Sustaining Effective Faculty Mentoring Programs." *Journal of Public Affairs Education* 22 (4): 483–506.

Gates, Margaret Jane, and Marjorie Fine Knowles. 1984. "The Inspector General Act in the Federal Government: A New Approach to Accountability." *Alabama Law Review* 36 (2): 473–514.

Ginsberg, Wendy, and Michael Greene. 2016. "Federal Inspectors General: History, Characteristics, and Recent Congressional Actions." Washington, DC: Congressional Research Service.

Government Accountability Office. 1983. "State Department's Office of Inspector General Should Be More Independent and Effective." GAO Publication No. 83-56. Washington, DC: US Government Printing Office.

————. 1985. "Compliance with Professional Standards by the Commerce Inspector General." GAO Publication No. 85-57. Washington, DC: US Government Printing Office.

————. 1987a. "Compliance with Professional Standards by the GSA Inspector General." GAO Publication No. 87-22. Washington, DC: US Government Printing Office.

————. 1987b. "Compliance with Professional Standards by the Transportation Inspector General." GAO Publication No. 87-28. Washington, DC: US Government Printing Office.

————. 1993. "Action Needed to Strengthen OIGs at Designated Federal Entities." GAO Publication No. 94-39. Washington, DC: US Government Printing Office.

————. 2007. "Activities of the Department of State Office of Inspector General." GAO Publication No. 07-138. Washington, DC: US Government Printing Office.

————. 2008. "Actions Needed to Improve Audit Coverage of NASA." GAO Publication No. 09-88. Washington, DC: US Government Printing Office.

————. 2009. "Survey of Governance Practices and the Inspector General Role." GAO Publication No. 09-270. Washington, DC: US Government Printing Office.

————. 2010. "Continued Actions Needed to Strengthen IG Oversight of the United States International Trade Commission." GAO Publication No. 115. Washington, DC: US Government Printing Office.

————. 2011. "Reporting on Independence, Effectiveness, and Expertise." GAO Publication No. 11-770. Washington, DC: US Government Printing Office.

————. 2014. "A Sample of the Treasury IG for Tax Administration's Audits Were Generally Consistent with Standards, but Additional Review Could Address Exceptions." GAO Publication No. 14-70. Washington, DC: US Government Printing Office.

————. 2018. "Inspectors General: Information on Vacancies and IG Community View on Their Impact." GAO Publication No. 18-270. Washington, DC: US Government Printing Office.

Grantmakers for Effective Organizations. 2016. "Strengthening Nonprofit Capacity: Core Concepts in Capacity Building." Washington, DC: GEO.

Haglund, Evan T. 2017. "Empty Seats: Vacancies, Vetting, and Nomination Delay in Presidential Appointments." In *Public Management Research Conference*. Washington, DC.

———. 2015. "Striped Pants versus Fat Cats: Ambassadorial Performance of Career Diplomats and Political Appointees." *Presidential Studies Quarterly* 45 (4): 653–658.

Henry, Gary T., and Melvin M. Mark. 2003. "Beyond Use: Understanding Evaluation's Influence on Attitudes and Actions." *American Journal of Evaluation* 24 (3): 293–314.

Hilliard, Nadia. 2017. *The Accountability State: US Federal Inspectors General and the Pursuit of Democratic Integrity.* Lawrence, KS: University Press of Kansas.

Hudak, John, and Grace Wallack. 2015. "Sometimes Cutting Budgets Raise Deficits: The Curious Case of Inspectors' General Return on Investment." Washington, DC: The Brookings Institution, Center for Effective Public Management.

Johnson, Charles A., and Danette Brickman. 2001. *Independent Counsel: The Law and the Investigations.* Washington, DC: CQ Press.

Linden, Russell M. 2002. *Working across Boundaries: Making Collaboration Work in Government and Nonprofit Organizations.* San Francisco, CA: Jossey-Bass.

Lewis, David E. 2008. *The Politics of Presidential Appointments: Political Control and Bureaucratic Performance.* Princeton, NJ: Princeton University Press.

Lewis, David E., and Terry M. Moe. 2009. "The Presidency and the Bureaucracy: The Levers of Presidential Control." In *The Presidency and the Political System*, edited by Michael Nelson, 9th ed., 425–457. Washington, DC: Sage Publications.

Light, Paul C. 1993. *Monitoring Government: Inspectors General and the Search for Accountability.* Washington, DC: Brookings Institution Press.

———. 1997. *Tides of Reform: Making Government Work, 1945–1995.* New Haven, CT: Yale University Press.

———. 2006. "The Tides of Reform Revisited: Patterns in Making Government Work, 1945–2002." *Public Administration Review* 66 (1): 6–19.

McCubbins, Mathew D., Roger G. Noll, and Barry R. Weingast. 1987. "Administrative Procedures as Instruments of Political Control." *Journal of Law, Economics, & Organization* 3 (2): 243–277.

Michaels, Judith E. 1997. *The President's Call: Executive Leadership from FDR to George Bush.* Pittsburgh, PA: University of Pittsburgh Press.

Moore, Mark H., and Margaret Jane Gates. 1986. *Inspectors-General: Junkyard Dogs or Man's Best Friend?* New York, NY: Russell Sage Foundation.

Mosher, Frederick C. 1979. *GAO: The Quest for Accountability in American Government*. Boulder, CO: Westview Press.

———. 1984. *Tale of Two Agencies: A Comparative Analysis of the General Accounting Office and the Office of Management and Budget*. Baton Rouge, LA: Louisiana State University Press.

Newcomer, Kathryn E. 1998. "The Changing Nature of Accountability: The Role of the Inspector General in Federal Agencies." *Public Administration Review* 58 (2): 129–136.

———. 1994. "Opportunities and Incentives for Improving Program Quality: Auditing and Evaluating." *Public Administration Review* 54 (2): 147–154.

Newcomer, Kathryn E., and George F. Grob. 2004. "Federal Offices of the Inspector General: Thriving on Chaos?" *American Review of Public Administration* 34 (3): 235–251.

O'Leary, Rosemary, and Lisa Blomgren Bingham, eds. 2009. *The Collaborative Public Manager: New Ideas for the Twenty-First Century*. Washington, DC: Georgetown University Press.

O'Leary, Rosemary, and Catherine Gerard. 2012. "Collaboration across Boundaries: Insights and Tips from Federal Senior Executives." Washington, DC: IBM Center for the Business of Government.

Radin, Beryl A. 2012. *Federal Management Reform in a World of Contradictions*. Washington, DC: Georgetown University Press.

Rivlin, Alice M. 1994. "Inspector General Vision Statement." *Government Accounts Journal* 43 (1).

Roberts, Patrick S., and Matthew Dull. 2013. "Guarding the Guardians: Oversight Appointees and the Search for Accountability in U.S. Federal Agencies." *Journal of Policy History* 25 (2): 207–239.

Rosen, Bernard. 1998. *Holding Government Bureaucracies Accountable*. 3rd ed. Westport, CT: Praeger.

Rosenbloom, David H. 2010. "Reevaluating Executive-Centered Public Administration Theory." In *Oxford Handbook of American Bureaucracy*, edited by Robert F. Durant, 101–127. Oxford, UK: Oxford University Press.

Schick, Allen. 1983. "Politics through Law: Congressional Limitations on Executive Discretion." In *Both Ends of the Avenue: The Presidency, the Executive Branch, and Congress in the 1980s*, edited by Anthony Stephen King, 154–184. Washington, DC: American Enterprise Institute for Public Policy Research.

Schickler, Eric, and Frances E. Lee, eds. 2011. *Oxford Handbook of the American Congress*. Oxford, UK: Oxford University Press.

Schmitz, Joseph E. 2013. *The Inspector General Handbook: Fraud, Waste, Abuse,* and Other Constitutional *"Enemies, Foreign and Domestic."* Washington, DC: Center for Security Policy Press.

Selin, Jennifer L. 2015. "What Makes an Agency Independent?" *American Journal of Political Science* 59 (4): 971–987.

Waxman, Henry A. 2005. "The Politicization of Inspectors General." Washington, DC.

Weiss, Carol H. 1998. "Have We Learned Anything New about the Use of Evaluation?" *American Journal of Evaluation* 19 (1): 21–33.

Notes

ACKNOWLEDGMENTS

1. A report from this grant was published in 2015 by the IBM Center as "Balancing Independence and Positive Engagement: How Inspectors General Work with Agencies and Congress," by Charles A. Johnson, Kathryn E. Newcomer, and Angela Allison, as part of the Improving Performance Series.

CHAPTER ONE

1. Lisa Rein, *Washington Post*, August 31, 2016.

2. Stephen Ohlemacher, Associated Press, *MSN News*, June 24, 2015.

3. Jim Carlton, *Wall Street Journal*, August 1, 2016.

4. Richard A. Oppel, Jr., *New York Times*, September 10, 2014.

5. Letter to Senator Ron Johnson, Chair, Committee on Homeland Security and Government Affairs, and Representative Jason Chaffetz, Chair, Committee on Oversight and Government Reform, July 23, 2015 (see https://www.oversight.gov/sites/default/files/oig-reports/IGAccess.JGlennLtr.072315.pdf).

6. CIGIE (2018), "Annual Report to the President and Congress, FY 2017" (see https://www.ignet.gov/content/reports-publications).

7. Michael E. Horowitz, Chair, CIGIE, and IG, U.S. DOJ, before the U.S. House of Representatives Committee on Oversight and Government Reform, November 15, 2017.

8. Empirical studies of IGs and their work are few in number. Among these few academic studies, books by Paul Light (1993) and Mark Moore and Margaret Gates (1986) discuss the initial development of OIGs in their first decade, and

articles by Kathryn Newcomer (1998) and Newcomer and George Grob (2004) report surveys of IGs regarding challenges they have faced since the 1990s. Additional insights about OIGs come from memoir-like books by three former IGs: Neil Barofsky (2012), TARP IG; Clark Ervin (2006), State and DHS IG; and James Schmitz (2013), DOD IG. Nadia Hilliard's (2017) recent volume reports on the role IGs play in democratic accountability and presents case studies of OIGs in three cabinet-level departments: State, Justice, and Homeland Security.

9. As we complete this volume, CIGIE announced the creation of a website (Oversight.com) presenting reports by U.S. IGs and summary data. Previously, individual OIGs published individual reports, which Congress required to be posted on the internet in 2008 legislation.

10. Radin (2012).

11. Eisenstein (1978, pp. 35–40, 72–75, 93–98, passim).

12. The IG Act of 1978, amended, includes exceptions to this broad independence for IGs in national security agencies where management may constrain IG activities for national security reasons.

13. Fisher (1998, p. 14).

14. Lisa Rein, "A 'largely toxic discourse' in Washington is hindering watchdogs, retiring IG says," *Washington Post*, July 15, 2015 (see https://www.washingtonpost .com/news/federal-eye/wp/2015/07/15/a-largely-toxic-discourse-in-washington- is-hindering-watchdogs-retiring-ig-says/?postshare=1561447185219352).

15. Ervin (2006, p. viii).

CHAPTER TWO

1. *Congressional Record—Senate*, vol. 154, no. 159 (October 1, 2008), pp. S10220–S10283.

2. Neil Barofsky, who served as the first TARP IG, gives a firsthand account of the mixed and sometimes conflicting expectations Congress and executive officials had for SIGTARP. See Barofsky (2012).

3. See Light (1993) and Gates and Knowles (1984) for full discussions of the 1978 IG Act's early legislative history. Francis (2019a) provides a summary of legislation establishing various OIGs under the IG Act of 1978 and separate legislation creating other permanent and special inspectors general with essentially the same responsibilities and authority. This book focuses exclusively on OIGs created under the IG Act of 1978 and those created by separate statutes. In 2019, each of these OIGs has a seat on the Council of the Inspectors General on Integrity and Efficiency and constitutes what we refer to as the IG community.

4. See "Operations of Billie Sol Estes: Report prepared by the Intergovernmental Relations Subcommittee of the Committee on Government Operations," October, 1964, Washington, DC, U.S. Government Printing Office, 1964.

5. See "Department of Health, Education, and Welfare (prevention and detection of fraud and program abuse), Tenth Report by the Committee on Gov-

ernment Operations," January 26, 1976, Washington, DC, U.S. Government Printing Office, 1976.

6. Light (1993, p. 31).

7. See Light (1993, pp. 28–31) for a discussion of the Department of State's IG and Schmitz (2013, pp. 9–33) for a discussion of the historical use of IGs in the military.

8. Now called the Government Accountability Office.

9. Light (1993, p. 35).

10. Hearings, Subcommittee of the Committee on Government Operations, "Establishment of an Office of Inspector General in the Department of Health, Education, and Welfare" (May 25 and 27, 1976, p. 8).

11. Subcommittee of the Committee on Government Operations, "Establishment of an Office of Inspector General in the Department of Health, Education, and Welfare" (May 25 and 27, 1976, pp. 1–2).

12. Hearings, Subcommittee of the Committee on Government Operations, on H.R. 2819 (July 27, 1977, pp. 449–452 and 468–469).

13. Hearings, Testimony by Mr. Morris, Subcommittee on Governmental Efficiency and the District of Columbia (June 14, 1978, pp. 53–56).

14. Committee on Governmental Affairs, "Establishment of Offices of Inspector and Audit General in Certain Executive Departments and Agencies, Report to Accompany H.R. 8588" (August 8 [legislative day, May 17], 1978, p. 8).

15. Hearings, Testimony by Representative Fountain to Senate Committee, Committee on Governmental Affairs, Subcommittee on Governmental Efficiency and the District of Columbia (June 14, 1978, p. 6).

16. Light (1993, p. 40, passim).

17. Discussions leading to passage of the IG Act of 1978 do not appear to have been substantially influenced by deliberations regarding the 1978 Ethics in Government Act, which passed at roughly the same time and created the Office of Independent Counsel. The latter was in response to executive misconduct surrounding the Watergate affair and created a process for appointment of independent counsel when the attorney general receives substantial allegations of wrongdoing by high-level executives. While the House Committee on Government Operations and the Senate Committee on Government Affairs held hearings on the Ethics in Government Act, the judiciary committees in both houses were the primary loci of most discussions for this act, especially the provision for appointment of independent counsel. For a thorough discussion of the development and implementation of the independent counsel legislation, see Johnson and Brickman (2001).

18. Mosher (1984, p. 21).

19. Mosher (1984, p. 2).

20. Mosher (1984, pp. 72–73). See also Light (1997, p. 27).

21. Mosher (1979, p. 120).

22. Mosher (1979, pp. 103–129).

23. Light (1997, p. 17).

24. Adair and Simmons (1988, p. 96, figure 1).

25. Light (1997).

26. Light (2006, p. 9, table 3).

27. Committee on Governmental Affairs (1994, p. 1).

28. Schick (1983, p. 154).

29. Rosenbloom (2010, p. 114).

30. Rosenbloom (2010, p. 114). See also, McCubbins, Noll, and Weingast (1987) for a discussion of the APA's importance in a principal-agent theoretical framework.

31. Quoted in Rosen (1998, p. 69) and Light (1993, p. 89).

32. Aberbach (1990, p. 30). Subsequent research by Aberbach demonstrated that congressional oversight activities had, in fact, increased after adoption of LRA 1970. See Aberbach (2001).

33. Schickler and Lee (2011, p. 727).

34. 84 Stat. 1156 (1970).

35. Frederick M. Kaiser, Walter J. Oleszek, and Todd B. Tatelman (2011), "Congressional Oversight Manual," Congressional Research Service, pp. 7–8.

36. Kaiser, Oleszek, and Tatelman (2011, p. 8).

37. The current edition of this manual is by Alissa M. Doland, et al., "Congressional Oversight Manual," Congressional Research Service, December 19, 2014 (https://fas.org/sgp/crs/misc/RL30240.pdf).

38. Kaiser, Oleszek, and Tatelman (2011).

39. Aberbach (1990, table 2-1, p. 35).

40. See *Vital Statistics on Congress: Data on the U.S. Congress*, updated September 2017, Brookings Institution, table 5-1, Congressional Staff, 1979–2015 (https://www.brookings.edu/multi-chapter-report/vital-statistics-on-congress/).

41. Light (1993, p. 52).

42. Quoted in Light (1993, p. 55).

43. Quoted in Light (1993, p. 56).

44. Epstein and O'Halloran (1999, pp. 117–120).

45. Light (1993, pp. 128–131).

46. This count includes agency IGs that were created by and operate under individual statutes other than the IG Act of 1978. These IGs are appointed by the agency director or leadership designated in legislation and essentially have the same responsibilities and authority as IGs operating under the IG Act of 1978. See Francis (2019a) for a discussion of statutes authorizing OIGs.

47. See Francis (2019a), Appendix A, pp. 27–30, for a 2019 listing of OIGs and authorizing legislation.

48. Inspector General Act of 1978, section 3(a).

49. Burrows (2009).

50. Inspector General Act of 1978, as amended, Pub. L. 111–259, section 6 (d)(1)(A)(i).

51. See Fong (2008) for a discussion of this and other changes in the 2008 act that enhanced the authority and independence of OIGs.

52. Inspector General Act of 1978, amended, section 6 (f)(2)(E).

53. The authority of IGs to initiate audits, investigations, and evaluations is not often questioned, and only designated national security agencies have the authority to stop an inquiry for national security reasons.

54. Testimony before the House Committee on Oversight and Government Reform on September 10, 2014, by Michael E. Horowitz, IG, DOJ, details his difficulties in obtaining information from DOJ (https://oig.justice.gov/testimony/t140910.pdf).

55. A copy of the letter is available at https://oversight.house.gov/wp-content/uploads/2015/01/IG-Access-Letter-to-Congress-08-05-20141.pdf.

56. See Public Law No: 114–317 (2016), section 5.

57. Hilliard (2017, pp. 53, 220).

58. Inspector General Act of 1978, amended, section 5.

59. Inspector General Act of 1978, amended, section 4 (b)(c)(d).

60. P.L. 101–576.

61. P.L. 103–356.

62. P.L. 106–531.

63. P.L. 107–347.

64. P.L. 112–199, sec. 117.

65. IG Act of 1978, amended, section 7 (a).

66. Government Accountability Office (2011). For recent criticism of IGs for underutilizing these letters and generally not keeping Congress informed of such matters, see Charles S. Clark, "Lawmaker Seeks More Frequent Alerts from Inspectors General," *Government Executive*, August 7, 2012 (https://www.govexec.com/oversight/2012/08/lawmaker-seeks-more-frequent-alerts-inspectors-general/57276/).

67. Analysis and recommendations regarding "Change the Focus of the Inspectors General" can be found in archives of the National Performance Review (NPR) (https://govinfo.library.unt.edu/npr/library/reports/smc03.html).

68. Rivlin (1994).

69. Rivlin (1994, p. 10).

70. Newcomer (1998, p. 133, and table 3, p. 134).

71. P.L. 95–452, section 6 (6).

72. Light (1993, pp. 175–186).

73. See Fong (2008).

74. See Inspector General Act of 1978 (amended), Section 11, "Establishment of the Council of the Inspectors General on Integrity and Efficiency.

75. Inspector General Act of 1978 (amended), Section 11, (a)(2)(A&B).

76. See Section 7 (d). As is discussed in chapter 3, the 2016 IG Empowerment Act imposes tighter deadlines for evaluation of misconduct allegations by the Integrity Committee in the face of congressional disappointment in the length of time such reviews were taking.

77. See CIGIE's website (https://www.ignet.gov/) for contemporary versions of these quality standards.

78. See Section 7 (c) (F), and see comments by CIGIE Chairs Fong and Horowitz on operation of the recommendation panel (Fong: https://www.ignet.gov/sites/default/files/files/CIGIE%20Testimony%20IG%20Vacancies_Final.pdf and Horowitz: https://www.hsdl.org/?view&did=794107).

79. For example, Council of the Inspectors General on Integrity and Efficiency (2012a).

80. Hilliard (2017, pp. 193–94). See also this group's final report, "Oversight of Gulf Coast Hurricane Recovery," a semiannual report to Congress, April 1, 2008–September 30, 2008, President's Council on Integrity and Efficiency and Executive Council on Integrity and Efficiency (December 2008).

81. Barofsky (2012, pp. 20–21).

82. Special Inspector General for TARP, "FY 2013: President's Budget Submission," 2013, p. 11 (https://www.treasury.gov/about/budget-performance/Documents/5%20-%20FY%202013%20SIGTARP%20CJ.pdf).

83. Barofsky (2012, p. 60, passim).

84. ARRA, 2009, sec. 1521.

85. Testimony, Kathleen S. Tighe, before the Committee on Homeland Security and Government Affairs Subcommittee on Emergency Management, Intergovernmental Relations and the District of Columbia, U.S. Senate, November 6, 2013 (https://cybercemetery.unt.edu/archive/recovery/20150830213628/http://www.recovery.gov/arra/About/board/Documents/TigheHSGAC-EMDCtestimony11.6.13.pdf).

86. See Charles S. Clark, "Historic Effort to Track Stimulus Spending Wraps Up," *Government Executive*, September 28, 2015 (http://www.govexec.com/oversight/2015/09/historic-effort-track-stimulus-spending-wraps/122129/).

87. P.L. 111–203.

88. P.L. 112-239, §848; listed in 5 U.S.C., Appendix (IG Act of 1978) §8L.

89. Lead IG reports are available via the internet (https://www.stateoig.gov/reports/overseas-contingency-operations).

90. Intelligence Authorization Act of Fiscal Year 2010, Section 405 (https://www.gpo.gov/fdsys/pkg/PLAW-111publ259/pdf/PLAW-111publ259.pdf).

91. This statutorily authorized forum was preceded by a group with the same name, created by the secretary of defense in 1994, which over time included IGs from federal agencies that had intelligence responsibilities. In 2005 the newly created Office of the Director of National Intelligence (DNI) created an OIG. This action was authorized by the Intelligence Reform and Terrorism Prevention

Act of 2004 and to be done at the discretion of the director "if [the director] determines that an Office of Inspector General would be beneficial to improving the operations and effectiveness of the Office of the Director of National Intelligence...." (Public Law 458.108, Section 1078, available at https://www.gpo. gov/fdsys/pkg/PLAW-108publ458/html/PLAW-108publ458.htm). The newly appointed DNI inspector general "assumed the chairmanship of the Intelligence Community Inspectors General Forum," which was characterized as a "meeting of all Intelligence Community agency Inspectors General or their designees" (see the DNI IG report for January 31, 2006, and subsequent reports through 2009 at https://www.dni.gov/index.php/who-we-are/organizations/ic-ig/ic-ig-features/1601-features-1). Passage of the Intelligence Authorization Act of 2010 created a statutory OIG for the intelligence community and authorized creation of the current Intelligence Community Inspectors General Forum.

Additionally, in 2015 the Department of Defense Office of Inspector General organized the Defense Council on Integrity and Efficiency, which includes the Defense IG and administrative (military) IGs. The charter creating this council indicates that its purpose is "to ensure effective coordination and cooperation between and among the activities of the Office of the Inspector General of the Department of Defense, the Defense Agencies, and the activities of the internal audit, inspection, and investigative organizations of the military departments with a view toward avoiding duplication." The charter for this council, which resides wholly in the Department of Defense, states that it is "modeled after the Council of the Inspectors General on Integrity and Efficiency." Accordingly, there are committees in such areas as auditing, inspection and evaluation, and criminal investigations, as well as intelligence. The latter committee, referenced as the Defense Intelligence and Special Programs Oversight Committee, "coordinates intelligence oversight" related to "Defense-wide issues and policies, identifies potential gaps in oversight coverage, and provides recommendations to the council on . . . training and development needs" (see Charter, Defense Council on Integrity and Efficiency, http://www.dodig.mil/programs/DCIE/DCIE_Charter_3-10-2015.pdf).

92. The forum includes IGs from the Central Intelligence Agency; departments of Defense, Homeland Security, Energy, Justice, State, and Treasury; Defense Intelligence Agency; National Reconnaissance Office; National Security Agency; National Geospatial-Intelligence Agency; and Federal Bureau of Investigation (see https://www.dni.gov/index.php/who-we-are/organizations/ic-cio/ic-cio-relat ed-menus/ic-cio-related-links/ic-technical-specifications/us-government-agen cy?id=367).

93. Intelligence Authorization Act of Fiscal Year 2010, section 405 (h)(2)(B).

94. Neil Barofsky is highly critical of the IG council associated with CIGFO, commenting that "whatever promise CIGFO might have had was squelched by Congress's choice for its chairman," who failed to press for IGs "being able to initi-ate and conduct independent audits" (2012, pp. 220–221).

95. An example of official unclassified minutes from a January 2012 meeting of the forum is posted on the website Governmentattic.org (http://www.governmentattic.org/18docs/MinutesIC-IGforum_2012.pdf). Activities of the forum are also discussed in the IC IG semiannual report to Congress. Copies of this report are available on the IC IG website (https://www.dni.gov/files/documents/FOIA/ICIG-SAR-Q3-4-FY15.pdf).

CHAPTER THREE

1. From Neil Barofsky's account of his first conversation concerning his eventual nomination and appointment as the special inspector general for the Troubled Asset Relief Program (SIGTARP). Barofsky (2012, pp. 1, 2, and 20). See chapters 1 and 2 for a full account of Barofsky's appointment process. Clark Ervin, IG for the Department of State from 2001 through 2003 and nominee as the first IG for the newly created Department of Homeland Security (DHS), details similar experiences in his book (2006, pp. 1–5). He reports that the possibility of an IG appointment in the State Department came from the newly appointed secretary of state, Colin Powell, while Ervin was being interviewed for a political appointment in George W. Bush's incoming administration. The DHS IG nomination was initiated in a phone call from PPO and was followed by the same sort of interviews reported by Barofsky.

2. For a discussion of politics and executive appointments, see Lewis (2008) and Michaels (1997). Both of these volumes discuss recent presidents' strategies for shaping the federal bureaucracy overall and in specific agencies.

3. Both noncareer SES and Schedule C appointments are technically made by the head of the agencies in which the appointees serve; in practice, however, the White House PPO is heavily involved in the recruiting, vetting, and selection of these appointees. Noncareer appointees to SES positions are limited by law to 10 percent of all SES positions. Schedule C positions are created at the request of agency heads for advisory roles to other PAS or SES appointees.

4. Lewis (2008) and Lewis and Moe (2009).

5. See, for example, the IG Act of 1978 (amended), section 3(a). A few other positions, such as U.S. Attorneys or ambassadorships, have similar requirements stressing independence from political influence and some qualifications for the position; but unlike with IG appointments, presidents have generally ignored these provisions (from the Foreign Service Act of 1980) relative to ambassadorships. See Haglund (2015) on characteristics of ambassadorial appointments and subsequent performance). For a broader discussion of specific restrictions or features of positions that might increase position or agency independence, see Jennifer L. Selin (2015), "What Makes an Agency Independent?" *American Journal of Political Science* 59 (October), pp. 971–987.

6. Roberts and Dull (2013).

7. This volume uses the term *PAS IGs* to clearly distinguish them from DFE IGs.

8. The list of agencies in table 2-2 in chapter 2 gives a breakdown of PAS IGs and DFE IGs. See also Burrows (2009) and Ginsberg and Green (2016).

9. This section relies heavily on Paul Light's discussion of how the IG Act of 1978 was implemented during the Carter, Reagan, and Bush presidencies. See Light (1993, pp. 81–145).

10. Light (1993, p. 82).

11. Light (1993, p. 88).

12. Light (1993, table 5-3, p. 88).

13. Anderson (1988, p. 247).

14. Light (1993, p. 104).

15. Light (1993, p. 107).

16. Light (1993, p. 118).

17. See table 2-2 for a listing of IGs by agency and the dates they were established.

18. Michaels (1997, p. 237).

19. Light (1993, p. 134).

20. Light (1993, p. 135).

21. CIGIE provides recommendations of candidates, but it is unclear whether these recommendations are for specific vacancies or just generally qualified candidates. Through interviews and Freedom of Information Act requests, we could not determine whether any of the candidates recommended by CIGIE were nominated and, if nominated, confirmed by the Senate or appointed by an agency head. In his statement to the Senate Homeland Security and Government Operations Committee, Michael Horowitz, DOJ IG and CIGIE chair, highlighted that CIGIE had made 114 recommendations for IGs to PPO, but he did not know how many of those recommendations were considered (https://www.hsgac. senate.gov/hearings/watchdogs-needed-top-government-investigator-positions-left-unfilled-for-years).

22. Quoted in Davis and Greene (2017, p. 2, footnote 6) citing *Congressional Record*, vol. 153, part I, January 9, 2007, p. 487. The Committee on Homeland Security and Government Affairs may be the sole committee for agencies over which it has primary jurisdiction, such as the Department of Homeland Security, General Services Administration, and the Office of Personnel Management.

23. The IGs of the intelligence community and the Central Intelligence Agency are referred to the Select Committee on Intelligence and then to the Committee on Homeland Security and Government Affairs; the IGs of the National Reconnaissance Office and the National Security Agency are referred to the Select Committee on Intelligence and the Committee on Armed Services. See Davis and Greene (2017, pp. 39–40).

24. See table 2-2 for a complete listing.

25. Light (1993, p. 131).

26. Inspector General Act of 1978, as amended, section 8 (a)(6)(c).

27. Inspector General Empowerment Act of 2016, section 4(a).

28. Government Accountability Office (2018, p. 11).

29. Government Accountability Office (2018, pp. 16–42).

30. For data comparing nomination delays for IGs and U.S. Attorneys, see Haglund (2017).

31. This lack of advocates and a consequent effect on pace of nomination and confirmation is similar to the situation for ambassadorial nominations; without focused and influential advocates, ambassadorial nominees are often seen by senators as easy bargaining chips to use in Senate–White House conflicts unrelated to that specific appointment.

32. Personal interview by Evan Haglund with Donald Gips, former Director of the Presidential Personnel Office, March 10, 2016.

33. See Inspector General Act of 1978, as amended, section 3 (a) for PAS IGs and section 8 (a)(6)(c) for DFE IGs.

34. Light (1993, p. 102, passim), quoting Reagan press secretary James Brady's explanation of the IG firings.

35. Light (1993, p. 104, passim).

36. Michaels (1997, p. 332, footnote 2).

37. Steven Mufson and Juliet Eilperin, "Trump transition team reverses course on warnings to oust inspectors general," *Washington Post*, January 19, 2017 (https:// www.washingtonpost.com/business/economy/trump-transition-reverses-course- on-warnings-to-remove-inspectors-general/2017/01/19/09312a12-ddfa-11e6- 918c-99ede3c8cafa_story.html?utm_term=.74585418bd21). See also letter dated January 31, 2017, to White House counsel from Representatives Elijah E. Cummings and Gerald E. Connolly (https://democrats-oversight.house.gov/ sites/democrats.oversight.house.gov/files/documents/2017-01-31.EEC%20 Connolly%20to%20white%20house%20counsel%20McGahn%20Re.Trump%20 Transition%20Team%20threats%20to%20IGs.pdf).

38. "The Politicization of Inspectors General," a report prepared for Representative Henry A. Waxman, U.S. House of Representatives, Committee on Government Reform—Minority Staff, Special Investigations Division, October 21, 2004, revised January 7, 2005 (pp. 3, 8–11). The analysis used a broad definition of "prior political experience," which included "having worked in the White House, having held a political position in a federal agency (except in an IG office), having worked for the Democratic National Committee or Republican National Committee, or having held a political position in state government for either President Bush or Present Clinton when they served as governors. For the purposes of this report, 'audit experience' means employment in an IG office, at the Government Accountability Office (GAO), or with a private accounting firm" (p. 13).

39. Data on time in office are for IGs who were appointed and subsequently left office from 1978 through 2016.

40. See Inspector General Act of 1978, sections 3(a) and 8G(d)(1) for PAS and DFE IGs, respectively.

41. Council of the Inspectors General on Integrity and Efficiency (2014, p. 4),

(https://www.ignet.gov/sites/default/files/files/IG_Authorities_Paper_-_Final _6-11-14.pdf).

42. Council of the Inspectors General on Integrity and Efficiency (2014, p. 4).

43. Council of the Inspectors General on Integrity and Efficiency (2014, p. 4).

44. See *United States Nuclear Regulatory Commission v. Federal Labor Relations Authority* [25 F.3d 229] (4th Cir. 1994, p. 20), (http://openjurist.org/25/ f3d/229/united-states-nuclear-regulatory-commission-v-federal-labor-relations-authority).

45. See Inspector General Act, section 3(b) and section 8G(e) for PAS and DFE IGs, respectively.

46. Ed O'Keefe, "Watchdog Fired by Obama Loses Appeal Case," *Washington Post*, January 4, 2001 (http://voices.washingtonpost.com/federal-eye/2011/01/ watchdog_fired_by_obama_loses.html).

47. Edward Walsh, "Inspectors General Ousted at 2 Agencies," *Washington Post*, April 3, 2002 (https://www.washingtonpost.com/archive/politics/2002/04/03 /inspectors-general-ousted-at-2-agencies/67a86a9c-ccac-45db-aefc-d1e464b 1336a/?utm_term=.e83ce8c7e700).

48. The IGs who reportedly resigned after an official investigation were: John Brachfeld, National Archives and Records Administration, resigned 2014 (https://www.washingtonpost.com/news/federal-eye/wp/2014/08/04/embat tled-national-archives-ig-to-retire-after-probe-finds-misconduct/); Robert Coff, IG, NASA, resigned, 2009 (http://www.nbcnews.com/id/30020406/ns/tech nology_and_science-space/t/nasa-inspector-general-resigns-post/#.V_gLy BDrtPY); Karla W. Corcoran, U.S. Postal Service, resigned 2003 (https://www .washingtonpost.com/archive/politics/2003/08/20/postal-service-ig-quits-as-inquiry-concludes/91b8668c-153a-421e-b209-48c77b562e79/); Johnnie E. Fra-zier, Department of Commerce, resigned 2007 (http://www.washingtonpost. com/wp-dyn/content/article/2007/06/07/AR2007060702228.html); and Rich-ard Mulberry, Department of Interior, resigned 1984 after GAO investigation (http://www.nytimes.com/1984/08/09/us/interior-dept-officialquits-in-coal .html).

49. "Administrative Allegations Against Inspectors General," Executive Order 12993, March 21, 1996, 3 C.F.R. 171 (1996 Comp.).

50. Congressional Research Service, "Oversight of the Inspector General Community: The IG Council's Integrity Committee," September 21, 2015 (https:// www.everycrsreport.com/files/20150921_R44198_ceaeead39431704eb909c0a 3e07c8bfb1a7c492c.pdf).

51. Inspector General Empowerment Act of 2016, section 3.

52. See Integrity Committee, "Policies and Procedures of the Integrity Com-mittee of the Council of the Inspectors General on Integrity and Efficiency," 2016 (https://www.ignet.gov/sites/default/files/files/Integrity%20Committee% 20Policies%20and%20Procedures%202016.pdf). The following paragraph sig-nificantly condenses processes and policies contained in this lengthy document.

53. Light (1993, pp. 115–120, data drawn from table 6-4 and text on p. 117).

54. This number includes a presumed IG appointment for the Community Development Financial Institutions Fund (CDFIF), an agency within the Department of the Treasury created in 1994 with provisions for appointment of a DFE IG. Legislation in 1999 closed the CDFIF IG office and brought the fund under the Treasury IG's jurisdiction. Information about the individual serving as CDFIF IG could not be retrieved by the authors. Except for the total count, this IG appointment is not included in any subsequent analysis.

55. Partial lists of IGs, including historical data on PAS appointees and DFE appointees, are available on the CIGIE website. "Inspector General Historical Data: DFE and Legislative Branch Members (Revised March 22, 2015)" is available at https://www.ignet.gov/sites/default/files/files/ig-historical-data-march-15.pdf. Lists were updated and corrected through the Obama administration as of March 2017.

56. We used printed and electronic versions of the *Federal Yellow Book: Who's Who in Federal Departments and Agencies* (New York: Leadership Directories), which provide information on previous positions held by some IGs.

57. Reagan's three DFE appointees are excluded from this DFE average—two were male, and one was female.

58. These averages mask significant variation in the race/ethnicity of appointments by Democratic presidents Carter, Clinton, and Obama.

59. Light (1993, p. 151, table 8-1).

60. Inspector General Historical Data (as of January 17, 2007): Designated Federal Entities and Other ECIE Members (https://www.ignet.gov/sites/default/files/files/dfehistory.pdf).

61. See Inspector General Act of 1978, as amended, section 3 (a) for PAS IGs and section 8 (a)(6)(c) for DFE IGs

62. See Light (1993, p. 85, table 5-2).

CHAPTER FOUR

1. Newcomer (1994).

2. For example, see Hudak and Wallack (2015).

3. Discussion of IGs' investigative authority engendered considerable debate after passage of the IG Act of 1978 regarding what authority IG investigators had, or should have, and who should grant that authority—the DOJ or Congress. See Light (1993), pp. 189–194. See also Hilliard (2017), pp. 121–145 for a discussion of the emergence of the DOJ IG's investigative authority after creation of that office in 1988.

4. We conducted an electronic survey of the Inspector General community in fall 2016 to follow up on the findings from our six case studies, broaden our understanding about activities OIGs pursue to fulfill their mission, and identify factors that led to their success. We pretested the survey with four sitting IGs and

then sent the survey to at least five officials in each of the seventy-four IG offices, including the IG, and where the office had other top officials, such as a deputy IG, assistant IGs, and IG general counsels, we included them. We received responses from a total of fifty-nine IG executives. Our analysis draws on the twenty-six responses of the IGs, which is most appropriate since we are primarily focused on interactions between IGs and leadership in the agencies and Congress. Taken together, the case studies and responses to the survey give us confidence in our observations and conclusions.

5. Respondents are located in agencies of varied sizes—85 percent of respondents work in OIGs with 100 or fewer staff, while 15 percent work in OIGs with between 101 and 1,000 staff.

6. Interview with Jeff Marootian, conducted on January 12, 2017.

7. Report, Committee on Homeland Security and Government Affairs, U.S. Senate, "Good Accounting Obligation in Government Act," September 4, 2018, p. 2.

8. Ginsberg and Greene (2016, p. 13).

9. Newcomer and Grob (2004).

CHAPTER FIVE

1. Inspector General Act of 1978, section 2.

2. Inspector General Act of 1978, section 4.

3. Public policy and public administration literature on cooperation and collaboration focuses almost exclusively on interagency or intergovernmental relationships—e.g., O'Leary and Gerard (2012), O'Leary and Bingham (2009), Crosby and Bryson (2005), and Linden (2002). The general principles and findings in this work may have application to the intra-agency relationship involving OIGs and their agencies; however, the overall dynamic involving an independent IG reporting to an agency and Congress creates a context not addressed in this literature.

4. Newcomer and Grob (2004, table 10, p. 248).

5. Newcomer and Grob (2004, p. 246).

6. The President's Council on Integrity and Efficiency (PCIE) and the Executive Council on Integrity and Efficiency (ECIE).

7. Council of the Inspectors General on Integrity and Efficiency (2012b, p. 30).

8. Council of the Inspectors General on Integrity and Efficiency (2012b, p. 32).

9. Council of the Inspectors General on Integrity and Efficiency (2012b, p. 34).

10. For example, see reports concerning NASA IG Robert W. Cobb, who resigned after multiple reports that he was too cooperative and protective of NASA Administrator Sean O'Keefe (http://www.nbcnews.com/id/30020406/ns/technology_and_science-space/t/nasa-inspector-general-resigns-post/#.V_gLyBDrtPY and http://www.washingtonpost.com/wp-dyn/content/article/2007/04/05/AR2007040501661_pf.html).

11. Barofsky (2012) and Ervin (2006).

12. So-called seven-day letters involve a process set forth in the original IG Act, which authorizes an IG to inform Congress of "particularly serious or flagrant problems, abuses, or deficiencies" (IG Act, section 5 [d]). The letter is sent to Congress through the head of the agency and must be forwarded to Congress within seven days. See "Inspectors General: Reporting on Independence, Effectiveness, and Expertise," GAO report, September 2011, GAO-11-770, pp. 8–9.

13. For examples, see criticism of IGs detailed by Light (1993, pp. 118–120); more recently, in 2013, Department of Commerce IG Todd Zinser resigned after being heavily criticized by members of Congress for ineffectiveness and mismanagement (http://www.govexec.com/oversight/2015/06/embattled-com merce-inspector-general-abruptly-retires/114469/).

14. This conclusion about the existence of some tensions in these two agencies is based on our interviews and on reports from various public sources, such as articles in the *Washington Post* and congressional hearings. Our commitment to maintaining confidentiality for the interviewees and their respective agencies means that we cannot give specific details or references to public sources that specifically cite individuals or agencies.

15. Ervin (2006, p. 39).

16. As discussed in chapter 2, the 2016 Inspector General Empowerment Act, enacted after we conducted our interviews, clarified that IGs have access to nearly all agency documents and established a process for review when agency management declines an IG's request for agency materials.

17. Subsequent to the authors' interviews in 2014, the Good Accounting Obligation in Government Act (GAO-IG Act) was approved by Congress and signed into law by President Donald Trump on January 3, 2019. This law, Public Law no. 115-414, requires all agencies to include information in their budget justifications on outstanding recommendations by the GAO and their respective OIGs. The act does not require reports from agencies overseen by four statutory OIGs: SIGAR, SIGTRAP, the CIA's OIG, and the IG for the intelligence community. These reports are to supplement the required OIG semiannual reports to Congress that also include the OIGs' listing of currently open recommendations.

A "CRS Insight" statement, authored by Kathryn A. Francis, explains features of this new legislation (see Francis [2019b]).

The implementation of this law on reporting and follow-through on OIG recommendations was not clear at the time of this book's publication. However, some agencies have issued reports in response to this new mandate (see Department of Justice [2019]).

18. Statement of Michael E. Horowitz, IG, U.S. DOJ, before the U.S. Senate Committee on the Judiciary concerning "Inspector General Access to All Records Needed for Independent Oversight" (https://oig.justice.gov/testimony/t150805 .pdf).

19. The IG Empowerment Act of 2016 responded to criticisms regarding

delays in investigations by IGs and senior IG staff. The 2016 act mandated deadlines for actions in response to allegations of misconduct. This process does not, however, address allegations of underperformance of responsibilities, poor management of the office, or ineffectiveness of reports or follow-ups.

20. By contrast, one IG we interviewed acknowledged pushing the envelope by issuing reports that made specific policy recommendations—recommendations that were not well received by the agency. Agency leadership and members of Congress publicly and privately criticized this OIG for overreaching its authority by making policy recommendations that they viewed as beyond the OIG's authority or expertise. This activity constrained the responsiveness and receptivity of OIG activities in that agency, and it lessened support for the office in some congressional offices.

21. See chapter 3 discussion of the appointment process.

22. None of the IGs we interviewed encountered the kind of challenges experienced by Clark Ervin, who served as acting IG for the Department of Homeland Security. He was permanently appointed as a recess appointee but never confirmed by the Senate, and left the office at the end of his recess appointment due to lack of support from the White House, the secretary of DHS, and relevant Senate committees. Ervin pointed to several instances of ineffectiveness and being ignored while awaiting confirmation for the permanent position. See Ervin (2006).

23. See Inspector General Empowerment Act of 2016, section 5. Legislative history can be found at https://www.congress.gov/bill/114th-congress/house-bill/6450.

CHAPTER SIX

1. Moore and Gates (1986, p. 70).
2. For an example, see Hudak and Wallack (2015).
3. Weiss (1998).
4. Weiss (1998, p. 24).
5. Henry and Mark (2003, p. 297).
6. Henry and Mark (2003, pp. 299–305).
7. Hilliard (2017, p. 180).
8. Brandon, Smith, and Grob (2012).
9. Grantmakers for Effective Organizations (2016, p. 6).
10. Government Accountability Office (2014).
11. Government Accountability Office (2007).
12. Government Accountability Office (1983).
13. Government Accountability Office (1985).
14. Government Accountability Office (1987b).
15. Government Accountability Office (1987a).
16. Government Accountability Office (2008).
17. Government Accountability Office (1993, p. 12).

18. Government Accountability Office (2010, pp. 12–13).

19. Data for fiscal years 2009 through 2016 are posted on the CIGIE's website under the tab "Resources: FOIA Reading Room" (https://www.ignet.gov/content/foia-reading-room-1). CIGIE leadership indicated in personal conversations with the authors that the data reported in the posted tables were standardized by CIGIE staff across OIGs, thus making possible meaningful comparisons across agencies and their OIGs.

20. Inspector General Act of 1978, section 5 (f).

21. Inspector General Act of 1978, section 5 (f) (4).

22. Inspector General Act of 1978, section 5 (f)(4)(A-F).

23. Memorandum for the Assistant Attorney General for Administration, DOJ, March 20, 1998 (https://biotech.law.lsu.edu/blaw/olc/fbuop2.htm).

24. Good Accounting Obligation in Government Act (2019) and Francis (2019b).

25. Lisa Rein and Emily Was-Thibodeaux, "Veterans Affairs improperly spent $6 billion annually, senior official says," *Washington Post*, May 14, 2015 (https://www.washingtonpost.com/politics/va-improperly-spent-6-billion-on-care-for-veterans-senior-agency-leader-says/2015/05/13/ab8f131c-f5be-11e4-b2f3-af5479e6bbdd_story.html?utm_term=.d442ffa4bea7).

26. Passage of the Good Accounting Obligation in Government Act (2019) indicates continued interest in seeing agencies consider and respond to IG recommendations—some of which may not involve estimated dollar values. Thus, this act focuses on remedying the large number of "open recommendations" that agencies have not decided on instead of differences between the actual dollar figures recommended and actually realized for questioned costs or better use of funds.

CHAPTER SEVEN

1. Newcomer and Grob (2004).

2. For examples, see Government Accountability Office (2009) and Government Accountability Office (2010).

3. See Burrows and Kaiser (2007).

4. Fountain and Newcomer (2016).

5. This number does not count those offices that have been decommissioned or merged by legislation affecting home agencies or the OIGs. See table 2-2 for a listing of OIGs that are no longer in existence.

Index

Aberbach, Joel, 33–34, 36

Accountability of IGs: budget increases and cutbacks, 11; case studies on, 124–34; and dismissal of IGs, 11, 79, 159; as expectation, 10–11, 56–58, 91, 116, 157–59; IG Act on, 3, 25–29, 122, 157; and implementation of recommendations, 112–14; independence vs., 121; key factors for, 146–54; peer reviews for, 159

Acting IGs, 71, 180, 195, 196

Adair, John J., 27

Administrative Procedures Act of 1946 (APA), 33

Agencies: accountability to, 158; audit liaisons for, 112, 131, 153–54; budgets of, 114, 179; collaborative engagement with IGs, 122–24, 144–46; confidence and trust in IGs, 149–50; conflict resolution, 15, 128–29; Congress, relationships with, 135; containing OIGs, 28–32, 38; draft recommendations and input solicitations for, 108, 119, 158; IGs balancing relations with Congress, 137–46; improving processes and policies of, 164–66, 168, 183, 195; and independence of IGs, 125–28; loyalty of IGs to, 147–48;

rejection of recommendations of IGs, 104, 108, 110; seven-day letters for, 45, 129; special offices for coordination with IGs, 131. *See also* Audits, investigations, and evaluations; DFE IGs; Impact of IG work; Recommendations of IGs; Stakeholders of IGs; *specific agencies*

Agendas for audits and investigations. *See* Work plans for audits and investigations

Agriculture Department (USDA), 19–20, 28, 177–78

American Recovery and Reinvestment Act of 2009 (ARRA), 52–53, 55, 190–93

APA (Administrative Procedures Act of 1946), 33

Appointment process for IGs: challenges in, 196–97; and CIGIE, 65, 68, 74, 204; congressional confirmations, 13–14, 66, 68, 70, 196–97; DFE IGs, 38, 62, 67–68, 176; IG Reform Act on, 65; and media, 73, 75–76; nonpartisan nature of, 3, 9, 39, 56, 61, 75–78; overview (1978–2016), 68–75; PAS IGs, 13–14, 19, 60–66, 68, 70, 196–97; and shared government powers, 13–14. *See also* Recruitment of IGs

259

backgrounds of, 86, 89; Congress, interactions with, 133; defined, 5–6; demographics of, 86–87; dismissal of, 79; educational background of, 88; Executive Council on Integrity and Efficiency, 46–47, 49; GAO report on, 170; and PAS IGs, 38–39; vacancies of, 68–75, 195–96

DHS. *See* Homeland Security Department

Dismissal of IGs: and accountability of IGs, 11, 79, 159; by Bush (G.W.), 79–80; and Congress, 11, 39, 56–57, 61–62, 79; of DFE IGs, 79; IG Reform Act of 2008 on, 39, 79; involuntary resignations, 79–80, 149; by Obama, 79; of PAS IGs, 63, 64, 70, 75, 79; politics of, 75–77; by Reagan, 63, 64, 70, 75; and supervisory authority, 78–80; turnover rates, 61

Dispute resolution mechanisms, 153

DOD. *See* Defense Department

Dodd-Frank Wall Street Reform and Consumer Protection Act of 2010, 53

DOE. *See* Energy Department

DOJ. *See* Justice Department

DOS. *See* State Department

DOT (Transportation Department), 70, 100

ECIE (Executive Council on Integrity and Efficiency), 46–47, 49

Education of IGs, 87–88

Eisenstein, James, 7

Energy Department (DOE), 28, 70, 96, 168, 190–93

Engagement. *See* Collaborative engagement of IGs

Environmental Protection Agency (EPA), 43

Epstein, David, 37

Ervin, Clark, 15–16, 124, 147–48

Estes, Billy Sol, 19–20

Ethnicity and race of IGs, 87

Evaluations by IGs. *See* Audits, investigations, and evaluations

Executive branch: congressional oversight of, 29, 33–38; congressional relations with, 25–38; continuity of IGs through executive changes, 3, 9, 201; dismissal of IGs, 63, 64, 70, 75, 79; federal budget authority, 26; IGs reporting to, 3, 13; records, IG access to, 117; shared powers of, 13–15, 117–18, 161. *See also* PAS IGs

Executive Council on Integrity and Efficiency (ECIE), 46–47, 49

Expectations of IGs: accountability as, 10–11, 56–58, 91, 116, 157–59; and audits, investigations, and evaluations, 116–17; balancing executive leaders and Congress, xi, 4, 13, 139–40; clarification of, 204; from Congress, 18; engagement as, 11–12, 56–58, 123–24, 160; and impact of IG work, 182; independence as, 3, 4, 9–10, 18–19, 56–57, 123–24, 157; and partisanship, 3; and role of IGs, 147–49, 197; vision statement on, 47–48

Export-Import Bank, 70

Fact-finding, 96–97

Federal agencies. *See* Agencies

Federal Bureau of Investigation (FBI), 81, 100

Federal Deposit Insurance Corporation, 70

Federal Financial Management Improvement Act of 1996, 44–45

Federal Information Security Management Act of 2002, 45

Federal Manager Financial Integrity Act of 1982, 28

www.ingramcontent.com/pod-product-compliance
Lightning Source LLC
Chambersburg PA
CBHW031413270326
41929CB00010BA/1437